Environmental Finance

Local Capital Markets for Environmental Infrastructure

PROSPECTS IN CHINA, KAZAKHSTAN, RUSSIA AND UKRAINE

OECD

ORGANISATION FOR ECONOMIC CO-OPERATION AND DEVELOPMENT

ORGANISATION FOR ECONOMIC CO-OPERATION AND DEVELOPMENT

The OECD is a unique forum where the governments of 30 democracies work together to address the economic, social and environmental challenges of globalisation. The OECD is also at the forefront of efforts to understand and to help governments respond to new developments and concerns, such as corporate governance, the information economy and the challenges of an ageing population. The Organisation provides a setting where governments can compare policy experiences, seek answers to common problems, identify good practice and work to co-ordinate domestic and international policies.

The OECD member countries are: Australia, Austria, Belgium, Canada, the Czech Republic, Denmark, Finland, France, Germany, Greece, Hungary, Iceland, Ireland, Italy, Japan, Korea, Luxembourg, Mexico, the Netherlands, New Zealand, Norway, Poland, Portugal, the Slovak Republic, Spain, Sweden, Switzerland, Turkey, the United Kingdom and the United States. The Commission of the European Communities takes part in the work of the OECD.

OECD Publishing disseminates widely the results of the Organisation's statistics gathering and research on economic, social and environmental issues, as well as the conventions, guidelines and standards agreed by its members.

This work is published on the responsibility of the Secretary-General of the OECD. The opinions expressed and arguments employed herein do not necessarily reflect the official views of the Organisation or of the governments of its member countries.

FOREWORD

Environmental finance is one priority area of work on environment policies in Central and Eastern Europe, the Caucasus and Central Asia (EECCA). Financial resources are scarce and are spread too thinly; priorities and objectives generally are not clearly defined in environmental programmes; inter-agency cooperation, particularly between environment and economic and finance departments needs to be improved; decentralisation of responsibilities needs to be matched by ensuring access to the resources needed to implement the new mandates devolved to local and regional jurisdictions. More skills and incentives are needed at both national and local levels to mobilize additional financing for environmental purposes.

In OECD economies, the financial sector (which consists of banks, the corporate debt market, and the equity market) provides the bulk of the investment finance. During the last 10 years of transition to market economy, none of the EECCA countries have been able to develop their financial markets to the level that would provide access to long-term debt finance at an affordable cost.

Available experience and empirical evidence suggest that high interest rates are not the major factor limiting the access to debt finance for environmental investments. This report examines opportunities beyond the public sector for financing water and other environmental infrastructure. Specifically, opportunities for accessing savings through private financial and capital markets have been examined. The report identifies bottlenecks to the development of local financial markets for environment infrastructure, and discusses policy recommendations to tackle them.

The publication of this report is one of the activities within the OECD programme of work with non-member countries, in the context of the Task Force for the Implementation of Environmental Action Programme for

Central and Eastern Europe, the Caucasus and Central Asia (EAP Task Force), for which the OECD Environment Directorate serves as a Secretariat.

It is directly related to a series of projects on municipal finance in EECCA countries, which advise governments in the region on policies aiming at strengthening municipal finance and the financial sustainability of environmentally-related utilities.

The project was initiated by Grzegorz Peszko, former Head of the Finance Team, Non-Member Countries Division, Environment Directorate, OECD, who developed the concept note. George Peterson, from the Institute for Urban Economics in Washington DC, USA, was commissioned as lead author. Mr. Peterson also co-ordinated and ensured quality of the inputs of the four country experts from Kazakhstan, Russia, Ukraine, and China. The final version was prepared by Xavier Leflaive, Head of the Finance Team, Non-Member Countries Division, Environment Directorate, OECD. Alexander Martoussevitch, Environmental Finance expert in the Finance team, provided valuable contributions.

TABLE OF CONTENTS

Tables

Figures

Boxes

ACRONYMS

AMA	Anti-Monopoly Agency (Kazakhstan)
CDB	China Development Bank (China)
CSE	Communal Service Enterprise
DFID	Department for International Development
EBRD	European Bank for Reconstruction and Development
EJF	Economically Justified Tariff
GDP	Gross Domestic Product
GKO	Federal Government Bond (Russian Federation)
IBRD	International Bank for Reconstruction and Development
IFI	International Financing Institution
IMF	International Monetary Fund
JBIC	Japan Bank for International Cooperation
MDLF	Municipal Development Loan Fund (Ukraine)
MSW	Municipal Solid Waste
MUE	Municipal Unitary Enterprise (Russian Federation)
PFI	Private Finance Initiative
PPP	Public-Private Partnership
PSP	Private Sector Participation
RKS	Russian Utilities System (Russian Federation)
RMB	Chinese currency
SEPA	State Environment Protection Administration (Russian Federation)
SSMSC	Securities and Stock Market State Commission (Ukraine)
UAH	Ukrainian Currency
UEI	Urban Environmental Infrastructure
USAID	US Agency for International Development
VAT	Value-Added Tax
WSS	Water Supply and Sanitation

EXECUTIVE SUMMARY

There are good reasons to investigate the issue of the development of local financial and capital market to finance investment in environmental infrastructures in EECCA now:

- With only one exception, these countries have engaged in a systematic devolution of responsibilities for the construction and maintenance of urban environmental infrastructure to sub sovereign levels of government;

- There is a pressing need to accelerate investment in environmental infrastructure at the local level;

- Alternative sources of finance are not very promising in the near future: State financing for environmental infrastructure investment is declining, and it is unlikely that direct private investment (including investment from domestic and international utilities) will play a significant role on the foreseeable future.

Moreover, although some EECCA countries have experienced the negative consequences of mismanaged local debt in the early 1990s, the macro-economic and institutional contexts have changed dramatically in the recent years, providing new opportunities to examine more market-based approaches.

China is a relevant benchmark, as this transition economy has engaged in an alternative strategy: sub-national credit has grown rapidly as a source of urban infrastructure investment financing, replacing a portion of direct expenditures from national and sub-national budgets.

The main objective of this project is not so much to create local markets, but rather to assess how local governments' access to local markets could be strengthened in order to finance investment in environmental infrastructure, allowing municipalities and municipal service enterprises to tap private savings market.

The focus is on the definition and implementation of sound financial policies for the decentralisation of environmental infrastructure and services. A particular framework should be established for the development of local financial markets, which should be consistent with the overall framework for local finance. The role of the central authorities is key in defining and implementing this framework, but it should be supplemented by actions taken at the local level.

As part of the process of fiscal decentralization, the policy and institutional obstacles that prevent the financial sector from playing a greater role in financing environmental projects should be removed; incentives for such an involvement include the right for local authorities to incur debt, support to the development of carriers of long-term savings (insurance companies, banks), regulation of the portfolio of these institutions (and the share that they are allowed to invest in local jurisdictions), etc. Experience from other regions could be applied in EECCA countries to enable local capital and financial markets to play a greater role in financing environmentally-related infrastructure.

A particular framework…

Local capital and financial markets cannot develop without the appropriate legal framework. This framework should clearly state:

- Who can borrow: local authorities, utilities (note that for the same service, public authorities will generate municipal debt, while private operators generate corporate debt; how do these two categories cohere?), special asset companies?

- For what purpose; long-term debt should be made available for investment only (and not current account deficit);

- Subject to what limitations (annual amount of borrowing, stock of accumulated debt);

- Which debt instruments are allowed (commercial banks, bonds issuance, access to foreign currency debt?);

- What collateral can be pledged by the local borrowers: revenue streams (this has to be legally accepted), real property. In addition, procedures have to be defined for enforcing revenue pledges in the event of default.

This framework should be made compatible with the related system of regulations for banks, pension funds, and insurance companies. In particular, such regulations should state how much these institutions can invest in municipal debt, creating incentive (or disincentive) mechanisms for the market.

This legal framework has to be supplemented by mechanisms that reduce risk to lenders. Such mechanisms rely on:

- Strengthened operation and maintenance capacity at utility levels,

- Project preparation facilities to develop projects on a financially viable basis,

- Guarantees, reserve accounts (which may be partially funded by donors),

- Ring fencing revenue flows, to ensure pay back,

- Establishing municipal banks and municipal development funds,

- Pooling debt of smaller municipalities,

- Secondary markets (securizing local loans, re-selling municipal bonds).

Again, the role of central government is key, as the steps have to be identified and planned on a country basis, depending on the current state of the infrastructure and the financial sector, the need for investments, and the political attitude towards future local credit markets. The main dimensions of the part played by central governments, both as direct implication and as facilitation, include:

- Effectively control sub-national borrowing, to mitigate the risk of bankruptcy of local governments, and the macroeconomic consequences of the decisions made at the local level;
- Support long term savings, for long term credit; this involves support the development of pension funds, and the insurance industry;
- Encourage the establishment of rating agencies, for sub-sovereigns, in order to disseminate reliable information on the financial situation of the borrowers;
- Support competition between types of lending (banks and bonds);
- Support market creation for environmental services;
- Facilitate market access, via such means as risk sharing, credit enhancement, subsidies.

… consistent with the broader context of public finance…

Any strategy concerning the development of local capital and financial markets must be compatible with the existing system on which other sources of finance are based, in particular intergovernmental transfers and fiscal autonomy. The objective should be to diminish uncertainties about the resources available to sub sovereign governments, to generate stable streams of revenues for these jurisdictions, and to allow these governments to adapt their revenues to their needs and financing strategies. This would significantly strengthen the creditworthiness of local governments, be they borrowers or providers of guarantees to other borrowers.

Other features of the financial context relate to the way governments, including environmental administrations, mobilize public funds and related means of intervention to stimulate commercial banks' involvement in environmental finance.

Central budget funds can be mobilized to facilitate local governments' access to local financial markets to finance investment in environmental infrastructure. Even very scarce funds can be used creatively to mobilize additional commercial co-financing of environmental projects. For instance, if the lack of access by banks to medium and long term capital is the binding constraint to financing investments, public funds could be used to provide banks with medium/long-term liquidity (e.g. master loans, deposits), earmarked for environmental, commercially-viable projects. In addition to public funds, governments can also use an array of non-financial instruments to facilitate market-based financing of environmental investments, such as commercialization of environmental infrastructure and certain environmental services, information campaigns and reduction of political and regulatory risks associated with environmental investments.

In addition, environmental administrations should carefully review the way they use public money to finance environmental investments in order to phase out practices and financing instruments that discourage banks from financing environmental projects. Indeed, environmental administrations in EECCA have tended to be part of the problem rather than part of the solution to the banking crisis. Public funds have sometimes been used to finance projects that could have been commercially viable. When financing environmental investments from the budget or extra-budgetary funds, administration at the national or regional levels usually preferred to offer grants covering 100% of project costs or direct loans, rather than using banks as co-financiers or intermediaries. None of the public environmental funds in the region has been encouraged or required to co-finance projects with commercial banks (e.g. by matching grants) or to lend through them in order to increase the leverage effect of public money. Instead, when environmental authorities or even external donors develop new financial products for public environmental funds, they generally chose financing instruments which do not facilitate bank credit to environmental sector, such as direct lending to replace matching grants.

… and with actions taken at the local level

In addition, action taken by central governments on the reform of the WSS sector in EECCA should be implemented in parallel with actions taken at the local level. Here, the focus is on the overall scheme of decentralisation, and on the institutional capacity of local authorities.

Excessive fragmentation can generate sub-optimal provision of public goods. In particular in the water supply and sanitation sector, it can typically fail to exploit economies of scale. In OECD countries, frequent solutions to these problems include:

- amalgamation of local authorities. Mergers lead to fewer authorities of larger size; the central government often contributes financially to improve the attractiveness of amalgamation, as it may benefit from lower costs at a local level through the grant system;

- a "two-speed" system, where spending responsibilities are assigned in an asymmetric way to jurisdictions with a critical mass and/or sufficient (human, technical) capacity;

- *ad hoc* cooperation agreements among levels of government. One approach relies on a purchaser/provider split: the supply of the service is concentrated in some jurisdictions, which receive some compensation from other jurisdictions benefiting from the service. Another approach is based on joint provision of public services, through jurisdiction associations. Financial incentives may be set out by the central government, as an additional percent of the central governments grants. Many countries have experienced the latter option to provide public utilities, including water supply and waste water treatment.

The impact of the policies envisioned in this paper would be very limited if the local authorities do not develop the capacities to accompany them. In particular, this relates to:

- Budgetary decision making at the local level; to make the best use of available resources, and to enhance creditworthiness and the capacity to attract more finance: appropriate planning, realistic strategies, competent management of financial resources, including debt;

- Capacity building. Local managers are often given new responsibilities without receiving appropriate training and without corresponding increases in their administrative budgets. Processes for ensuring the prompt flow of resources from the centre to the periphery need to be streamlined, as severe bottlenecks have impeded the local use of allocated funds.

SYNTHÈSE

Il y a de bonnes raisons d'étudier maintenant la question du développement des marchés financiers et de capitaux locaux dans les pays d'Europe Orientale, du Caucase et d'Asie Centrale (EOCAC) et de leur contribution au financement de l'investissement dans les infrastructures environnementales :

- Dans tous ces pays, sauf un, la responsabilité de la construction et de l'entretien des infrastructures environnementales urbaines a été transférée aux collectivités locales ;
- Il est urgent d'accélérer l'investissement dans les infrastructures environnementales au niveau local ;
- Les autres sources de financement resteront modestes dans un avenir proche : les finances publiques que l'état central consacre au secteur de l'environnement sont en baisse, et il est peu probable que l'investissement privé (qu'il provienne d'opérateurs nationaux ou internationaux) joue un rôle majeur à court ou moyen terme.

De plus, même si, au début des années 1990, certains pays de la zone EOCAC ont souffert des conséquences d'une mauvaise gestion de la dette des collectivités locales, les contextes macroéconomiques et institutionnels ont connu des changements très significatifs depuis quelques années. Cela offre de nouvelles opportunités pour considérer des approches fondées sur les marchés.

La Chine constitue un point de comparaison pertinent, car ce pays en transition s'est engagé dans une autre voie de réforme : le crédit aux collectivités régionales et locales s'est développé rapidement pour financer l'investissement dans les infrastructures urbaines, se substituant en partie aux ressources provenant des budgets nationaux ou provinciaux.

Par ce document, l'objectif n'est pas tant de créer des marchés locaux, que de voir comment l'accès des collectivités locales aux marchés locaux pourrait être renforcé pour financer l'investissement dans les infrastructures environnementales, en permettant aux collectivités et aux opérateurs d'utiliser l'épargne privée.

Le document est centré sur la définition et la mise en œuvre de politiques financières adaptées à la décentralisation des infrastructures et services liés à l'environnement. Un cadre particulier doit être créé, propice au développement de marchés financiers locaux, et cohérent avec le contexte général des finances locales. L'état central a un rôle clé à jouer, dans la définition et la mise en œuvre de ce cadre, mais il doit être relayé par des actions au niveau local.

Dans le processus de décentralisation fiscale, il convient d'éliminer les obstacles politiques et institutionnels qui empêchent le secteur financier de jouer un rôle plus important dans le financement des projets environnementaux ; les facteurs qui favorisent une implication du secteur financier incluent la capacité des collectivités locales à s'endetter, l'appui au développement de porteurs d'épargne longue (compagnies d'assurance, banques), la régulation des portefeuilles d'actifs gérés par ces institutions (et la part qu'elles ont le droit d'investir auprès des collectivités locales), etc. L'expérience accumulée dans d'autres régions pourrait être utile aux pays de la zone EOCAC pour permettre aux marchés financiers et de capitaux locaux de jouer un rôle plus important dans le financement des infrastructures environnementales.

Un cadre particulier…

Les marchés financiers et de capitaux locaux ne peuvent pas se développer sans un cadre légal adéquat. Ce cadre doit clairement spécifier :

- Qui a le droit d'emprunter : les collectivités locales, les opérateurs de services publics locaux (on remarque que pour le même service une municipalité va générer de la dette publique, alors qu'un opérateur va générer une dette *corporate* ; comment s'articulent ces deux catégories ?), des sociétés de gestion d'actifs ?

- Pour quelle utilisation ; les financements longs ne doivent financer que des projets d'investissement (et non des déficits d'exploitation) ;

- Dans quelles limites (plafond d'endettement annuel, stock de dette accumulée) ;
- Quels instruments de financement sont autorisés (prêts bancaires, obligations, emprunts en devise ?) ;
- Quelle garantie peut être apportée par les emprunteurs locaux : des revenus réguliers (cela doit être confirmé par la loi), des actifs immobiliers ; des procédures doivent être définies pour appuyer les demandes du créditeur en cas de défaut de paiement.

Ce cadre doit être compatible avec le système de régulation des banques, des fonds de pension et des compagnies d'assurances. En particulier, il doit préciser quelle part de leurs actifs ces institutions peuvent investir dans la dette des collectivités locales, créant ainsi des incitations (ou des désincitations) pour le marché.

Ce cadre légal doit être complété par des mécanismes qui réduisent le risque pour le prêteur. Ces mécanismes reposent sur les éléments suivants :

- Renforcer la capacité de gestion et de maintenance des opérateurs de services publics locaux ;
- Concevoir des projets viables financièrement, avec le soutien de structures d'appui à la préparation de projets ;
- Mettre en place des garanties, ou des comptes de soutien (qui pourraient être en partie financés par l'aide internationale) ;
- Circonscrire des flux de recettes, pour garantir le remboursement ;
- Créer des banques et des fonds de développement municipaux ;
- Mettre en commun les dettes de petites municipalités ;
- Développer des marchés secondaires.

Rappelons que le rôle de l'état central est essentiel, car les mesures à mettre en œuvre doivent être identifiées et planifiées au niveau national, en tenant compte de l'état actuel des infrastructures et des marchés financiers, du besoin d'investissement, et du climat général envers les instruments financiers locaux. Le rôle de l'état, qu'il intervienne directement ou agisse en facilitateur, comprend les dimensions suivantes :

- Contrôler l'endettement des collectivités locales, pour prévenir le risque de faillite et pour maîtriser les conséquences macroéconomiques des décisions prises au niveau local ;

- Encourager l'épargne longue, pour les prêts à long terme ; cela passe par le développement des fonds de pension et du secteur de l'assurance ;

- Encourager la création d'agences de notation qui travaillent sur les collectivités locales, afin de diffuser une information fiable sur la situation financière des emprunteurs ;

- Veiller à la concurrence entre les modes de financements (prêts ou obligations) ;

- Soutenir la création de marchés de services environnementaux ;

- Faciliter l'accès des collectivités locales aux marchés financiers, en partageant les risques, bonifiant les taux, ou par des subventions.

… compatible avec le cadre plus large des finances publiques locales…

Une stratégie pour le développement de marchés financiers ou de capitaux locaux doit être compatible avec le système sur lequel reposent les autres sources de financement, en particulier les transferts budgétaires entre niveaux de gouvernement et l'autonomie fiscale des collectivités. L'objectif doit être de réduire les incertitudes qui existent quant aux revenus des administrations locales, de générer des flux financiers stables pour ces collectivités, et de leur permettre d'adapter leurs revenus à leurs besoins et à leurs stratégies de financement. Cela renforcerait sensiblement le crédit des administrations locales, qu'elles soient directement emprunteurs, ou cautions pour d'autres emprunteurs.

Une autre caractéristique du contexte financier doit être prise en compte : la manière dont le gouvernement (y compris les administrations en charge de l'environnement) mobilisent les finances publiques et autres moyens d'intervention pour inciter les banques à s'impliquer dans le financement de projets environnementaux.

Les ressources budgétaires du gouvernement central peuvent être utilisées pour faciliter l'accès des administrations locales aux marchés financiers locaux pour financer leurs investissements dans les infrastructures environnementales. Des fonds publics, mêmes limités, peuvent être utilisés de manière imaginative pour lever des cofinancements issus du secteur concurrentiel pour des projets environnementaux. Par exemple, si le principal facteur qui freine le financement de l'investissement est la difficulté qu'éprouvent les banques à accéder à l'épargne longue, les fonds publics peuvent être utilisés pour offrir aux banques des liquidités à moyen / long terme, dédiées au financement de projets environnementaux attrayants. En plus des fonds publics, les gouvernements ont également accès à une gamme d'instruments non financiers pour faciliter le financement par le marché de projets environnementaux : commercialisation d'infrastructures et de certains services environnementaux, campagnes d'information, et réduction des risques politiques et réglementaires associés aux investissements dans le secteur de l'environnement.

En même temps, les administrations en charge de l'environnement doivent être attentives à la manière dont elles utilisent l'argent public pour financer des investissements dans le secteur de l'environnement, afin d'éliminer les pratiques et les instruments qui découragent les banques. En effet, dans les pays de la zone EOCAC, les administrations en charge de l'environnement ont eu tendance à contribuer à la crise bancaire, plutôt qu'à la résoudre. Les fonds publics ont pu être utilisés pour financer des projets qui auraient intéressé des banquiers. Lorsqu'elles finançaient un projet par des ressources budgétaires ou extrabudgétaires, les administrations nationales et régionales préféraient proposer des financements (dons ou prêts) qui couvraient la totalité des coûts du projet, plutôt que d'utiliser les banques comme co-financeurs ou intermédiaires. Dans la région, aucun fond public pour l'environnement n'a été incité à, ou obligé de, utiliser des banques pour financer des projets, ou pour relayer des prêts, ce qui aurait accru l'effet de levier des finances publiques. Au contraire, lorsque les administrations en charge de l'environnement, ou même des donneurs, mettent au point de nouveaux produits financiers pour les fonds environnementaux publics, ils tendent à privilégier des instruments qui n'incitent pas les banques à investir dans le secteur de l'environnement.

… et avec les mesures prises au niveau local

Les actions des gouvernements centraux pour réformer le secteur de l'eau et de l'assainissement dans la zone EOCAC doivent être mises en oeuvre en même temps que les actions réalisées au niveau local. Ici, l'éclairage est mis sur le schéma général de décentralisation, et sur la capacité institutionnelle des collectivités locales.

Une fragmentation excessive peut dégrader la production d'un bien public. En particulier dans le secteur de l'eau et de l'assainissement, elle peut nuire à la réalisation d'économies d'échelle. Dans les pays de l'OCDE, les réponses les plus fréquemment apportées à ce problème sont les suivantes :

- Regroupement des collectivités locales. Les fusions conduisent à un plus petit nombre de collectivités, plus grandes ; le gouvernement central met souvent en place une incitation financière au regroupement, puisque que ces regroupements devraient lui faire économiser des dépenses au niveau local ;

- Un système à deux vitesses, selon lequel les responsabilités en matière de dépenses sont concédées de manière asymétrique aux collectivités en fonction de leur taille et / ou de leur savoir-faire (humain, technique) ;

- Des accords de coopération sur mesure entre niveaux administratifs. Une approche repose sur un partage client / fournisseur : l'offre de service est limitée à certaines collectivités, qui reçoivent une compensation de la part des autres collectivités qui bénéficient du service. Une autre approche consiste à produire conjointement un service public, dans le cadre d'associations de collectivités. Des incitations financières peuvent être proposées par le gouvernement central, en augmentant la part de subventions. Cette option a été retenue par un grand nombre de pays, pour les services publics locaux, y compris l'eau et l'assainissement.

Les impacts des mesures discutées dans ce rapport seront très limités si les collectivités locales ne renforcent pas leur capacité à les accompagner. En particulier, cela concerne :

- L'élaboration des choix budgétaires au niveau local ; cela passe par les outils suivants, pour faire le meilleur usage des ressources disponibles, améliorer la crédibilité des collectivités locales et leur capacité à attirer des ressources complémentaires : la planification, des stratégies réalistes, une bonne gestion des ressources financières (y compris de la dette) ;

- La compétence institutionnelle. Souvent, les cadres locaux se voient conférer de nouvelles responsabilités sans recevoir la formation nécessaire et sans voir leur budget augmenter de manière cohérente. Des procédures doivent être définies qui favorisent un transfert rapide de ressources du centre vers la périphérie, alors que des freins considérables ont ralenti l'usage local des fonds alloués.

PART I. LOCAL CREDIT MARKETS AND ENVIRONMENTAL INVESTMENT: LESSONS LEARNT FROM ECONOMIES IN TRANSITION

Introduction

In Almaty in 2000, Economic/Finance and Environment ministers of EECCA acknowledged that structural reform was needed to raise the financial resources necessary to modernise the water supply and sanitation (WSS) sector in the region. They identified an urgent need for a new institutional framework. This entailed devolving responsibility for water service provision from national to local level, and strengthening the related capacity of local authorities, in particular locally-elected governments, to assume their new responsibilities.

As owners of the communal service infrastructure, municipalities are responsible for its rehabilitation, modernisation, and development. But most municipalities in EECCA do not have sufficient funds to carry-out these responsibilities, because they are not financially autonomous or sustainable. Rather, the municipalities are still largely dependant on fiscal transfers from central or regional budgets. For that reason, they often have to coordinate their infrastructure development plans and capital expenditure budgets with national/regional plans and budgets. This makes the strategic planning and investments at local level dependant on the policies at the national/regional level, and generates a risk that local investment plans will not be implemented due to budgetary constraints.

In this context, local authorities can rely on a limited number of sources of finance:

- Tariff. Tariff levels must provide sufficient incentives for the efficient use of water and discourage excessive use. They must also enable the development of sustainable financing systems so that water services can be provided on a commercially viable basis (taking into account affordability considerations). The price people pay for water supply and sanitation services is a criterion that directly impacts on the creditworthiness of local authorities; indeed, financial institutions confirm that the general attitude of a municipality towards tariffs and their reform is the most important criterion to assess the reliability of the municipality to re-pay any debt that it incurs.

- Local taxes. Exploiting the local tax base may conflict with national objectives and raise serious distributive concerns. Generally, there is only limited scope for fiscal autonomy, and EECCA is no exception. Moreover, this issue relates to the wider agenda of fiscal reform, which is beyond the scope of this paper;

- Intergovernmental transfers. National public funding is expected to remain a major source of finance for the water and sanitation sector in most EECCA countries for the foreseeable future. This is even more so in the context of the MDGs which requires investment which cannot be financed exclusively by user charges or other sources of finance;

If investment levels are to accelerate, it will be critical to tap the private savings market to help in investment financing. There is increased recognition that developing and transition countries need to find ways of accessing local capital and financial markets in order to achieve their water and sanitation objectives (see, for instance, the Camdessus Report). These mechanisms are widely used in OECD countries, in contrast to the situation in EECCA countries and other transition economies.

Some of this financing will come in the form of direct private investment in municipal environmental facilities like water distribution systems or wastewater treatment plants. However, the recent record of private investment in the water supply and sanitation sector has been disappointing. The most important mechanism for accessing private savings is likely to be borrowing by public authorities, either directly from the capital market or through intermediary financing institutions like banks or special infrastructure funds.

As devolution is shifting the principal investment burden from the State budget to local budgets, the credit systems required to finance urban environmental investment therefore will be local credit markets, in which the borrowers are sub-national governmental units or municipal utilities. The task of a well-functioning local credit market is to access domestic (and, sometimes, international) savings on a sustainable basis, then lend these funds to creditworthy local institutions to invest in urban environmental infrastructure. Given that many urban environmental services, like wastewater treatment or water supply, are highly capital intensive and involve long-lived assets, the ability to generate longer-term credit is one requirement of a successful local credit market.

So the adequate question is how to create markets that generate finance of long-term credits, from the perspective of local authorities? And what part can be played by central states to support the development of such markets?

The question is all the more relevant that a renewed context has generated new opportunities to consider the development of local capital and financial markets in EECCA countries and other economies in transition.

A few years back, the mismanagement of debt by local authorities, and its consequences for the national economies in EECCA seemed to have disqualified the issue of sub sovereign debt. National *and* sub national debts have played a major role in the financial crisis in EECCA in the 1990s. As a consequence, central authorities in most EECCA countries have banned sub sovereign debt, or put heavy administrative burden on it, so as to discourage potential borrowers.

The slow recovery of the financial sector, impaired by modest bank restructuring, limited sophistication in local credit markets, and the lack of municipal credit infrastructure, has failed to provide new opportunities, until recently. The situation is even more acute in rural areas, plagued with the difficulty to raise users finance, with the financial/fiscal weakness of municipalities, and with relatively higher transaction costs.

In recent years, this ban on municipal debt seems to have been relaxed. Local credit markets were recently revitalised in Ukraine (in the case of Odessa). The situation of the financial sector has evolved, with the recent growth of the bank assets, the expansion of accumulators of long term savings (pension funds, insurance companies), and the increasing orientation of banks towards servicing business.

Borrowing by local governments, municipal utilities, or private operators of course, is not an end in itself. The IMF among other international organizations has repeatedly warned against excessive sub-national borrowing as a potential de-stabilizing influence on fiscal management.[1] At least three of the countries covered in this study experienced sub-national debt crises in the 1990s, resulting, *inter alia*, from excessive, unregulated local borrowing, frequently to cover current account deficits unrelated to capital spending. The debt crises serve as potent reminders that the purpose of a local credit system is to generate financing for capital investment that can prudently be repaid from recurring revenues. The creditworthiness of borrowers provides the basic underpinning of a sustainable credit market.

This paper addresses the strengthening of local credit markets to help in the financing of urban environmental infrastructure investment. It focuses on four countries - China, Kazakhstan, Russia, Ukraine - and complements the country papers that were prepared as part of the overall study.

The study is founded on the premise that increased use of market-oriented credit is both necessary and desirable in the financing of local environmental infrastructure. The four countries covered in this study have made varying degrees of progress in developing local credit markets, and have embraced quite different strategies for mobilizing funds in the future for urban environmental investment.

The first section of the paper, following this Introduction, summarizes current local credit market activity in each country and the policies that have been announced for developing future financing sources. Subsequent sections examine the key elements that are necessary for building a sustainable local credit market in the urban environmental sector, and assess how these issues are being addressed. The final section draws overall conclusions about the status of local credit market development in the four countries, and provides country-specific assessments about next steps regarding initiatives that could assist in strengthening local credit markets, taking into account the activity that donors and International Financing Institutions already have underway.

---

[1] For example, "Public Debt in Emerging Markets: Is It Too High?" Chapter 3 in *World Economic Outlook* (IMF: September 2003).

Local credit market development in countries that have recently devolved responsibilities for urban environmental infrastructure to local authorities, or are still deciding how to incorporate market orientation in their laws and institutions, is necessarily an iterative process. The legal and institutional framework for local borrowing needs to be clearly established. At the same time, practical experience has to be gained in the process of borrowing, credit assessment, and debt repayment. In fact, the attempt to put together bankable deals often reveals which elements of the legal framework need to be clarified or revised if credit financing is to be viable. Credit market development cannot be a strictly deductive exercise, where local borrowing does not commence until the full set of desirable institutional and fiscal relationships has been written into law. Accordingly, in this paper, we look at countries' credit market development from two perspectives: first, what has been done and what more can be done to promote lending to local government units for environmental infrastructure investment under the current legal and institutional framework; second, what are the priorities for legal, regulatory, and institutional reform if local credit market activity is to be expanded significantly on a sustainable basis?

This synthesis paper draws heavily throughout on the four country papers that were prepared as part of the overall effort. It also utilizes other sources of information to update recent developments. The country papers were prepared following a common set of guidelines and a common set of descriptive and analytical questions. This common approach has facilitated country comparisons. In many cases, however, desired data simply are not available. One of the fundamental lessons of this endeavor, in fact, is the need for more systematic monitoring and reporting of local credit market activity by national authorities, and the need for meaningful public disclosure about local government and municipal utility finances, the specific revenue sources that support local debt obligations, and the specific investment purposes that local borrowing is used to finance.

Local borrowing in support of urban environmental investment

The four countries in this study vary greatly in the status of existing urban environmental infrastructure (UEI) and in the priority they now assign to investment in these infrastructures, as well as the way they use credit to help finance local capital expenditures and the strategies they have announced for future UEI financing. This section provides an overview of country practices, before examining in greater detail some of the critical obstacles to local credit market development.

China

Starting in the mid-1990s, China substantially elevated the importance of UEI in its overall investment planning. It has assigned particular priority to construction of wastewater treatment plants to handle domestic discharge and to sanitary disposal of urban solid wastes. The Tenth Five Year Plan (2001-2005) set ambitious targets for wastewater treatment coverage. By 2005, cities with more than 500,000 population were to have wastewater treatment capacity able to handle 60% of their discharge, up from an urban average of 36.4% coverage at the beginning of the period.

The scale of investment implied by this target is even more impressive, taking into account the continuing high rates of urban growth that add to domestic discharge levels. It is estimated (see China Case Study) that in the next five years, under the 11th Five Year Plan, 2006-2010, some 170 billion RMB (or roughly USD 21 billion) will be required to finance investment in domestic wastewater treatment plants and solid waste sanitary disposal facilities alone.

Sub-national credit has grown rapidly as a source of urban infrastructure investment financing in China, displacing a portion of direct expenditures from national and sub-national budgets. These trends are summarized in Table 1. As can be seen, the two dominant sources of local credit for infrastructure financing have been bank loans and on-lending from the national government of funds raised from State Infrastructure Bonds. On-lending of the proceeds of State Infrastructure Bonds has been concentrated in China's laggard regions—Western and Central regions in the last five-year plan, the rustbelt Northeast in the upcoming five-year plan. Proceeds typically have been disbursed as a mix of grants and loans, and have been highly concentrated on urban environmental projects. Approximately 1,000 separate UEI projects, implemented at the local level, were financed between 2001 and 2004 through Infrastructure Bond financing passed through to sub-national government budgets. State bond issuance for this purpose totaled 150 billion RMB (USD18 billion) in 2001. However, the political nature of inter-governmental lending has led to a very spotty repayment record for the portion of Infrastructure Bond financing originally planned for debt repayment by local authorities.[2]

Bank loans are divided between longer-term financing provided by the China Development Bank, a policy bank, and shorter-term credits provided to local borrowers by commercial banks. Infrastructure loans from the China Development Bank range from 10 years to 20 years, and finance large investment projects. Commercial bank loans, which many mid-sized municipalities rely on for infrastructure financing, have three to five year maturities, and typically have to be rolled over to be viable sources of infrastructure finance. At present, all of the banks in China are state-owned. The credit instruments available to local authorities therefore have served as extensions of the State-controlled financial sector. Banks' lending patterns have been heavily influenced by State investment policy.

Table 1.China: urban environmental investment (UEI) and sources of finance

Item	1990	1995	2000
Urban Infrastructure Investment As % GDP	0.65%	1.4%	2.1%
Sources of Financing for Urban Infrastructure Investment (%)			
Bank loans to local authorities	NA.	14%	25%
State Infrastructure Bonds, Passed to Local Authorities	0	0	19%
Central and Local Government Regular Budgets	NA	62%	32%
UEI % of All Environmental Investment	33%		55%

Financing sources do not add to 100% because of excluded "other" sources.

Source: Constructed from China Case Study.

In his report to the recent 10th Peoples Congress (March 2005), Premier Wen Jiabao reiterated the priority that the government would give to

2 For a discussion of the political considerations leading to non-repayment of Infrastructure Bond "loans" in Sichuan Province, see OECD (2004a).

environmental improvements and urban environmental investment in the next five-year period. In an accompanying detailed presentation of financing plans, the Ministry of Finance indicated that it would reduce State Bond issuance as a source of local infrastructure financing, because of inefficiencies revealed in the use of proceeds transferred to the local level (China Ministry of Finance, 2005; also China Case Study).

The government has indicated that it is committed to developing a diversified set of market-oriented sources of credit and private investment financing for the urban environmental sector. The implications of this policy approach for tariffs, on the one hand, and possible expansion of the small-scale local government bond market, on the other, are examined in later sections. The entry of foreign banks into China, under the WTO agreement, promises to increase the scrutiny given by banks to the creditworthiness of borrowers, including municipal borrowers and municipal enterprises, which account for a large share of total borrowing. In anticipation of opening the financial sector to market competition, the government has relieved banks of a portion of their bad loans (mostly loans to state-owned enterprises), has reduced its policy guidance regarding sectors that commercial banks should finance through lending activity, and has stepped up pressure for market-oriented risk assessment in banks' lending decisions. Some commercial banks are now being prepared for partial privatization and listing on international stock exchanges.

In sum, sub-national credit figures significantly in China's announced plans for future urban environmental infrastructure financing. State policy banks will continue to play a major role in the financing of large-scale projects. Borrowing from commercial banks and the capital market will have a stronger market orientation.

Kazakhstan

At an opposite extreme of present experience from China lies Kazakhstan. Kazakhstan's urban environmental investment needs consist less of expansion of coverage rates than repair and replacement of aging infrastructure. According to a recent report by the United Nations Development Program (UNDP, 2004), over 70 percent of the country's water supply pipelines have exceeded their planned useful lives and approximately 30% fail to meet minimum sanitary requirements. Investment in UEI has been slow to respond to these needs, and remains at low levels. Local credit financing for urban environmental investment also has been sparse, consisting largely of international donor-financed loans that have been on-lent to the local level. Commercial banks routinely lend to municipal utilities in the water and wastewater sector, but much of this lending is used to finance short-term operating needs.

Two principal obstacles have been identified as hindering greater use of sub-national credit in general and for the urban environmental sector in particular (Kazakhstan Case Study; EBRD, 2004). First, Kazakhstan has an intergovernmental finance system that captures "excess" funds from surplus municipalities for re-distribution to other locations. Although based in principle on expenditure norms, this system is frequently adjusted and neither predictable nor transparent in its impact. The effect is to introduce a large element of uncertainty into the revenue side of municipal budgets, as well as to reduce incentives for local revenue collection, since local "surpluses" are captured by the national government for re-distribution and lower local "deficits" reduce local governments' eligibility to receive re-distributive transfers. Both the uncertainty of their revenue streams and the disincentives for own-source revenue collection weaken local governments' creditworthiness as borrowers.

Second, Kazakhstan lacks a stable, predictable and commercial tariff regime for local utilities. Formally, according to the current regulation in Kazakhstan, the tariff covers all operating costs and provides return on capital. Now, because of problems related to collection efficiency, actual consumption (*versus* norms), and methods of cost calculation, local environmental utilities are unable to recover full operating costs, much less capital costs, from user charges; cannot enter into longer-term agreements with municipal governments defining how future costs of service delivery and debt service will be shared between municipality and utility; and cannot identify for lenders the revenue streams that will be used to pay debt service. The inability to adjust tariffs autonomously at the local level, coupled with the unpredictability of municipalities' general revenues, has caused EBRD to cancel all three of its municipal-level environmental financing projects in Kazakhstan as financially unviable. Domestic banks, however, have been active lenders to water and wastewater utilities under arrangements whereby the general oblast government supplements tariff-based revenue flows.

The government does not appear to assign high priority to developing a "local government" credit market in the future. Its Program Statement, "Drinking Water" (see Kazakhstan Case Study) indicates that future investments in the water sector should be financed primarily from direct national and sub-national budget expenditures, and enterprises' own resources. Local government borrowing is expected to take place through intergovernmental arrangements. Central government controls on other types of local government borrowing are very stringent. Government policy does, however, appear to allow for growth in lending activity to local utilities.

Russia

Russia's financial sector has recovered fully from the 1998 financial crisis. Commercial bank liquidity has improved, and domestic bank financing has expanded rapidly. A well-functioning bond market has emerged, in which municipalities and regional authorities play a significant role. In 2003, sub-national governments accounted for 11% of outstanding bonds in the Russian market (Russia Case Study). The largest cities--Moscow and St. Petersburg--are regular issuers in the domestic bond market. A January 2005 bond issue by the City of Moscow raised the equivalent of USD170 million, for a seven-year bond, at an average yield of 7.3%, indicating the quality of access to the capital market that large, well-financed cities with transparent accounting enjoy (The Banker, 2005). Moscow's State Debt Committee has announced plans to lengthen bond maturities by issuing 15-year bonds in the fall of 2005. In all, some 30 oblasts have received authority from the Russian Ministry of Finance to issue bonds; approximately half currently have bonds outstanding. Outside of Moscow and St. Petersburg, few cities tap the bond market for significant financing.

Unfortunately, it is difficult to quantify how much credit financing is being generated to support local environmental infrastructure investment. The expenditure purposes for which bond proceeds will be used are not spelled out in bond prospectuses. The terms and financing objectives of bank loans are not a matter of public record. According to the Russia case study and other sources, however, UEI credit financing from bond issuance is meager. The bulk of bond financing has been used to re-finance outstanding debt. To the extent new investment is financed by municipal bonds, it appears to be concentrated on the urban transport and housing sectors.

Municipal utilities in Russia are active borrowers from commercial banks, but primarily for operational purposes or to finance operating deficits. The financial condition of local environmental utilities is weak. In the early 2000s, more than 60% of local environmental Municipal Unitary Enterprises (MUEs) operated in deficit conditions, a higher proportion than found in any other sector (Chernyavsky, 2003). The poor financial condition of utilities makes them credit risks for lending and has become a major obstacle to generalized development of a local credit market for environmental finance. At the root of this financial weakness is the inability to establish commercial tariff rates for water, wastewater, solid waste and district heating companies, compounded by interlocking debt obligations from utility non-payers to utilities and from utilities to their suppliers.

The financial weakness of municipal environmental utilities has forced participants in the local credit market to exercise ingenuity in structuring arrangements that can adequately secure local borrowing. A number of IFI loans for local water sector investment have established a de facto model for such lending. Loans either are made to the local municipality, which enters into its own contractual agreement with the water utility (Vodokanal) covering tariff rates and revenue payments the utility will make to the municipality, or loans are made to the utility with a municipal guarantee to cover revenue shortfalls. This model insulates the lender from direct involvement in tariff disputes. It also reduces the lender's exposure to a utility's general finances. Variants of the model have been used by banks to finance construction of wastewater treatment plants by special purpose companies as well as by private investors in environmental infrastructure (OECD, 2004b). IFIs have been able to use this structure of lending to support long-term loans, but domestic banks have limited themselves to short-term financing of capital investment.

The scheme developed by EBRD and widely applied in Russia addresses this gap between short-term domestic lending, and long-term international finance: EBRD issues bonds (recently) or promissory notes (before 2005) nominated in RUR, local banks buy the securities, EBRD on-lends the funds to local municipalities for UEI investments.

Given the growth of Russia's financial sector and the precedents for local lending, via both bond issues and bank loans, it would be reasonable to look to local credit market growth as a prime financing instrument to tackle Russia's large backlog of urban environmental investment needs. Government policy appears to be ambiguous regarding future credit market direction, however. The Government has announced its priority is to attract private investment financing into the local environmental sector (Russia Case Study). This approach is viewed partly as a financing solution and partly as a vehicle for achieving management reforms. It has the effect of transferring to private investors the task of obtaining credit financing. It remains to be seen to what extent private sector participation can diminish local public authorities' borrowing needs for UEI. Some of the initial applications of the private participation model involve the creation of joint ventures between a municipal utility and private sector partners, in which the partners jointly assume liability for borrowing.

Ukraine

Ukraine has developed a small market for local infrastructure credits, consisting of a blend of short-term bank loans, intermediate-term domestic bond financing, and long-term on-lending of IFI loans, especially for the local water supply sector. As elsewhere, the volume of long-term lending is limited by the lack of long-term deposits in the banking system. However, the proportion of bank loans made for one year or longer is steadily and rapidly rising. A special survey carried out as part of the Ukraine Case Study found that 20% of municipal environmental utilities in oblast capitals had used bank financing to finance capital investment, and that such loans often extended to three-year maturities. As the Case Study points out, some investment opportunities—especially in energy saving or repairs to reduce distribution losses—have high rates of return, which make it possible to obtain investment paybacks in short periods. Under these conditions, even relatively short-term borrowing can be a realistic component of investment financing.

Ukraine's biggest cities have been able to obtain somewhat longer-term financing. The Odessa Water Utility obtained a 5-year UAH 15 million loan in 2004 to finance infrastructure investment. The lending bank reported that the utility's special institutional arrangements made it a viable candidate for a longer-term loan (Genz, 2004). The utility has entered into a 49-year outsourcing agreement for utility management, involving a domestic firm that the bank respected. Odessa's mayor did not appoint the utility director, an unusual political distancing between municipality and water utility in Ukraine. The utility has put in place a tariff program that recovers operating costs as well as debt service and a return to capital. The Municipality of Kyiv issued a 5-year bond on the domestic market in 2004, following a large Eurobond issue in 2003.

Ukraine has specifically identified the sub-national credit market as an instrument it intends to develop to assist in UEI financing. In late 2003 an Inter-Agency Working Group was established, representing the Government as well as international donor agencies and international financing institutions, to provide guidance on development of a prudent local borrowing market that would not require sovereign guarantees. A draft National Program emphasized the role of local credit, both in financing environmental infrastructure investment and in enhancing the efficient use of energy and other resources (Ukraine Case Study). The World Bank has supported with the Government the creation of a Municipal Development Loan Fund that would provide commercial banks with access to long-term lines of credit, for on-lending at commercial rates to local authorities (municipalities or utilities) to finance infrastructure projects, with commercial banks performing credit analysis and assuming credit risk. The objective of this program is to introduce banks to municipal infrastructure finance as a regular line of business, and to gradually extend loan maturities. USAID is supporting a complementary program to further develop the local bond market as an instrument for environmental infrastructure finance.

Three key requirements

Institutional Clarity: Who Is the Borrower? Who Bears Contingent Liability?

In all four countries covered by this study, urban environmental services are provided primarily by municipal utilities. These are variously known as municipal unitary enterprises, vodokanals (in the case of water and wastewater utilities), communal services enterprises, or local state-owned enterprises. Investments in the urban environmental sector, however, as well as the borrowing to finance such investment, may be undertaken by the utilities themselves, by the general-purpose municipal or regional government, or (in the case of China) by a third type of local institution that owns the municipality's physical assets and has the sole authority to borrow for new infrastructure investment.

Financial relations among these institutions, and between them and national oversight institutions, typically are opaque. The legal framework does not fully spell out the obligations of different parties. There are inconsistencies in the various laws covering borrowing, asset ownership, and budgetary relations, as well as differences of opinion within the national legal professions as to the interpretation of the laws. Even when the law appears to be clear, actual practice may deviate from the law.

These conditions pose fundamental obstacles to credit market development. They raise both practical and legal questions as to whether the borrower has the power to generate revenue on its own sufficient to cover debt service, and, if not, which party, if any, bears contingent liability. The difficulty of identifying a clear chain of responsibility for debt service makes lenders less willing to lend for environmental investments.

Municipal Utilities

In the countries of the Former Soviet Union (Kazakhstan, Russia, and Ukraine), municipalities generally own the assets utilities operate, and they are in charge of the bulk of investment finance. However, utilities are allowed to write these assets on their balance sheet, and to borrow to finance capital investments (mostly capital repairs, or, under certain circumstances, new investments presented as capital repair). When they do so, they function under corporate laws, which impose much less stringent conditions on borrowing than do the laws governing municipal government borrowing. Municipal utilities, however, are not autonomous commercial entities. They are dependent upon external bodies for approval of their tariff rates. In Russia, the municipal duma and/or administration must approve municipal utility tariffs; in Kazakhstan, approval is required from the national Anti-Monopoly Agency. In China, municipal environmental utilities must receive tariff approval first from the municipal government, then from the next higher level of government. In the case of provincial capital cities, this means approval from the provincial government and eventually from the Provincial Peoples Congress. Political considerations can intervene at every stage of the rate-setting and approval process.

The uncertainty surrounding tariff revenue streams makes most municipal environmental utilities weak credits as standalone entities. There are some exceptions in Russia and Ukraine, where tariff decisions have been delegated to the local level, and where, in larger cities, the tariff system can be structured for commercial-industrial and residential users to generate a more reliable but politically acceptable income stream. In general, however, the weak financial condition of municipal environmental utilities raises the question, 'Who bears contingent liability for debt service in the event that the utilities cannot repay borrowing on their own?' Here, the laws typically are opaque. In all three countries where utilities are borrowers, municipalities in fact make large budgetary contributions to the operations of water and wastewater utilities, and utilities may use these contributions to repay debt. However, it usually is unclear as to whether, and to what extent, general-purpose governments bear will accept liability for honoring the debt service obligations of municipal utilities.

Municipal General Governments

Municipal governments in the Former Soviet Union also borrow and use the proceeds of borrowing to invest in environmental infrastructure systems. When they borrow, they are subject to specific restrictions imposed at the national level on municipal governments' debt. Regional governments also help finance local environmental investments, and can raise financing through debt. They are subject to similar borrowing restrictions. General-purpose governments' borrowing is typically "general obligation" borrowing—i.e., debt that is secured by the full faith and credit of the municipality, and all of its sources of revenue.

The inter-relation between municipality and municipal utility is subject to several ambiguities that can weaken the creditworthiness of both borrowers. One issue that commonly arises is 'Who owns the utility property that is financed by municipal borrowing? When important income-generating property is transferred without compensation to a utility, this may weaken a municipality's own finances, as the municipality remains responsible for the debt liability but has no corresponding asset on its balance sheet. Ongoing operating deficits on the part of the municipal utility add a further dimension of potential liability. If borrowing is used to expand municipal utility coverage, but operating income fails to cover operating expenses, system expansion only magnifies the operating losses that the municipality may have to cover through budgetary transfers. On the other hand, as in Russia, municipalities may be entitled to share (to an undefined extent) in the 'profits' of utility enterprises. Many of the financial relationships between general-purpose governments and municipal utilities have evolved over years of practical experience. These de facto relationships may seem adequately defined to the parties responsible for service delivery and annual budgeting. However, a well-functioning credit market requires more explicit commitments of future budgetary support and contingent liability.

Asset Ownership Companies

China employs a quite different institutional arrangement for asset ownership and borrowing for capital investment. Both municipal governments and municipal utilities are prohibited from borrowing on their own. Instead, a special type of local state-owned enterprise, known generically as Urban Development Investment Companies (UDICs), was created starting in the late 1990s at central government instruction. UDICs are owners and managers of all of the infrastructure assets of the municipality, and are responsible for obtaining financing for new infrastructure investments. They are the sole local institution empowered to borrow. They also can arrange financing for infrastructure investment through other means, by creating joint ventures with domestic or foreign private companies, or by selling or leasing existing assets and re-investing the proceeds in new asset formation.

As owners of the infrastructure assets, UDICs enter into financial agreements with municipal service suppliers, such as water and wastewater utilities. The separation of asset ownership and management from service supply emulates institutional arrangements introduced in other countries, like New Zealand, Australia, and the United Kingdom, and, in principle, is intended to obtain more efficient use of the capital embodied in public investment. Depending in part on the size of city government, a single UDIC may hold all local infrastructure assets, or UDICs may be organized by asset type. The Shanghai Water and Wastewater Asset Ownership and Operations Company, for example, specializes in owning, managing, investing in, and financing water and wastewater facilities.

As borrowers, UDICs are structured to be balance-sheet borrowers. They operate subject to (non-public) guidelines on liability/asset ratios, and in principle borrow for new financing against the value of the assets they already hold. This institutional arrangement, however, is subject to vast legal and practical ambiguities. First, the separation between "municipal government" and "municipal asset-owning enterprise" is largely a fiction. (see China Case Study) The municipal government through the Development and Reform Commission and the Construction Commission still decides on investment priorities, and the UDIC acts as its financing agent.

Second, the assets on UDIC balance sheets cannot in fact be attached or foreclosed upon by lenders. They are infrastructure facilities essential to municipal operations, and it is inconceivable in the Chinese system that a lender would seize them for non-payment of debt service. In reality, essentially all borrowing by UDICs is secured by a "comfort letter" from the municipal government, stating that the municipality will take the steps necessary to see that the UDIC can pay its debt service. A comfort letter of this kind is tantamount to an implicit general obligation guarantee, indicating that the municipality will transfer budgetary revenues or income-earning property to the UDIC if necessary to service debt obligations.

An implicit guarantee of this kind may suffice in a government-controlled credit market, in which state-owned banks lend to municipal authorities, and UDICs occasionally issue bonds, based on generalized faith that the intergovernmental system will not let local borrowers fail or, if in the case of bank lending municipal authorities actually do default (as has occurred with some frequency), the intergovernmental system will bail out the banks. However, as China moves toward market-based lending, through quasi-privatized banks, this kind of opaqueness regarding institutional relationships will become a more severe hindrance to local credit market development.

What Is at Stake: the Scale of Potential Contingent Liabilities

The need for clear identification of borrower, and clear identification of the nature and bearer of contingent liabilities, may seem an abstract issue. However, the amounts at stake are large, and a clear pinpointing of debt service exposure is important to credit market development.

The World Bank's Atyrau Pilot Water Supply and Sanitation Project in Kazakhstan illustrates the magnitude of potential municipal liability (World Bank, March 2005). The project financed rehabilitation and replacement of water mains and sewer pipelines. The loan was to be repaid by the Vodokanal from tariffs that would be adjusted to recover operating costs and debt service costs. However, as the evaluation report states, "the lack of management and financial autonomy on the part of the vodokanal" made it impossible to implement the planned cost recovery. Tariff decisions were "highly political." The national Anti-Monopoly Agency, in fact, did not approve any tariff adjustments over the lifetime of the project (2000-2004), necessitating large transfers from the Atyrau oblast to cover operating expenses (See Table 2). Debt service on the USD12.0 million loan did not become effective until February 2005. These costs will have to be absorbed by the oblast, as well. The experience of the Atyrau project actually is more favorable than most similar projects, in the sense that a specific level of government, in this case the regional oblast, stepped forward to cover the operating shortfall. More typical of on-lending experience for environmental projects, as the World Bank evaluation report points out, have been unresolved disputes between municipal utility, municipality, regional government, national government and regulatory agency, about who should absorb the utilities' debt service costs and operating deficits. International financing institutions have the advantage of a fallback sovereign guarantee to protect them from the financial repercussions of these disputes. Domestic and private-sector lenders do not have such protection.

Table 2. Finances of the Atyrau water treatment and supply administration

Year	Operating Income	Operating Costs	Operating Deficit	Transfer from Atyrau Oblast	Surplus Available for Investment and Debt Service(a)
2002	NA	NA	NA	10.5	Positive
2003	2.1	5.0	2.9	9.9	7.0
2004	2.1	6.1	4.0	4.3	0.3

(a) debt service under loan commences in February 2005.

Source: World Bank (2005).

The ambiguities of implicit guarantees and contingent liabilities can be addressed in either or both of two ways. One option involves preparing a mutually consistent set of laws that more clearly defines the financial and legal interrelationships between institutions, and either expressly identifies or prohibits what are now implicit liabilities subject to different interpretations. Russia through a series of laws has moved in this direction, as has Ukraine, which for the past two years has been drafting and exposing for comment a broad legal framework that would establish clearer rules for borrowing and institutional relationships. Meanwhile, in the absence of a revamped comprehensive framework, a practical option is to incorporate in individual loan contracts or bond covenants explicit statements regarding the income streams, collateral, and guarantees that protect a credit, while also making explicit that no other back-up guarantees of any kind, not expressly identified, are available to the lender. The countries of the Former Soviet Union included in this study already have made clear that there are no implicit guarantees on the part of national government. Parallel clarity regarding implicit guarantees from municipalities and other levels of government is conspicuously lacking.

Revenue streams and collateral

Underlying a successful local credit market is the creditworthiness of borrowers. Creditworthiness, in turn, depends upon access to adequate and predictable revenue sources that can be used to cover debt service, and the availability of collateral or other types of guarantees to protect the lender in the event of revenue shortfalls.

In building a local credit market for environmental infrastructure investment, the initial foundation block is the revenue stream that a municipal utility generates from user charges or tariffs. It is well recognized that, with a few conspicuous exceptions, the revenue streams of municipal environmental utilities currently are insufficient to support intermediate- or longer-term loans on their own. Local credit market development for the urban environmental sector therefore requires a twofold strategy: strengthening tariff flows and making the improved revenue streams available as pledged security for borrowing, while also identifying ways within the current legal and regulatory structure to support borrowing by supplementing tariff revenues with specified budgetary transfers or back-up collateral that reduces lender risk. Some progress is being made on both fronts.

Strengthening Revenue Streams as Debt Service Support

In a revenue bond model of credit financing, the sole source of debt service support is a project's or institution's revenue stream from operations. At an early stage of credit market development, it may be unrealistic to rely solely on pledged revenue streams as support for debt service. However, the revenue stream remains a basic building block of debt repayment capacity.

The ability to convert a municipal utility's future revenue stream into up-front borrowing for capital investment may be broken down to three essential elements. Each of these is the subject of reform debate in the countries covered by this study.

Definition of Costs to be Included in Tariff Rate

All four countries have inherited an historical legacy, in which debt service and capital costs were not recognized as costs to be recovered through service charges for water supply, wastewater discharge and treatment, or sanitary disposal of solid wastes. A first step toward commercialization and revenue-based borrowing involves formal recognition of these costs in tariff-setting formulas.

Ukraine represents an example of tariff policy that has developed in a way that can potentially support revenue-based debt financing. National rules for water and wastewater tariffs allow utilities to recover all justifiable costs, expressly including debt service costs, which are identified as the costs of repaying borrowing from bank loans, issuance of bonds, and financial leasing (Ukraine Case Study). Based on the terms of agreement between lender and borrower, debt service costs can be specifically incorporated into the cost basis for tariffs. The tariff-setting rules also allow for including costs of capital replacement and system expansion in the rate base. Responsibility for reviewing and approving tariff schedules rests with the local municipality. Therefore, a reform-minded municipality and utility can legally establish tariffs that cover total costs, including debt service at a designated rate.

This procedure provides a more stable revenue stream to support debt service, at least in situations where household income levels and the industrial-commercial mix make it socially feasible to charge cost-recovery tariffs. A 2004 assessment prepared by USAID of prospects in Ukraine for municipal utilities' access to credit markets concluded:

Overall, the environment for increased penetration by CSEs (communal service enterprises) into credit markets is considered favorable, since the regulatory basis for approving cost-recovery tariffs is sufficient, and local government owners of CSEs have the power to approve such tariffs and enforce payment collection, the two most important factors contributing to the creditworthiness of potential CSE borrowers (cited in Genz, 2004).

Tariff procedures in Russia[3] illustrate the difficulties of converting municipal utilities' revenue streams into reliable sources of credit market support for debt incurred to finance system-wide improvements[4]:

- There is almost no individual metering of consumption; instead, consumption is estimated based on "norms."
- According to the recommended methodology, costs for tariff recovery are supposed to be based on norms for utility expenses as well as norms for user consumption.

[3] It should be noted that a framework Law on Tariffs has been introduced in December 2004, which anticipates substantial improvements and addresses some of the problems mentioned in this paper.

[4] See the Russian Case Study

- In practice, tariffs are usually based on actual costs, with lagged adjustments to changes in input prices like electricity, many of which are subject to state pricing, plus a percentage markup for "profit."

- Investment in system replacement and expansion is supposed to be financed from "profit" so identified, which is typically insufficient to cover true capital costs, even when the other elements of the tariff formula are priced realistically.

- Debt service is not specifically recognized as a cost to be recovered through tariffs.

- There is no regularly prescribed review of tariff rates. Typically, tariff rates stay in effect for undefined periods, and fall well behind levels required for cost recovery.

As in Ukraine, the process of municipal utilities' tariff approval in Russia has been decentralized to the local level.[5] Local authorities are not obligated to follow the recommended tariff methodology. Under the Law of Local Autonomy, municipal dumas must approve tariff structures. On the one hand, this delegation allows reform-minded governments the flexibility to introduce greater commercial orientation into their environmental utility charges. On the other, it exposes intermediate- or longer-term lenders to the risk that future political authorities will alter the tariff structure, even in these cities. Because there is no independent regulatory body, and no required methodology for setting tariff rates, the entire revenue stream becomes uncertain.

China has adopted an interesting third approach to tariff setting. Joint proclamations in 2000 and 2002 by several state ministries (including the ministries of finance, environment, construction and the State Development and Reform Commission) established the principle of full cost recovery for certain elements of environmental services' infrastructure networks. All cities were instructed to move toward full-cost pricing of water treatment

[5] In both Russia and Ukraine, municipal utility tariffs are regulated at the local level. Tariff regulation for privately owned utilities in the same sectors is carried out at higher levels of government.

plants, drinking water supply, and sanitary solid waste disposal. Cities that already charged fees for these services were supposed to adopt a system of full cost recovery, including recovery of debt service costs and a return on equity, by 2005-2006. The pricing guidance forms part of an explicit strategy to attract more market-based capital into the environmental sector, by identifying segments of infrastructure systems that can appropriately be priced so as to generate income streams that can support market-rate borrowing or private equity investment. The guidance for wastewater systems, for example, applies only to wastewater treatment plants, where new investment is being sought, not to network wide costs of collection and transmission.

Political realities have dictated that, even in China, local implementation of full-cost tariffs lags well behind national policy schedules. In fact, China's central authorities seemingly countermanded the order to move toward full cost recovery pricing when, in 2004, it ordered municipalities to freeze service charges as part of an effort to control incipient inflation.

Pledging Revenue Streams in Support of Debt Service

The legal ability to pledge future revenue streams in support of debt service is central to the revenue financing approach. In the absence of specific legislation stating that revenue streams can be offered as collateral for debt, the legal status of such pledges remains in doubt. Legal authorities often take the position that, unless modified, current laws permit only existing assets to be offered as loan collateral, not future revenues. Indeed, Russian prudential standards set by the Central bank rule that revenue streams should not be considered as appropriate collateral for bank loans. There are examples in Ukraine (Ukraine Case Study) of lenders accepting revenue pledges from municipal utilities as collateral for one-year loans, but no examples of longer-term pledges being acceptable as collateral to domestic lenders. International agencies working to develop the local credit market in Ukraine have made the express ability to pledge future revenues as debt security a priority for inclusion in new debt framework legislation.

Explicit Blending of Budgetary Support and Tariffs

Countries in all parts of the world blend general budgetary support with tariffs to produce combined revenue streams that can support market-based borrowing. Blending of this kind is most appropriate for environmental services, like waste collection and treatment that have externalities that benefit the population at large. In some models, the blending of budgetary support occurs at the lending stage. State Environmental Revolving Funds in the United States, for example, blend market-rate borrowing through bond issues with budgetary contributions from state governments to lower the interest costs of on-lending to local governments to finance selected environmental investments. Some Environmental Funds operate in a similar manner.

Alternatively, budgetary contributions can be blended with tariff revenue streams at the loan repayment stage. All of the countries in this study make large contributions to environmental utilities from municipal or oblast (provincial) governments. These contributions, however, are made on a voluntary, ad hoc basis, in part adjusted to the financial condition and priorities of the general-purpose government. In this form they cannot serve as adequate security for loan repayment in a successful local credit market. The commitment to provide supplementary budget support to the municipal utility must be formalized in a legal contract, with provisions that guarantee that the combined income stream will be sufficient to repay debt service with an adequate cushion of safety now and in the future. The legal system must recognize as binding the commitments that a municipality makes about its future behavior. Laws must allow the blended revenue stream to be pledged as debt collateral. Practical experience must be accumulated in actually combining revenue streams, as promised, and using them to service debt.

Physical Collateral

The first line of defense for a lender to the sub-national sector is to secure marketable collateral for its loan. At the present stage of market development, according to the country case studies, lenders prefer real property as collateral; EBRD is a clear exception, as it avoids accepting fixed assets owned by a municipality as collateral for loans to that municipality. It is typical for bank lenders to require collateral appraised at anywhere from two to three, and occasionally as much as five, times the value of a loan. The requirement that physical collateral support loans can slow growth of the credit market, as municipal borrowers may exhaust suitable collateral or be reluctant to limit their ability to sell property by pledging it as loan collateral.

However, as long as real property collateral reduces lenders' perceived risk, it can be used as back-up security to introduce new forms of primary loan repayment that do not yet have a track record of reliability, such as commercial-rate tariff revenue streams or blended revenue streams of the kind described above.

One practical impediment to development of a local environmental credit market has been the difficulty of identifying appropriate collateral to secure loans for investment in the water, wastewater, or solid waste sectors.[6] Infrastructure elements are part of an interconnected network of vital service provision. In most countries, the law specifically prohibits pledging property essential to public service provision as loan collateral. Even where the law is ambiguous, it is politically and practically impossible for a lender to break up an infrastructure network by foreclosing on part of that network, and either selling the capital item or operating it as a receiver in possession.

Borrowers and lenders have found ways around this limitation to finance specific investment opportunities, where the capital element in question can be functionally and economically separated from the network. In Russia, for example, a local vodokanal may form a special purpose company with a joint venture partner, typically a commercial bank, to carry out a specific investment project, such as a wastewater treatment plant, or a water purification plant. The newly formed company then receives credits from the sponsoring bank to help finance construction. The physical infrastructure serves as collateral for the loan, and the bank's participation as equity partner makes it easier for it to foreclose on the collateral should that be necessary.

This approach to physical collateral typically is combined with a loan structure that relies on a tariff revenue stream as the primary source of debt servicing, but in a manner that insulates the lender from direct exposure to tariff uncertainties. In effect, a municipality or other entity promises to internalize the blending of utility revenues and budgetary contributions that is

[6] The importance of physical collateral as security also has been an impediment to early development of the bond market. In many countries, it is legally undefined how numerous different bondholders could foreclose on physical collateral backing a municipal or utility bond. This is one reason among many for establishing the practice of intervening trusteeships, which can act on behalf of bondholders as a group in the event of default.

necessary to cover debt service. Physical collateral provides additional protection. When this model was applied to the city of Ekaterinburg in Russia it had the following features[7]:

- The municipal unitary enterprise, Vodokanal, joined with the Ecological Foundation, "Water Eurasia," and the commercial bank, "Interregional Investment Bank," to form a Special Purpose Company to build a wastewater treatment plant in a new area of city expansion.

- The Bank provides investment credits to the SPC.

- The SPC and Vodocanal enter into a tariff agreement, according to which all expenses of the project are incorporated into the tariff rate.

- Vodokanal transfers the corresponding revenue collection to the SPC to cover debt service, other costs of the SPC, and a return on equity investment.

- The SPC in turn services the debt to the Bank.

- In the case of default, the Bank has the contractual right to seize the assets of the SPC. In this case the assets include expensive foreign technological equipment with a ready market value.

This model illustrates a basic approach repeated with variants throughout the region. A Special Purpose Company is formed to invest in a separable piece of capital. An agreement is struck with the municipal environmental enterprise to recover the cost of capital and debt service through tariffs. The lender protects against the uncertainty of the tariff revenue stream by lending for a relatively short period, to finance construction, and by taking the capital investment as collateral. Special purpose joint ventures of this kind combine equity investment by private investors with market-rate borrowing. Arrangements of this type are clearly makeshift adjustments to a poorly defined institutional and legal framework for securing debt. Nonetheless, they build practical experience with credit financing and can lay the groundwork for future market development.

---

7 Source: Russia Case Study; follow-up communication with author.

Risk Mitigation

Other strategies to reduce lender risk are employed. Throughout Central and Eastern Europe, in the early stages of local credit market development, one of the most common types of loan collateral has been municipal accounts held and managed by the lending bank. The fact that the lending bank manages the municipality's accounts, or the accounts of a municipal utility, makes it much simpler for the bank to ensure that debt service obligations are treated as a priority. The acceptability of this form of collateral implies that when—as in Ukraine, and, some years ago, in Hungary—the government changes treasury rules, to require that local governments maintain all of their accounts in the state treasury system, rather than with private banks, there is an initial adverse impact of banks' willingness to lend.

Attempts to introduce more 'modern' forms of risk mitigation into the local water and sanitation sector have met with mixed results, at best. A World Bank assessment (Baietti and Raymond, 2005) concludes that "Experiences in the use of risk mitigation instruments in water supply and sanitation have not been at all encouraging." Less than 1% of the value of all guarantees extended by International Financing Institutions in 2001 was targeted to the water and sanitation sector. This pattern reflects the fact that the obstacles to private sector investment in, and private sector lending to, the water and sanitation sector are deep-seated ones not easily remedied through cost-efficient guarantees. The political and social pressures resisting commercial tariff rates, the lack of independent or well-defined regulatory processes, the long payback periods for environmental infrastructure investment (implying that guarantees must be extended many years into the future), and the lack of legally binding instruments for pledging revenue streams or identifying contingent liability all constitute significant risks. Until political and institutional issues are resolved, it is difficult to introduce formal risk-mitigation instruments that can focus on the remaining obstacles, such as protecting out-year payments for an otherwise well-structured loan.

The experience with international donors' risk mitigation instruments suggests that primary emphasis in building local credit markets should be placed on the policy and legal reforms necessary to reduce underlying risk. Once true risk has been lowered, the role of risk mitigation instruments becomes clearer. They are most effectively used to demonstrate to the market that true risk is lower than commonly perceived, and to accelerate lenders' willingness to lend under new arrangements.

National Controls on Local Borrowing

Three of the countries in this study experienced sub-national debt crises during the 1990s—the exception being Kazakhstan, which has always operated a much more centralized fiscal and financial system. These crises exposed the weakness of unregulated local debt markets. Much of the borrowing that occurred at that time, especially through bond issues, and especially in Russia and Ukraine, was used to finance operating deficits, without reasonable prospect for debt repayment out of future municipal savings. As the Ukraine Case Study points out, bond issues were favored as debt instruments precisely "due to the lack of defined legal provisions." In China, borrowing often financed extremely ambitious local capital investment plans that exceeded municipalities' ability or willingness to pay. A wave of defaults followed in Russia and Ukraine, and de facto defaults on bank loans in China. The consequences extended beyond sub-national government finances, as they raised fundamental questions about the contingent liabilities of national governments that either authorized or permitted sub-national government borrowing.

National authorities responded to these events by imposing strict controls on sub-national borrowing, while attempting to construct legal and institutional frameworks that would assure that local debt was used for beneficial purposes and was within localities' capacity to finance. National oversight of the local credit market has involved dual objectives, not always acknowledged, and sometimes in conflict with each other: (i) the desire of national authorities to prevent excessive local borrowing and insulate national-level finances from local debt problems, and (ii) the desire to build a responsible local credit market, in which local borrowing has an important role to play in prudent financing of environmental and other types of local investment. The first objective gives priority to national *controls* over local borrowing. The second objective gives equal priority to *building* a local credit market.

The current set of national controls contains a mix of provisions designed to serve one or the other of these twin objectives of *control* and *market-building.* On balance, however, they are weighted toward control—often to an extent that discourages responsible growth of the sub-national credit market. There has been some movement away from a strict control orientation recently, as the SNG debt crises recede in memory, and as local governments and municipal utilities build a more stable track record of loan repayments. Still, as summarized below, the combination of debt limit rules and procedural requirements for local borrowing approval remain an impediment to responsible market expansion. In contrast, the framework elements that would encourage prudent development of the local credit market have been slow to be put in place.

Controls on Municipal Debt

The debt controls described below apply to municipalities' own debt. In Kazakhstan, Russia, and Ukraine municipal utility debt is treated separately, under the body of corporate law, and is subject to much less stringent controls. In the case of municipal utility debt, lenders are allowed to make their own market-based decisions as to whether it is prudent to lend. As discussed earlier, the local state-owned asset companies in China (UDICs) are in effect proxies for the municipal government. The municipal controls described for China are those that apply to UDICs, as the only institution legally permitted to borrow.

Long-Term Borrowing for Capital Investment Only

All four countries now apply the "golden rule" of capital financing, by requiring that long-term borrowing (debt of more than one year) be used exclusively to finance capital expenditures. The precise instruments used to achieve this purpose vary slightly. The Russia Case Study suggests that the rules in effect in Russia—that operating costs be financed entirely from regular budget revenues, not borrowing—have not been entirely effective in eliminating debt financing of operations, including debt that is rolled over from year to year. Nonetheless, sub-national governments' long-term borrowing is now much better matched with capital investment. This is an essential building block both of the sub-national credit market.

No Implied National Guarantees

Russia, Ukraine and Kazakhstan now clearly state, as is true in most developed countries with active sub-national credit markets, that there is no implicit guarantee by national government of sub-national debt. On occasion, national authorities may choose to provide explicit guarantees for sub-national borrowing, but, in the absence of explicit bond or loan covenants to this effect, the national government bears *no* liability for repayment of sub-national debt obligations. This express statement of law insulates central fiscal authorities from irresponsible local debt management. It also is a building block for a responsible sub-national government credit market, as it requires both borrower and lender to make realistic assessments of the borrower's capacity to repay loans rather than speculate about the probability of bail-out by central government.

China's approach to implicit guarantees reveals a sub-national credit market at the incipient stage of distinguishing itself from the general government credit market. In truth, all sub-national borrowing in China *does* operate on the basis of implicit guarantees. Banks, capital market lenders, credit rating companies and others do not have access to the information necessary to make true credit judgments about the capacity of UDICs or municipalities to repay loans on their own. In interviews, even the most sophisticated investors, like China's largest insurance companies, stated that they would purchase Shanghai UDIC bonds, if and when issued, on the basis that the government would never allow a publicly marketed bond from Shanghai to fail. In provincial cities, commercial banks reported the same thing—the "comfort letters" provided by the municipality were the true security behind UDIC borrowing. The banks were confident that municipalities in the end would see that loans were repaid, or, at worst, higher level governments would intervene either to see that the loans were paid or to relieve the banks of bad loans made to municipalities under government priority investment programs. "Implicit guarantees"—i.e., faith that the government will ensure that the loan obligations of its agents are honored--underlie the Chinese financial system. The system has resulted in high levels of non-performing loans that have become the government's responsibility to handle. This system is now being transformed into one where credit risks are spelled out much more clearly, and where government guarantees for some types of lending are no longer implied. These changes will reach the sub-national government sector in the near future, but not in the first wave of banking sector reform.

Debt and Borrowing Limits

Table 3 summarizes the debt and borrowing limits in effect in each country. The table reveals in more detail the different strategies that countries have adopted toward control of the sub-national credit market. Ukraine and Russia have tried to move toward a moderate number of rule-based limitations on borrowing and debt, thereby accepting in principle the role of independent local credit markets. Kazakhstan has created a maze of severe limitations on local debt, as well as case-by-case compliance audits by central authorities. These rules are consistent with an approach that views local governments primarily as part of a single intergovernmental state, not participants in an independent local credit market. China has essentially no rules—or at least none that are disclosed publicly. Local governments and the banking sector as currently constituted are both extensions of the state. Lending is a matter of political priority-setting and negotiation rather than rules-based limitations.

Table 3. Borrowing and debt limits

Country	Limit on Debt Service Ratio	Limit on New Borrowing (Annual)	Limit on Stock Of Debt	Other Limits
China	None	None	None	Only UDICs can borrow
Kazakhstan	10% of Total Local Revenue	10% of Total Local Revenue	25% of Total Local Revenue	Municipalities cannot borrow from banks, only from republic budget and bonds (Almaty and Astana)
Russia	15% of Total Local Expenditure	None	None	Restrictions on Debt Maturities; Limit on Local Budget Deficit (10% of Own-Source Revenues)
Ukraine	10% of General Fund Expenditure in Any Year with Debt Service	None	None	

Source: Country Case Studies.

Restrictions on Bond Issuance

China, Russia and Ukraine have additional restrictions on local bond issuance. Bonds have been singled out for further controls, in part because of the past history of abuse in bond issuance and the financial crises that erupted as a result, and in part because national regulatory authorities have less control over the buyers of bonds than they do over the banks that extend municipal loans, and therefore cannot introduce prudential standards on the suppliers of credit. This is particularly true because bonds sometimes are marketed on a "communal" basis to individual citizens, who are less equipped to assess risk. Many of the controls on bond issuance are procedural controls, which do not limit total borrowing, but which add significant amounts of time and cost to preparation of a debt issue.[8]

Table 4 summarizes selected additional controls on bond issues in each country. This is a snapshot of a frequently changing regulatory environment. For example, at the time the Kazakhstan Case Study was prepared a draft law was pending which would prohibit local bond issuance completely.

Measures to Encourage Local Credit Market Development

In contrast to the swift adoption of local debt limits and other controls, the national governments in this study have been slow to mandate disclosure standards, reporting procedures, and other measures that would help build a responsible local credit market. This situation is perplexing, given that, next to overall financial and economic strength, financial transparency is the primary distinguishing characteristic of responsible and active participants in the sub-national credit market. The region has numerous examples of municipalities and municipal utilities with high standards of disclosure—including websites that provide public access to full, up-to-date financial

[8] There often is a difference of opinion within legal and financial circles as to whether a requirement for national certification of local bond issues involves only verification that proper procedures were followed in preparing a bond issue, and the appropriate debt limits were adhered to, or whether national "approval" of the bond issue also is involved. This question has been the subject of extended debate within Ukraine, for example, with different opinions being voiced both by local experts and international advisors. The prevailing opinion now is that procedural verification, not approval, is required.

statements, balance sheets, and debt records. These are very much the exception to common practice, however.

Table 4.Selected national controls on local bond issuance

China	All bond issues must be approved by the State Development and Reform Commission on a case-by-case basis. Numerous applications have been rejected or left pending for more than a year on policy grounds. All bond issues must be approved by the Peoples Bank of China, which also fixes the interest rate. Individual bonds must be approved for purchase by the Insurance Regulatory Commission before insurance companies can purchase them. Other regulatory approval is required on a case-by-case basis for pension fund purchases. No municipal or UDIC bonds have been approved for purchase. Credit rating required.
Kazakhstan	Only oblasts and oblast level municipalities (Almaty and Astana) are authorized to issue bonds. Local bonds must be approved by the Ministry of Finance and identified in the Republic budget. The Ministry Finance must approve the purpose of borrowing and the interest rate. Pension funds are restricted to holding no more than 5% of their assets in sub-national bonds Credit rating required
Russia	Credit rating required Registration required with national authorities
Ukraine	Procedural certification by Ministry of Finance Registration with national authorities (20 working days for Ministry of Finance; 30 calendar days for Securities Commission Credit rating required Up to 10% of State Pension Fund assets can be invested in municipal bonds Up to 20% of non-state pension funds can be invested in municipal bonds

Source: Country Case Studies.

A checklist of disclosure standards illustrates the shortfall in performance:

- None of the four countries requires effective public disclosure of municipal financial statements, or the financial statements of municipal utilities.
- In China, even credit rating agencies do not have access to bond issuers' financial statements or balance sheets.

- In Russia, China, and Ukraine, bond issuers are not required to identify the specific investment purposes for which bond proceeds will be used.
- In Russia, municipalities must maintain a Debt Book listing municipal debts, but there is no requirement that this information be publicly disclosed.
- National registries of collateral—necessary to ensure that local borrowers do not offer the same collateral to different lenders—either do not exist, are not properly maintained, or are not subject to public disclosure

Financial and other disclosure is the most fundamental requirement of a successful local credit market. It is a necessary pre-condition for informed market competition and for an effective system of local credit ratings. It is a prerequisite for early warning systems of financial trouble. International assistance in building credit markets too frequently has jumped forward to introduce specific credit-market instruments, without giving adequate attention to the foundation of disclosure standards.

Developing local credit markets for environmental investment

This section summarizes the logical next steps in each country to strengthen local credit markets and their ability to finance urban environmental investment. It also briefly assesses the potential value of additional external assistance in building local credit market capacity, given the advisory activities and pilot projects already underway.

China

China has announced its intention to further diversify financing sources for UEI and to strengthen the market orientation of its infrastructure financing. In terms of local credit market development, this agenda fits several themes.

Bank Lending

China Construction Bank has a well-functioning model of policy-based, longer-term loan financing for urban environmental investment. Commercial bank lending to municipalities via UDICs, on the other hand, is likely to be subjected to major overhaul. At present, banks do not undertake true risk analysis for municipal loans. Loans are secured either implicitly by the "comfort letter" that the municipality provides to the UDIC, or by land lease and development rights that the UDIC controls. Land development rights are the most valuable and most readily marketed asset in China's public sector. At present, however, they are used primarily to secure borrowing for investments in local growth projects that directly increase land values, such as highway construction and city re-development.

In the next stage of commercial bank credit market development, domestic banks will be partially privatized and, under the WTO agreement, foreign banks will be allowed to enter the domestic market. These events will raise the standard of credit analysis, and will exert pressure for greater disclosure and transparency if the local public sector is to have access to significant commercial bank financing.

The appropriate vehicle for implementing these changes is competition within the banking sector, which already is a major policy commitment of China's government. For the UEI sector specifically to be able to compete successfully for financing in a more market-oriented banking system, the economic returns from environmental tariff streams will have to be strengthened by supplements from other sources (China Case Study). Such supplemental revenue may take the form of agreements regarding budgetary transfers. However, China's most fully market-tested instrument for augmenting economic returns is land leasing and development rights. As the China Case Study points out, one option for the next step in UEI credit market development is to make additional returns from land development (or highly profitable asset investment) available to support lower-yielding investments in the UEI sector. This can be achieved by giving the borrower, the municipal UDIC, land development and investment rights which it can market to cross-subsidize environmental revenue streams, thereby gaining the capacity to service market-rate borrowing for UEI even in the face of inadequate tariff revenue streams. Or development rights can be granted to the investor, allowing him to supplement low-return mandatory investments in wastewater treatment plants, for example, with other high-return projects. The first option—strengthening UDICs' capacity to borrow at market rates by providing them with high-return property assets—already is followed to some degree. In the next stage of market development, the supplementary revenues and assets backing UDIC borrowing will need to be made more explicit and transparent, so as to facilitate risk assessment.

Bonds

China has all the economic and financial pre-conditions for expansion of a bond market. Domestic and international analysts agree that one of the greatest macroeconomic risk factors is the concentration of debt in the banking sector, much of it of low credit quality. China's national savings between 1998 and 2002 grew at 21% per annum rate, reaching 1.02 times GDP in 2002, indicating a large capital market absorption capacity. (China Case Study) To significantly diversify the local credit market for UEI financing, China will need to revise its approach to the "municipal" bond market. At present, all local bond issues are subject to case-by-case review and approval by national authorities. The approval process can take well over a year and often results in rejection, for national policy reasons rather than because of the financial or economic inadequacies at the local level. As a result, few bond issues are proposed.

Reform of local bond market regulation has been under active discussion in China for at least four years. Agreement has been reached on what is needed for market expansion. One key element is conversion from the current procedure of case-by-case state review of bond issues, based on unspecified and non-transparent policy criteria, to rules-based limits on bond issuance, established to ensure prudential financial management. Second, development of an active local bond market will require much greater financial and risk disclosure. At present, local bond issuers do not make public their balance sheets, their income statements, their debt obligations, or the specific project purpose to which bond proceeds will be put.

Technical expertise is not the missing element for bond market development. Experts under a United States Trade Development Agency program worked with Shanghai municipality and Shanghai UDIC to develop a structure of local bond issuance in support of local environmental infrastructure investment, but the concept eventually was rejected for broader policy reasons. At heart, the issue involves how much discretion over financing options the government wants to delegate to the local level, free from strict national controls, and how much openness it wants to introduce into what is now a state-controlled financial sector. If the elements of bond market regulatory reform, under discussion for several years, were approved, a local bond market would grow quickly to diversify local infrastructure credit financing.

Kazakhstan

The fundamental distinction to draw in assessing Kazakhstan's future local credit market development is between "municipal" or general-purpose local government credit, on the one hand, and municipal utility or environmental enterprise credit, on the other.

Kazakhstan has decided, for the time being, that it does not want to encourage development of a "municipal" credit market. The priority requirements for development of such a market are quite clear: reform of the intergovernmental finance system that redistributes local surpluses to deficit governments in a way that weakens local creditworthiness; modification of the national revenue system, which does not allow local authorities to introduce new taxes or differentiate local tax rates (except for a land tax); and relaxation of the very stringent controls over local debt and local borrowing. These reforms have been recommended by various donor agencies and IFIs. However, Kazakhstan has chosen to implement a more centralized and unitary intergovernmental financing system with strict controls over local borrowing.

Significantly more latitude has been allowed for municipal utility borrowing under corporate laws. The principal impediment to expanded utility borrowing is the inadequacy of tariff revenues. The Kazakhstan Case Study estimates that at present tariff revenues cover 67%-75% of costs. As shown in Table 2 of this report, detailed ex-post analysis of Atyrau water and wastewater utility's financing reveals an even larger shortfall from tariff revenues. Development of the next stage of local credit market utility financing will require more formalized, more explicit, and more legally binding commitments as regards the source and magnitude of future revenues that will complement tariff income to pay for debt service. It will also require a more transparent and well-defined tariff regulation procedure than currently found in the national Anti-Monopoly Agency.

Russia

Russia's future development of the local credit market raises interesting issues because of the policy path the country appears to have chosen. In a series of program statements and legislative initiatives in 2004 (Russia Case Study) national authorities laid out the framework they foresee for investment in the water and wastewater sector. First, future investment by municipal governments in utility infrastructure is supposed to be minimized. Such investment is to be financed by enterprises operating under corporate law. In the view of the case study author, this policy posture greatly reduces the scope of the "municipal" credit market—banks or bonds—as a source of environmental infrastructure financing.

Second, the government has stated clearly that its priority is to attract private sector investment and management into municipal utilities. Materials prepared for an OECD-World Bank conference (September 2004) estimated that in the water sector 8% of Russia's urban population now is served by private operators and that, if current negotiations underway are successfully consummated, this proportion will rise to 16%. The job of obtaining credit financing for new sectoral investment might then become the responsibility of private investors, or, perhaps a more likely outcome, the joint responsibility of municipal utilities and private operators/investors. In fact, the responsibility for investment financing and credit under the private participation model that Russia is developing is still in the process of being clarified. There is a need to establish the legal and institutional framework for private sector participation in the WSS sector, including specifically the parties' respective responsibilities for obtaining credits to finance investment and pay debt service. At the same time, private companies have shown interest in serving no more than 20% of Russian municipalities (OECD-World Bank, 2004), which leaves unanswered the question of how other cities will gain access to financing.

Under any institutional model of future utility management, credit market development will require predictable implementation of tariff rules that allow for recovery of investment and debt service, and reduction in the political risk involved in tariff regulation. At present, municipal utilities are subject to tariff regulation at the local level, while private enterprises are subject to tariff regulation at a higher level of government—an inconsistency that also needs to be normalized. Better regulation will require implementation of clear methodologies for calculating and approving tariffs. These issues are being addressed by the Gosstroi (which was recently attached to the Ministry of Regional development).

Ukraine

Ukraine is farther along than the other countries in this study toward framing and adopting a comprehensive legal and institutional framework for borrowing in the local infrastructure sector. Draft legislation has been circulated, discussed, and revised for the last two years. International experts are currently (April 2005) providing advice on the full array of legal and regulatory provisions needed to support local credit market development within this policy framework. Adoption of a single, coherent policy framework that applies both to local governments and local utilities, and to bond issues as well as to bank loans, will constitute a fundamental step forward in credit market development.

Ukraine also is benefiting from external assistance in the development of both commercial bank lending and bond issuance as financing devices. The World Bank has been cooperating with the government in the creation of a local government on-lending program, in which commercial banks would be able to access longer-term credits, then on-lend funds for infrastructure investment by municipalities or municipal utilities. Under the program, banks would perform credit analysis and assume all credit risk. The design follows a structure that was successfully used to introduce commercial banks to longer-term environmental infrastructure lending in the Czech Republic and Bosnia. Several banks have already signed on to participate in the program in principle, although the program's start-up has been, and continues to be, delayed at the World Bank. USAID simultaneously is assisting municipal utilities in developing access to local bond markets.

Ukraine has made the clearest statement of its intention to develop the local credit market as a sustainable financing tool for the water and sanitation sector. Credit market development has become a priority as a result of Ukraine's commitment to reach EU environmental standards, and its recognition that the costs of doing so cannot possibly be financed from government budgets alone.

References

Baietti, Aldo and Peter Raymond. 2005. *Financing Water Supply and Sanitation Investments: Utilizing Risk Mitigation Instruments to Bridge the Financing Gap.* World Bank: Washington, DC.

The Banker. March 2005. "Moscow's Muscle in Bond Market," pp. 62-63.

Chernyavsky, A.V. 2003. *Review of the Municipal Finance Development in Russia in 1992-2002.* Institute for Urban Economics: Moscow.

China Ministry of Finance. 2005. *Report on the Implementation of the Central and Local Budgets for 2004 and the Draft Central and Local Budgets for 2005.* Beijing.

EBRD. 2004(a) *Strategy for Kazakhstan,* London.

. 2004(b) *Strategy for the Russian Federation,* London.

Genz, Richard. 2004. "USAID Access to Credit Initiative: Rapid Assessment of the Municipal Bond Component." Urban Institute.

Hall, David and Vladimir Popov. 2004. "Privatisation and Re-Structuring of Water Supply in Russia and Ukraine," paper presented to regional meeting on water and energy. Moscow.

OECD. 2004a. Task Force for the Implementation of the Environmental Action Programme for Central and Eastern Europe. *Financing Strategy of the Urban Wastewater Sector in Selected Municipalities of the Sichuan Province in China.*

OECD. 2004b. OECD-World Bank Conference on Private Sector Participation in Municipal Water Services in Europe and Central Asia, 20-21 September, Moscow.

OECD. 2004c *Overview of Domestic and International Private Companies Operating in the Water Utilities Sector in the Russian Federation.*

Peterson, George E. 2005. "Intergovernmental Fiscal Systems and Sub-National Growth: China," paper prepared for DFID and World Bank.

Swianiewicz, Pawel. (ed.). 2004. *Local Government Borrowing: Risks and Rewards.* Open Society Institute: Budapest.

UNDP. 2004. *Water Resources for Kazakhstan in the New Millennium.*

World Bank. 2005a. "Implementation Completion Report, Atyrau Pilot Water Supply and Sanitation Project."

2005b. "Ukraine—Municipal Credit Market Development."

PART II. COUNTRY CASE STUDIES

China[9]

UEI Investment and Financing in China

Urban infrastructure normally divides into four parts due to the different sector management system in China:

- Urban public utilities including water supply, gas, heating system, public transportation, etc.;
- Urban public work construction: including road, bridge, pipeline, sewerage treatment, flood, and light, etc.;
- Urban environment and sanitation: public toilet, public cleaning, and solid waste collection and disposal;
- Urban park, garden, and greens.

This report focuses on water supply, sewerage treatment, and municipal solid waste (MSW) disposal, defined as urban environmental infrastructure (UEI).

Insufficiency of Total Investment to Meet Needs

The development of urban infrastructure was increasing in last two decades, but the level of facilities and urban infrastructure investment scale is still behind its economic development in China compared with the target recommended by World Bank World Development Report 1994: Infrastructure for Development. World Bank report recommended that the rate of investment in urban infrastructure to social fixed-assets investment

9 The country case study was written by Mr. Fu Tao, Department of Environmental science and engineering, Tsinghua University, Beijing, China.

might be from 9% to 15%, and the rate to GDP might be from 3% to 5% in developing countries (see below) (World Bank 1994).

Table 5.Investment in urban infrastructure in China

Year	Investment for urban infrastructure	The rate to social fixed-assets investment	The rate to GDP
1978	8.35	1.20	0.23
1979	13.15	1.90	0.32
1980	13.54	1.50	0.30
1981	19.53	2.00	0.40
1982	27.16	2.20	0.51
1983	28.17	2.00	0.47
1984	41.66	2.30	0.58
1985	63.99	2.50	0.71
1986	80.07	2.70	0.78
1987	90.31	2.50	0.75
1988	113.24	2.50	0.75
1989	106.97	2.60	0.63
1990	121.20	2.70	0.65
1991	170.88	3.10	0.79
1992	283.17	3.50	1.06
1992	521.83	4.00	1.50
1994	666.04	3.90	1.42
1995	807.63	4.00	1.38
1996	948.62	4.13	1.40
1997	1142.65	4.60	1.56
1998	1477.61	5.20	1.89
1999	1590.84	5.33	1.98
2000	1893.65	5.76	2.12

Source: Construction Industry Publisher of China 2002.

In the 1990s, China fulfilled the 8th and the 9th Five-year Plans and the national economy sustained rapid and sound development. At the same time, China experienced rapid urbanization and the level of urbanization increased by 0.63% annually. The urbanization rate has reached about 31% in 2002.

Household wastewater drainage is increasing rapidly with expansion of urban population and improvement in living standards, and in 1999, it started to exceed the amount of industrial effluent, polluting both surface water and ground water. Although the amount of garbage is increasing rapidly, the rate of collection and treatment has remained low. In some cities, the reclamation of garbage is transported to dump yards without appropriate treatment. Even in cities that are exceptionally implementing sanitary treatment of solid wastes, the treatment processes are short of standards, causing secondary pollution around the landfill areas. Since the cost and technology are insufficient, garbage incineration has not gained momentum.

Thus, in China, the needs for UEI development are increasing rapidly, and financing UEI has been the central concern of the national and local governments. The Chinese government pursues a strategy of sustainable development and continuously devotes its efforts to improve the environment, and accelerates the construction of UEI that are related with urban drainage, urban municipal solid waste disposal and treatment. The measures have helped improve the quality of urban environment substantially. UEI is one area in which investment is growing rapidly; its share of overall environmental investment rose from 33% in 1991 to 55% in 2002 (see the next two tables and the figure below).

Table 6.Water infrastructure development in Chinese cities

Item	Unit	1985	1990	1995	1999	2000	2001
Water supply capacity	100 million liter	128	382.3	496.6	467.5	469	466
Per capital daily consumption of tap water for residential use	Liter	55.1	100.1	158.1	189.6	220	216
Ratio of water supply	%	81	89.2	93	96.3	96.7	72.3
Length of sewer pipelines	Kilometer	31,556	57,787	110,293	134,486	141,758	158,128
Per capital length of sewer pipelines	Kilometer	2.7	3.9	6	6.7	6.8	-
Ratio of sewerage treatment	%	-	14.9	20	31	34.2	36.5

Source: National Bureau of Statistics of China 1986-2002.

Table 7.Increasing water infrastructure capacity in China

Item	Unit	1979-85	1986-90	1991-95	1996-99
Urban Infrastructure fixed capital investment	100 million	207.2	511	2,449.6	5,066
Urban Infrastructure Fixed capital investment/ Total social fixed capital investment	%	2.2	2.6	3.8	5.2
New capacity for water supply	10,000 m3	1,490	1,677	2,974	2,500
New capacity for sewerage treatment	10,000 m3	272	540	1038	1,000

Source: National Bureau of Statistics of China 1986-2002.

Figure 1. Change of the ratio of municipal solid waste disposal in China

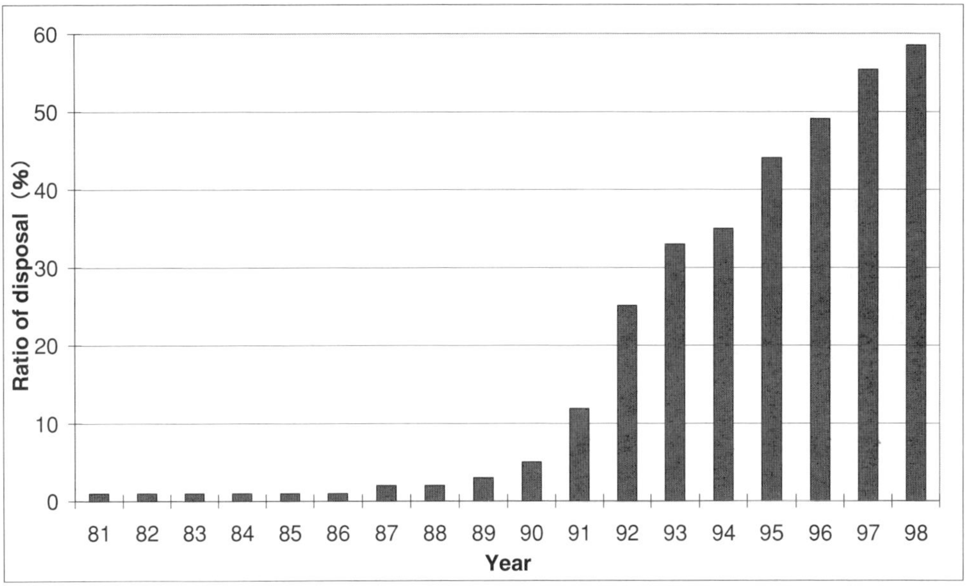

Source: Wang 1999.

By 2010 and 2020, the urbanization rate of the population is expected to increase to 46% and 55%, respectively. Growth in the number of cities and an expansion of existing cities will result in a corresponding increase in the volume of urban domestic wastewater and solid waste. Over the past decade, discharges of urban domestic wastewater have increased by 5% annually. In 2002, the amount of urban domestic wastewater discharged reached 23.22 billion tons, accounting for 52.9% of China's total emissions of wastewater, and urban domestic solid waste increased by between 5% and 8%. In 2002, the amount of urban domestic solid waste generated reached 1,360 million tons. It is anticipated that, by 2020, the production of urban domestic wastewater and solid waste will increase the volumes discharged in 2000 by between 1.3 and 2 times.

Existing facilities for treating urban domestic wastewater and solid waste, however, are seriously deficient, and new construction is lagging behind. By the end of 2001, the rate of primary treatment of urban domestic wastewater was merely 36.4% of the total amount produced, of which only

18% received secondary treatment. The municipal solid waste disposal rate was 58.2%, of which only 10% received sanitary treatment and disposal.

According to China's environmental protection plan for the Tenth Five-Year Plan period (2001-2005), the treatment rate of centralized urban domestic wastewater is targeted at 45% by 2005, and the rate in cities with populations larger than 500,000 is targeted at 60%. Under the plan, the increased capacity of sanitary treatment and disposal of urban solid waste is supposed to be 150,000 tons per day. In order to realize the above objectives, China will need hundreds of billions of RMB to construct treatment facilities for urban domestic wastewater, and 45 billion RMB to invest in the construction of domestic solid waste treatment facilities. The Task Force expects that during the Eleventh Five-Year period, the investment required in these two fields will be around 170 billion RMB.

Under the current investment mechanisms and capabilities, it will be very difficult to satisfy these demands. For some local areas, the problem of insufficient funding for construction of urban environmental infrastructure will be very serious.

Low Investment Efficiency

Due to the growing demand for financing, and despite inefficiencies nationwide, China has started to introduce market-based approaches for pollution prevention and control. The low efficiency of environmental investment in China is mainly reflected by inefficiencies and problems in the construction, operation, and management of urban wastewater treatment and solid waste disposal facilities.

For years, the government has been the main source of funding for construction of UEI facilities, with non-profit organizations[10] responsible for their operation and management. This type of government monopoly excludes institutional competition, which in turn contributes to the problem of low investment efficiency.

---

[10] In brief, *government affiliated non-profit organizations* refers to a category of public services operated according to government mechanisms, whose finance is provided by the government, and whose human resources are managed by the government.

With the advancing reforms of the market economy system and the ongoing development of the environmental service industry, a pattern of so-called "marketization" emerged in China for pollution treatment at the end of the 1990s, based on international trends favoring practices such as public-private partnership (PPP) and PFI (Private Finance Initiative). Marketization[11] is contributing to a break-up of the government's monopoly structure. This was carried out at four levels:

1. levying urban residents for household wastewater treatment and waste disposal and opening up the development of urban environmental infrastructure through public bidding;

2. demolishing the system of government-dominated construction and operation by introducing competitive mechanisms (i.e., enterprises[12] take over commercialized management of existing facilities);

3. encouraging the participation of other economic entities[13] , apart from government agencies, in the construction and operation of the facilities, attracting capital that has accumulated in the society; and

4. establishing a management system, under which various entities participate in facility construction. The corporate operation of those facilities is also based on market mechanisms.

Since market-based patterns could increase investment efficiency and secure financing, active reforms have been undertaken in recent years in

[11] The term "*marketization*" derives from the process of a planned economy to a market-based economy in specific circumstances in China. This includes the "utilization of economic instruments based on market mechanisms," the "corporatizaiton/privatization of public and or government run sectors", "introduction of profit-oriented capitalistic management" and so forth.

[12] The enterprises referred to here include those established on the basis of reformed government-affiliated non-profit organisations (e.g., state-owned, or state holding enterprises) and other types of enterprises.

[13] In China, economic entities other than the public sector include state-owned enterprises, collective enterprises, private enterprises, foreign-funded enterprises, and joint ventures, etc., whose content exceeds the private sector, as frequently mentioned in the global forum.

China. Ground-breaking progress has been made in both shifting policy and practices for the marketization of pollution treatment, although these are still at their initial stages in the context of China's overall situation.

Lack of Sound Investment and Financing Mechanisms

The shortcomings of existing investment and financing mechanisms are the most significant causes of insufficient investment in environmental protection today. As the country develops a clearer picture of its needs for environmental protection, and as China makes progress with reforms of its economic system (including overall national investment and financing systems), the future structure for environmental investment and financing is taking shape in China, with the involvement of multiple investment entities, financing channels, and instruments. The multiple entities include governments, environmentally-liable social entities (e.g., polluting enterprises), and non-environmentally-liable social entities (e.g., enterprises and other profit-oriented and non-profit organizations). The multiple channels and instruments include public budgets, environmental levies (from enterprises and non-profit organizations for pollution discharge and from urban residents for wastewater treatment and waste disposal), treasury bonds, government loans, funds from enterprises, enterprise loans, and private funds, etc.

In terms of the roles played and contributions made by the entities and various instruments, however, the current mechanisms reflect the following characteristics: (1) they mainly rely on measures and channels under governmental plans, e.g., public budgets, environmental levies, and treasury bonds, etc.; (2) measures related to non-environmentally-liable social entities and public fund-raising approaches are either insufficient or non-existent; and (3) levy systems for urban domestic wastewater treatment and waste disposal are still at an initial stage and they have not been fully utilized. According to initial estimates, about 60 per cent of urban solid waste is subject to a levy to pay for treatment, with the price ranging between 0.2 to 1.2 RMB per ton, while only about 16% of waste is subject to a levy for solid waste treatment and disposal.

The above-mentioned problems in investment and financial mechanisms are the main causes for the insufficient investment in environmental protection, particularly in UEI. Although financing has been increasing significantly in recent years, mainly through governmental channels, the huge need for investment in urban infrastructure construction in China has barely been satisfied. Investment in UEI mainly relies on tax revenues, local financing, and treasury bonds. Over the past decade, investment in UEI increased rapidly. It is necessary to immediately develop a strategy for designing competitive municipal credit market.

Credit financing for UEI and its challenges

Demand and Supply Analysis of Municipal Credit Markets

As mentioned above, from 2000 to 2020, China is invited to the UEI construction boom. UEI development plan of the central government is driver of municipalities and municipal utilities to borrow for financing of UEI projects. In China, municipality is the major investor for UEI. The financial environment for UEI of local governments is changing with development of social capital, improvement in administrative management capability, and accumulation of capital practical use know-how.

Local government investment mainly includes urban maintenance and construction tax, surtax for public utilities, state Treasury bond, and budget allocation from the central and local governments, etc. Investment via the market mainly includes domestic bank loan, utilization of foreign investment, funds raised by enterprises themselves and other sources. Statistic showed that from 1990 to 2000, the ratio of governmental investment decreased from 64.23 per cent to 12.75 per cent; at the same time, however, the ratio of investment via the market increased from 35.74 per cent to 87.26 per cent.

Figure 2. Investment sources from the government and from the market

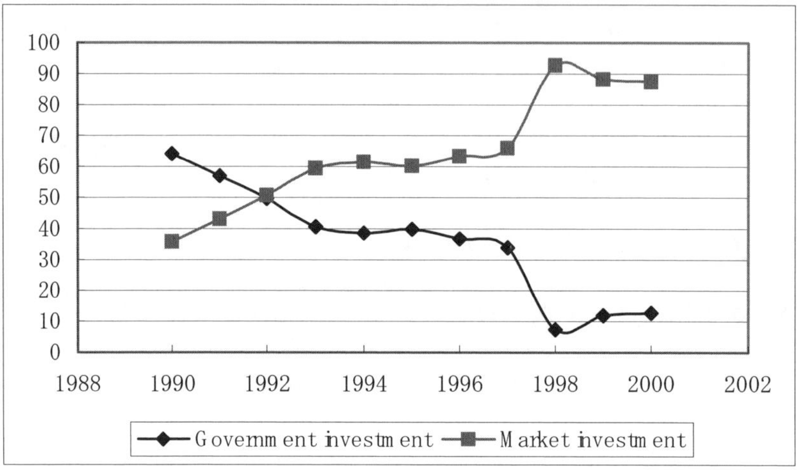

Source: Song, XT 2003.

Table below shows over five years time series data and indicators of social capital investment in urban infrastructure in China. State-owned enterprises, collective enterprises, private enterprises, foreign-funded enterprises, and joint ventures, etc. are investors. State-owned enterprises account for a large share of the market and are the leading player of UEI investment. Collective enterprises, in particular the joint venture companies established between state-owned enterprises and multinational companies, are stronger than private enterprises, and their management system is more advanced than the one of state-owned enterprises.

Table 8.Social capital investment in urban infrastructure (1996-2000, million yuan)

Year	Total investment	Government		Social capital				Ratio of social capital (%)
		National budget	Local financing	Domestic bank	Bond	Foreign investment	Others	
1996	87,119	3,481	48,613	12,219	494	10,556	11,753	40.2
1997	105,667	4,301	55,433	16,528	305	12,954	16,144	43.5
1998	134,645	10,023	60,042	28,476	4,031	11,012	21,059	48.0
1999	145,326	17,384	59,515	35,780	5,594	6,863	20,188	47.1
2000	174,354	21,855	68,572	42,853	3,252	7,674	30,146	48.1

Source: Ministry of Construction.

Much social capital has turned its attention to long-term and stable investment projects by reaction to the burst of the internet bubble in 2001. This has partly benefited UEI, which has become a target for social capital investment. The table below shows the regulation situation of social-capital participation in UEI. Most of companies find it difficult to enter the stock or bond market for financing, because of the high requirements and lack of capacity.

Table 9. Regulation social-capital participation in UEI

Service sector		Open-markets grade	Note
Water supply	Clean water	With no restriction	
	Waterworks pipe system	Participation with restriction	Restriction of the shareholding in the large and middle city
Sewerage treatment	Sewerage treatment	With no restriction	
	Drain pipe system	Participation with restriction	Restriction of the shareholding in the large and middle city

Source: Construction Industry Publisher of China 2002.

Current Situation and Challenges of Financial Sources for UEI

The current situation of local credit market is as follows:

- Treasury bond investment has played a significant role in accelerating the construction of UEI, but there are problems with the use of treasury bonds, as the supervision of projects funded by treasury bonds is not effective;

- The budget Law prohibits the issuance of municipal bonds; corporate bonds are used to finance UEI projects instead;

- Bank loans play a key role in China`s financial system, but only a small share concern UEI, and there is clear limitation to their increase. The policy based method of "Public Environmental Trust Fund." raising money through the Social Security is still under review;

- The stock market and corporate bonds play an increasing part.

Treasury Bond

From 1998 to 2002, the central government issued a total of 660 billion RMB in long-term treasury bonds, of which 65 billion RMB was invested in the construction of 967 UEI projects, covering 95% of cities and some counties in western China. Treasury bonds not only accelerated the construction of UEI in some cities in China, but also played a positive role in boosting economic growth. During 1998 to 2002, the accumulated total of long-term treasury bonds directly produced about 2,500 billion RMB in investment from local governments, relevant departments, enterprises, and bank loans. One study showed that projects funded by treasury bonds led to a 2% increase of GDP in 1999.

During 1998-2001, 32.6 billion RMB were invested in 404 UEI projects. Specifically, 20.8 billion RMB was used to support 214 clean water projects, increasing the national capacity of urban sewerage treatment by 1.4 times; 69 MSW disposal projects were launched, raising the level of innocent treatment of MSW from 57% to nearly 70% nationwide.

In 2001, the Chinese government issued 150 billion RMB long-term construction treasury bonds, and funds supported about 1000 projects of urban water supply, sewerage treatment, MSW disposal, etc., and launched the project of water pollution prevention and control in the Three Gorges area. In the Three Rivers and Three Lakes area (Liao River, Hai River, Huai River, and Tai lake, Dian Lake, Chao Lake), which covers twelve provinces and autonomous regions, treasury bond funds supported the construction of 117 treatment plants, with a total treatment capacity of 9.8 million tons/day. Treatment plants in operation in the Three Rivers and Three Lakes area can reduce pollution load by more than 200,000 tons annually in term of chemical oxygen demand.

However, due to lack of experience, problems occur in the management of treasury bond and its implementation. Some local governments make false project proposals to snare treasury bond funds; in some projects, treasury bond funds are misappropriated, reallocated without permission or directed to other uses; project management does not conform to norms, and the project entity responsibility system, public tendering system, construction supervision system and contractual management system are not fully implemented; some local governments for not provide matching funds fully and timely (Wang, YX et al. 2003).

Loans from Commercial Banks

The majority of commercial financing in China, exclusive of treasury bond, is indirect financing via banks. In the instance of corporate finance, the ratio of indirect financing via banks against direct financing is about 9:1; in 1991-2001, bank loans increased by ten trillion RMB, while corporate financing via stocks and bonds amounted to one trillion RMB.

Chinese government encourages banks to extend loans to support the development of UEI. But according to the financial system reform, the People`s Bank of China will not assign plans for special loans to commercial banks. The table below shows bank loans for urban infrastructure construction in China.

At present, only relatively small amount of capital are made available in commercial bank loans to support UEI projects. There are four main reasons for this:

- UEI projects require long-term investments with a lower profit, as revenue charges fail to generate a high return on investment, compared with other infrastructures;
- revenue charges can not be pledged effectively;
- municipal governments are already heavily indebted. Municipalities usually set up an Investment Company for urban construction, which is contracting with the banks as a representative of municipal government. Such companies are heavily indebted, and debt payment has been a problem.

Table 10. Bank loans for urban infrastructure construction in China (M yuan)

Year	Urban infrastructure construction	Domestic bank loans	Domestic bank loans / urban infrastructure investment
1986	13,142	317	2.41%
1987	14,422	616	4.27%
1988	18,451	758	4.11%
1989	18,356	444	2.42%
1990	21,048	884	4.20%
1991	26,611	2,292	8.62%
1992	39,347	3,225	8.20%
1993	58,119	4,456	7.67%
1994	67,480	4,133	6.13%
1995	77,437	4,766	6.16%
1996	84,764	9,568	11.29%
1997	111,034	16,574	14.93%
1998	143,331	30,696	21.42%
1999	162,712	37,419	23.00%
2000	198,893	41,469	20.85%

Source: Construction Industry Publisher of China 2002.

Loans from Policy Banks

The policy banks have largely supported the UEI sector. They are the major financing source for the development of UEI, although UEI is only one small component in there activities, compared to power, telecommunication, railway, highway, petroleum and petrochemical.

The China Development Bank (CDB) plays a particular part here. It was established in March 1994 as a policy bank under a Special Decree of the State Council, with its registered capital of RMB 50 billion:

- It is wholly owned by the Government; it reports directly to the State Council.
- It is the largest of the three policy-oriented banks in China, and the only financial institution with ministerial status besides the PBOC.
- Its primary function are

    1. To foster the construction of infrastructure, basic industries and pillar industries through financing;
    2. To support the nation's regional development policy;
    3. To on-lend loan from the international financial institutions.

Figure 3. Forecasts of Bond Issuance and Lending Activities

(USD billion, 1USD = 8.28 RMB

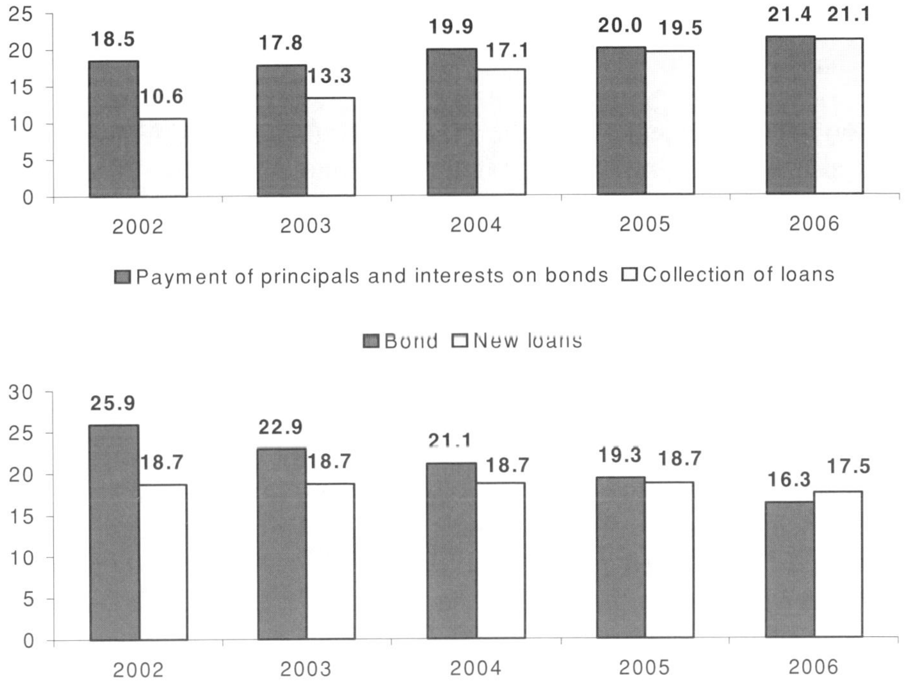

Source: China Development Bank 2004.

CDB has already carried out loans on the UEI projects of a hundred cities. The amount of fund went up to 100 billion yuan, and encouraged the investment of 100 billion yuan from the local government. The loans for infrastructure construction including UEI amounted to 73,992 million yuan, and 115,636 million yuan in 2001 and 2002 respectively. CDB is particularly supporting local water infrastructure construction (for instance, 60% of the loans provided to Heibei province by the Heibei branch of CDB was dedicated for maintaining water infrastructure and its pipeline system).

CDB is considering a pilot project to support private sector participation in UEI (Dongjiao Sewerage Treatment Plant, Xinhui City, in Guangdong province).

CDB will play a key role in the development of central and western China which is clearly identified in its development strategy for the next 5 Years. 60% of the loaned disbursed since CDB was established were committed to the central and western region. CDB is also supporting UEI development in central and western region through acting as underwriter of corporate bond, investment and financing adviser, industrial fund investment, and technical support.

Another instrument of public finance is under consideration, which would also be policy oriented: "Public Environmental Trust Fund", which would raise money through the Social Security.

Municipal Bond and Corporate Bond

In the case of municipal bonds, the debtor is the local government or a state-owned enterprise (such as a wastewater treatment plant, water supply company, or urban infrastructure construction and management company) which issues bonds on the capital markets. Funds raised by municipal bonds are usually used for the construction of urban infrastructures or public utilities, including roads, bridges, water supply, wastewater treatment, solid waste disposal and other public facilities. UEI is one of the components of overall urban infrastructure. With the support of local governments, the repayment of municipal bonds can be guaranteed by several sources. Also, profits gained from other development projects can be used to compensate for UEI projects. These characteristics make municipal bonds a promising tool for financing UEI projects. Indeed, it is a common approach in developed countries.

Chinese municipalities are prohibited from issuing municipal bonds, except for special regulation and regulation of the State Council under the Budget Law. However, local domestic companies under local public sector have managed to issue bonds for the construction of urban infrastructure. The profit generated by the project is used to pay back the loan. Although the company takes the responsibility and the risk associated to the issuance, it gets the support and the assistance from the local government. Such an operation is not a genuine corporate bond; it is similar to municipal bonds financing public goods.

For example, the Water Supply Company of Jinan city issued Water Supply Bond of 150 million Yuan for building storage-of-water dam for water supply in 1999. Changsha city Beltway Construction Company issued bonds for 180 million Yuan for constructing the second beltway. The bonds were issued by the company, but used in the same way as municipal bonds. It is the specific product of financial mechanism in China now.

Box 1. Chengdu: Municipal Bond in planning for private capital

At a municipal meeting on urban governance and management held in 2004, Chengdu city officials announced they will make more financing channels accessible for UEI construction. The city will create and provide conditions for the issuance of municipal bonds. At present, local government still have no permission for the issuance of municipal bonds openly, however a number of bond investment groups have emerged. The relative organizations will discuss on the feasibility of the annual issuance of municipal bonds based on the credibility guarantee of local government, value of urban infrastructure project and prospective cash flow.

Chengdu city has experienced various financing tools, such as collective consignation loan and corporate bond. The first collective consignation loan project of Sichuan province was launched in Chengdu on 16 Jan. 2003. The Construction Bank of China, working as depositary, issued a new investment service named treatment of water resource with RMB 200 million. The consignation loan interest will be paid on a yearly basis, and the capital at expiration. In addition, Chengdu Xingrong Investment Ltd. plans to issue corporate bonds in 2004. According to the bonds project drafted by the agency, Chengdu Xingrong Investment Ltd. could issue 10-year corporation bonds, amounting to 1,000 million. Xingrong plans to sell the corporate bonds by main underwriters. It is also hopeful to make transactions in the Shanghai Stock Exchange.

In Shanghai, the World Bank has approved a loan of 200 million US dollars for urban planning. Part of the loan will be used by local government for financing and institutional reform of urban infrastructure, especially for developing long term municipal infrastructure bonds as new financing tool.

Source : H2O China 2004.

At present corporate bond financing is nearly nonexistent, and the corporate bond market stagnates. This is so for two reasons:

- Compared with bank loans, corporate bond financing is subject to more strict requirements. It takes more time to raise funds, and it generates higher costs; thus, enterprises qualified for bond financing prefer bank loans, and qualify for them.
- The administrative framework for corporate bond financing is not straightened out.

In addition, very few UEI companies meet the requisites to issue bonds, because few of them have gone all the way to reorganizing the firm and its governance structure, to severe the jurisdiction and the corporation. Apart from the bond issuance approved by the central government for particular reasons, corporate bonds issuance by local enterprises has almost come to an end in the past two years.

Table 11. Volume of corporate bond issuance in recent years (billion RMB)

Year	1995	1996	1997	1998	1999	2000	2001	2002
Volume	30.1	26.9	25.5	14.8	15.8	8.3	14.7	27.0

Source: The State Development Planning Commission 2003.

Since the central government imposes tight control over the issuance of corporate bonds, there has been no precedent of issuing corporate bonds for UEI. Nevertheless the issuance of corporate bonds has a number of favorable conditions.

First, the revised Regulations over the Administration for Corporate bonds will facilitate corporate bond financing for UEI:

- A ratifying system will replace the current examination and approval system for issuing corporate bonds;

- The interest rate of corporate bond will be set through public tender, which will facilitate the reduction of the cost of corporate bond financing;

- It will be allowed to issue foreign currency or RMB corporate bonds to commercial banks located in China with a view to restructuring foreign debt projects. This will make it possible to repay the foreign loans to environmental projects through issuing corporate bonds.

Second, in recent years, with strengthened administration and strict control, local governments were able to pay back matured corporate bonds.

Third, the interest rates of corporate bonds are lower than those of bank loans. This scenario makes the option of corporate bond attractive to both investors and enterprises.

Box 2. Corporate bond issuance in China

In case a company issues corporate bonds, it should comply with the regulation of corporate bond management:

- central government's companies need to be examined by the People's Bank of China and the National Development and Reform Commission;
- local government's companies need to be examined by the branch of People's Bank of China and the local Development and Reform Commission.

The company has to comply with the following conditions to issue corporate bonds:

1. the size of the company should be compatible with national regulation;
2. the financial accounting system of the company must coincide with national regulation;
3. the company should be able to pay back the debt;
4. the management of the company should be appropriate, and the company ought to have generated profits for the last three consecutive years prior to bond issuance;
5. the use of the raised fund should coincide with national industrial policy.

Private Sector Participation

The following reasons suggest that private sector participation should develop in China:

1. Local governments are playing an increasing role in UEI construction and operation, but their financial capacity can not meet the huge demand due to the lack of subsidy system from central government, and to the limited flexibility of independent fiscal management.
2. Trends in government monopoly have been institutionally squeezing out competition and, hence, lack efficiency. The existing UEI are not operated properly, and deteriorate.

3. Deregulation and privatization should support the introduction of advanced environmental technology from foreign countries, and the development of domestic environmental technologies. China has a large-scale market of UEI, environmental industry will increase with 14-17% per year during 2000 -2015. It creates good business opportunities for foreign and domestic companies. In particular, as domestic companies are facing the saturation of industrial pollution control equipments market, UEI is considered as a new market that is responsive to private sector initiatives.

The policies which encourage private sector participation in UEI construction and market-oriented operation have made substantive progress in recent years, especially tariff policies for sewage and garbage treatment, and the promotion of their industrialization. Progress is manifold:

- Formulating tariff policies for sewage and garbage, creating the necessary conditions for PSP;

- Reforming the management system, implementing franchise operation, initially creating a fair and competitive market for environment-related services;

- Formulating priorities, fostering industrialization of urban sewage and MSW treatment;

- Working out supervision and management structures and procedures, normalizing market, and guaranteeing a healthy and ordered industrialization path.

Six reference documents provide guidance to support PPP:

- 1999, Notice concerning trial implementation of sewage fee in the cities of Huai He River;

- 2000, Notice of the State Council on strengthening urban water supply, water saving, and water pollution control;

- 2000, Notice concerning further promotion of price reform of water supply;

- 2002, Notice concerning levy of garbage treatment fee and facilitation of industrializing garbage treatment;
- 2002, Opinions on facilitating industrialization of sewage and garbage treatment.
- 2002, Industrial catalogue guidelines for foreign investment.

Table 12. The major policy issues on construction and market-oriented operation of UEI, since 1999

Policies	Time of issue	Issuance department	Main contents
Strengthing Collection of Sewerage Treatment Charges, Setting up Sound Operation Mechanism of Urban Sewage Discharge and Centralized Treatment	May 1999	State Planning Commission; Ministry of Construction; SEPA	Collect sewage disposal fee besides the water supply fee; establish the principle and extent of authority for the sewage disposal charging standard; set up and improve the supervision mechanism of management of sewage disposal charging and operation of sewage treatment in order to ensure healthy implementation of sewage disposal charging.
Strengthening Urban Water Supply, Saving and Pollution Control	Nov. 2000	State Council	Cities all over China should start collecting sewage disposal fees according to relevant regulations. Priority should be placed on adjusting the sewage disposal charging to the level of maintaining break-even and making meager profit in order to meet the need sewage treatment facility construction and operation; Value added taxes should be exempted from the sewage disposal fees charged and the depreciation process can be accelerated for equipment purchased for wastewater disposal projects.
Promoting and Guiding Non-Governmental Investment	Dec. 2001	State Planning Commission	Change old concepts; gradually broaden investment fields; widen financing channels; implement fair and equitable taxation and fee policies; and establish socialized services systems.

Table 12. The major policy issues on construction and market-oriented operation of UEI, since 1999 (continued)

Policies	Time of issue	Issuance department	Main contents
Industrial Guidance Category for Foreign Investment	March 2002	State Planning Commission; State Economic and Trade Commission; Ministry of Foreign Trade and Economic Cooperation	Municipal sewage treatment equipment at a capacity of 10,000 ton/day or above, industrial wastewater film treating equipment and other waste water bio-treatment equipment, other garbage burning treating equipment production; construction and management of sewage treatment and MSW disposal plant, hazardous waste disposal plant (garbage burning plants and landfills) and other environmental pollution treatment facilities.
Charging System for Garbage Treatment and Promotion of Industrialization of Garbage Treatment	June 2003	State Planning Commission; Ministries of Finance; Construction; SEPA	Establish proper garbage charging standards and scientific calculation and collection methods; strengthen charging management; reform garbage disposal operation mechanism and promote garbage disposal industrialization.
Promoting Industrialization of Urban Sewage and Garbage Treatment	Sept. 2002	State Planning Commission; Ministry of Construction; SEPA	Set targets to promote the industrialization of municipal sewage and garbage disposal; Reform the old systems and establish innovated mechanism to create the fundamental conditions for the industrialization process of municipal sewage and garbage disposal with market-orientation and policy support; Strengthen the supervision and control to guarantee the healthy industrialization development of municipal sewerage treatment and MSW disposal plant.
Speeding Up Market – Oriented Operation of Municipal Public Utility Sectors	Dec. 2002	Ministry of Construction	Open up municipal public utility sector market, set up the public utility sector franchising system, change the old government regulation practice, strengthen the leadership in order to steadily promote its market-oriented operation process.

Source: Pei, X.F., et al 2003.

BOT (Build – Operate – Transfer) and TOT (Transfer – Operate – Transfer) are the most popular PPP options adopted in Chinese cities (see next two boxes).

Box 3. Wenzhou Dong Zhuang Power Generation Plant

Wenzhou City has an annual production of 400,000 tons of MSW, which is still increasing at an annual rate of 8-10%. While the first two landfills already reach full capacity, there is no more place in the city for new landfills. Wenzhou decided to build an incinerator, and to use BOT. The gross investment of this project is RMB 90 million yuan, financed by a private enterprise, Wei Ming Environmental Protection Engineering Co., Ltd. This company will build, manage and operate the plant for the next 25 years (not including the two-year construction period), and return the plant to the government without any compensation. This plant is designed to process 320 tons of municipal garbage per day, and to generate some 25 million kW annually.

The total investment for the first phase of construction is RM 6.5 million yuan. With this phase, the daily treatment capacity is about 160 tons, and the power production capacity is 9 million kW annually, out of which 7 are sold on the market (while 2 are used internally). Besides, a compensation of RMB 73.8 yuan per ton was collected from the government. The investment should be payd back within 12 years.

Source: Field survey.

Box 4. TOT project of Henggang sewerage treatment plant

Henggang, located in the upstream of Longgang River, is a fast growing town of the Longgang District in the direction of urbanization. At present, its daily sewerage discharge volume has already exceeded 90,000 tons. The construction of Henggang Sewerage Tretament Plant began in December 2000. The treatment capacity of the first phase of the project was 10,000 tons/day with a total government investment of RMB 129 million. Upon completion, the first phase of the project was successfully audited in February 2003.

In order to realize fast return of government investment and to activate the cash flow of construction funds, the pattern of TOT was adopted by the Government of Henggang District. The franchise rights for operating the sewerage treatment plant were transferred to Shenzhen Hanyang Investment Holdings Co., Ltd. at RMB 120 million for a period of 20 years. In the contract, it was stipulated that the company must possess at least 30% of the total funds needed. The tax on sewerage disposal granted by the government to the company was RMB 1.05 per ton. If the inflation rate exceeds 5%, this rate may be adjusted after proper public hearings. Aside from various financial expenses, it was initially anticipated that the annual revenue rate of the company will be 3%. The returned funds will be used for the construction of new sewerage treatment installations.

Source : Pei, X.F., et al. 2003.

Investment Organization

The role of investment organization, like pension funds and insurance companies, in long-term capital market is not much developed in China. Recently, trust and investment companies like the China Foreign Economy and Trade Trust & Investment Co., Ltd. have been quite active in the urban environmental field. There are discussions about the feasibility and the appropriate model of UEI trust and investment funds. Both public and private sectors want to learn the know- how and international experience of establishing such funds.

International Development Agencies

International development agencies have played an important part from 1980`s to 1990`s. There were few UEI facilities in China at that time, and the UEI plants aided by international development agencies were considered as model projects. International development funds are attractive for local governments due to their low interest, and long maturity. But their availability decreases as the economy develops, in particular in coastal areas. Japan Bank for International Cooperation (JBIC), the World Bank, and the Asian Development Bank are the major players.

JBIC pledged support for environmental conservation measures as part of sector-specific policies in its Medium-Term Strategy for Overseas Economic Cooperation Operation. Accordingly, JBIC is enhancing and expanding financial provision for projects which contribute to environmental conservation and improvement in the borrowing countries (environmental projects). Since 1995, JBIC had offered lower interest rates for loans to environmental projects (standard environmental interest rates) than other projects (JBIC 2004). In the former subcategory, water supply and sewerage projects accounted for a large share. The borrowing countries for living environment improvement projects (in the narrow sense) are a diverse set of countries in Asia, Africa and Latin America. Among them, China ranked first with the greatest number of projects (see table below).

Table 13. List of UEI projects for improving the living environment in China (1990-2001, million Yen)

Project Name	Date of L/A	Amount of Environmental Project
Three Cities Water Supply Project (Tianjin, Hefei, Anshan)	19-Nov-90	8,866
Urban Water Supply Project (Xiamen, Chongqing, Kunming)	4-Oct-91	10,403
Qingdao Development Project (Water Supply and Sewerage)	25-Aug-93	2,513
Xi'an Water Supply Project (1)	25-Aug-93	4,587
Xi'an Water Supply Project (II)	2-Nov-95	2,552
Hohhot Water Supply Project	26-Dec-96	5,446
Beijing No.9 Water Works Expansion Project	26-Dec-96	14,680
Guiyang Water Supply Project	26-Dec-96	5,500
Zhanjiang Water Supply Project	26-Dec-96	5,519
Dalian Water Supply Sistem Rehabilatation Project	12-Sep-97	5,500
Shandong Yantai Water Supply and Water Induced Disaster Management Project	25-Dec-98	6,008
Guangxi Water Supply Project	28-Mar-00	3,641
Kunming Water Supply Project	28-Mar-00	20,903
Chengdu Water Supply Project	28-Mar-00	7,293
Chongqing Water Supply Project	28-Mar-00	6,244
Jiangxi Water Supply Project	28-Mar-00	4,147
Tianjin Wastewater Treatment Project	30-Mar-01	1,480
Dalian water Supply and Wastewater Treatment Project	30-Mar-01	1,591
Changsha Water Supply Project	30-Mar-01	4,850
Yingkou Water Supply Project	30-Mar-01	2,504
Tangshan Water Supply Project	30-Mar-01	2,841
Xi'an Environmental Improvement Project (portion of expanding sewage network)	29-Mar-02	4,577
Anshan Environmental Improvement Project (water supply portion)	29-Mar-02	3,398

Source: JBIC 2004.

Future directions of JBIC for financing UEI include:

- The provision of safe water and facilities for improving public health. As access to such goods and services are often inadequate or lacking for the poor, their improvement will play an important role in poverty reduction. Demand for clean water is rising sharply in many developing countries because their populations are increasingly concentrated in urban areas. Thus increased provision of safe water is indispensable to improve the quality of urban life;

- Unaccounted-for water (loss of water due to leakage and pilferage), advance recycling, and demand management. Since increased water supply will inevitably lead to increased sewage, an approach combining both water supply and sewerage must be further pursued.

As for the World Bank, the aid agenda for the next decade (2006-2010) in sewerage treatment in China focuses on efficiency improvement(assets management and treatment efficiency, secondary connections, leakage detection, optimizing discharge standards, low cost technologies), institutional arrangement (demand management, regulation, benchmarking, tariff reform, long term planning), and technical aspects (sludge management and water reuse). The following recommendations were issued by World Bank experts to facilitate PSP in water/wastewater sectors:

- at national level, systems for information sharing and benchmarking (to compare utility costs and performance), strengthening the legal base for PPP projects, for the continuum of PPP options, clarifying roles of various ministries and agencies, and allowing pilot projects for full water and sanitation systems, including distribution networks;

- at local government level, tariff policy (to be oriented towards full cost recovery), reliable financial data, market-oriented provision of service (as regards asset ownership, tariff revenues, enterprise accounting, etc.), the separation of regulatory functions from service provision.

The Maturity and Costs of Bank Credit, Bonds, and Other Sources of Credit

There is an example of financial structure of Beijing Capital Co., Ltd which is one of the major company of UEI field.

Table 14. Debt structure of Beijing Capital Co., Ltd

Item	Interest	Period
Domestic bank	5.76%	3-5 years
Trust loan	4.5%	3-5 years
Overseas bank	3.4%	10 years

Source: Pan, WT. 2004.

The competition of different sources of credit (banks, bonds, on-lending) in UEI investment is not developed yet. How to access the lower interest loan has become the key of a company's development strategy.

Conclusions and Policy Recommendations

Making the Best Use of Public Money

The Reform of Treasury Bonds

Treasury bond investment has played a significant role in accelerating the construction of UEI and boosting economic growth in China. Now, there are problems with the use of treasury bonds. For instance, the required counterpart funding to be provided by local governments is not always available. In addition, treasury bond issuance has two problems peculiar to China:

- local governments ask for a "lease" from the central government, or they attempt to have their projects approved by the central government and have them mentioned in the object of treasury bond investment;

- the issuance of treasury bonds relies on administrative tools that do not take advantage of market mechanisms for effective resource allocation.

Therefore, the reform of issuing treasury bonds is urgently needed. The following steps seem appropriate:

1. The use of treasury bonds should be focused on priority projects in major regions. As regards environment, priority should be given to major environmental protection projects in specific regions proposed in the Tenth-Five Year Plan for Environmental Protection. Particularly, the Government should increase the proportion of treasury bond investment in some poor regions, where the financing capacity is usually low and counterpart funding cannot be ensured by local governments.

2. Market mechanisms should be employed for issuing treasury bonds. Two reforms could be considered.

   – to diversify the treasury bonds. Special treasury bonds for the construction of UEI could be an option. In issuing the special treasury bonds, the central government should clearly define the issuer and the borrower, as well as the responsibilities and rights of the central government and the local governments. The issuing of special treasury bonds should make use of market mechanisms. Referring to practices in other countries, part of the treasury bonds can be replaced gradually by municipal bonds.

   – a trust management structure should be experimented for treasury bonds. Detailed management procedures should be specified.

Trust Investment

Trust investment funds are widely used in China, however, not to finance UEI projects. In addition, trust investment agencies do not play a major role in China's financial sector. Neither their scope nor their capacities can make them a major financing channel for UEI projects.

The Government of China has had clear policies on using trust investments to finance environmental projects. It is necessary to study the feasibility of establishing a "Public Environmental Trust Fund." The method of raising money through the Social Security Fund could be used as a reference. The foundation of such a fund should get approval from the State Environmental Protection Administration (SEPA). The Public Environmental Trust Fund should be established by means of trust investments, and should be managed and operated by qualified trust investment agencies.

Optimizing the Recourse to Commercial Finance

Bank credits and corporate bonds are the most important tools coming from the area of commercial finance.

Bank loans play a key role in China's financial system, accounting for 90% of the total volume of finance. The Government should invite banks to offer credit to finance UEI projects. In addition, governmental policies to support environmental protection should be integrated with the requirements of risk management for bank credits. This would include:

- implementing a pilot system which allows levy authority for environmental projects to be used as a mortgage for loans;
- to integrate environmental projects, such as wastewater treatment and municipal solid waste disposal facilities, into the master plans for the construction of urban infrastructure (taking advantage of combined bank credits), and adopt the system of integrated loans for urban development; similarly, more environmental projects could be included into comprehensive urban development programs financed by the National Development Bank;
- to implement the system of initial fund requirement for environmental projects;
- to make full use of governmental investment as a facilitator in the financing of commercial banks. For example, combining governmental funds with commercial bank credits, in such ways as paying interest for bank loans and subsidizing the initial funds required for environmental projects, is likely to increase the attraction for environmental projects;
- State-owned corporations involved in urban infrastructure development, not the juridical person of the UEI project, could be

made eligible for bank loans. The borrower should be different from the owner of the project;

- The main shareholder should provide security for the borrower. Also, state-owned corporations involved in urban infrastructure development (which can be supported by local government) could qualify as warrantors or loan guarantors.

From a macro-perspective, however, commercial bank loans face some problems. The future development of China's financial sector requires reducing banks' risks and increasing direct investment, two dynamics which contradict the reliance on commercial bank loans to finance UEI projects. Indeed, at the moment, financial risks are too concentrated in banks, and the share of financing through bank loans should be reduced gradually, and superseded by direct, private investment.

The issuance of corporate bonds complies with the general direction of China's financial reforms. While revising the Ordinance for Corporate Bonds, the government should facilitate recourse to corporate bonds to finance UEI projects. Relevant policies include:

- incorporating environmental projects into the bond issuance plan for comprehensive urban development;

- selecting urban construction enterprises as borrowers, with high credit and strong repayment capability;

- granting the borrower the right to develop other, non-environmental, urban infrastructure projects, and allowing them to use profits from non-environmental projects as a revenue to pay back the debt incurred for UEI;

- providing favourable land-use policies for UEI projects;

- subsidizing the bond interest when the corporate bond interest rate is higher than that of the treasury bonds;

- facilitating the circulation of corporate bonds used for the construction of urban infrastructure.

Introducing Municipal Bonds

Based on the current trend, there is a growing notion that local governments will be given permission to issue municipal bonds.

Municipal bonds are consistent with the nature of UEI as a public good. Since the objective of municipal bonds is to provide financing for public facilities, their issuance and trading are often tax-free. The application of municipal bonds is often limited to pure public goods or quasi-public goods that have difficulty or are incapable of recovering their costs in the short term. UEI is a clear example.

Compared to other financing mechanisms, municipal bonds can better help realize local governments' objectives, relate governmental responsibilities with their credibility, and strike a balance between responsibilities and resource availability.

The funding conditions and financial environment necessary for issuing municipal bonds now exist. From 1998 to 2002, the national savings showed an increase of 21% annually, to reach about 1 trillion RMB by the end of 2002, equivalent to 1.02 times the country's GDP. The increase of national savings represents the rapid growth in the national economy, but has restricted the channels available for private investment. Under such circumstance, they provide a solid basis for direct financing through municipal bonds. In addition, China has set up a comprehensive system of financial institutions in the context of a market economy, including a financial market and supervision and management systems, which provide the necessary conditions for issuing municipal bonds.

Issuing municipal bonds will help to not only establish a stable channel for financing UEI projects, but also to adjust the structure of local governments' debt, in an attempt to share the central government's debts with local governments. This would allow to reduce the amount of treasury bonds and their risks, since the financial burden can be partly shared with local governments. The central government can provide the necessary support to local governments, including budgetary transfers and other preferential policies.

The following points should be taken into account while considering and designing an implementation scheme for issuing municipal bonds:

- conduct pilot projects in selected major cities in China's developed regions. The volume of issuance should be strictly controlled, and the types of projects which use municipal bonds should be limited. For example, the construction of facilities for the 2008 Olympic Games in Beijing and for the Horticulture Expo in Shanghai could be good candidates for experimentation;

- develop supplementary policies:

  – tax incentives (including tax reduction and exemption policies) could attract investment from financial organizations and private investors;

  – the market of municipal bonds should be accessible to commercial banks, which would be invited to invest;

  – municipal bonds should be tradable in and beyond nationwide bond markets, to reduce risks;

  – effective issuance and assurance mechanisms should be established for municipal bonds. It is important to promote the issue of municipal bonds through the market and properly select issuers and sellers as well as the method of issuance;

  – it is necessary to construct a rational guarantee structure and implement guarantors' responsibilities and investors' liabilities for bearing the risks.

- Set up mechanisms which ensure preferential use of municipal bonds to UEI construction projects; for instance, the government could create a special environmental budget for buying bonds and offer preferential guarantee policies.

In addition, it is necessary to establish a system to rate the creditworthiness of local governments, as well as a supervision system and monitoring mechanisms. Note that long-term saving pools and institutional investors are the key element to issue municipal bonds. The establishment of long-term capital market including pension funds and insurance funds is important in this perspective.

The risks associated with issuing municipal bonds can be effectively controlled, but this depends on a number of aspects:

- the creditworthiness of the issuer. Municipal bonds are issued or guaranteed by municipal governments that have stable revenues from taxes and assumes the responsibility of providing public facilities.

- the low risks associated with the projects financed by municipal bonds. Municipal bonds can only be used for investment in urban infrastructure. Generally speaking, if UEI facilities can be operated and managed properly, their operating risks are far lower than those associated with other commercial projects.

- an incentive to control and mitigate risks. The issuer of municipal bonds also assumes the responsibility for their management. Sustaining financial stability and reducing financial risks are important responsibilities of municipal governments. A municipal government is both the issuer and the municipal governor. In this context, the risks associated to municipal bonds have a social dimension as well.

Use FDI to Transfer Know-How and Reduce Costs

Low interest of loans from overseas is attractive for the Chinese domestic enterprises. Some Asian countries experienced the foreign exchange rate risk while accessing the international capital markets. But that risk is not a big issue in the Chinese context, as the government tends to promote a high valuation of RMB.

Encourage Domestic PPP

It is necessary to encourage strong domestic banking and domestic companies to take a leading role in the PPP based initiatives

The role of International Development Organisations

Based on previous experience, institutional capacity building, at both national and local levels, should be the focus of future assistance. This includes institutional design and decision making, fiscal reform. An array of methods could be considered: information on international experience and best practices, advice for project design, training, pilot projects.

Donor agencies may also help local governments in contract management and negotiations, as some governments may not have the expertise to match their private sector counterparts. The funds from International Development Organisations can be used as seed money to start a revolving fund for encouraging social investment, or play the role of guarantee (Chang et al. 2004).

Related Policy Issues

Related Public Finance Issues

To promote investment at the local level, and to support the development of local capital markets, the national government should reform the intergovernmental transfer mechanisms, securing grants to sub sovereign governments, and strengthening their autonomy for tax policy.

Establishment of a special fund for the UEI sector could be an effective incentive, which has worked well in the USA (see the Clean Water State Revolving Fund).

However, such policies may crowd out money coming from the capital markets to finance investment in UEI projects. So, the support from the central government should be targeted to projects related to network extension, tariff transition, demand management, wastewater treatment and municipal solid waste disposal. The objective and process of support should be transparent and publicly known.

Public funding needs to shift from input based to output based financing. A cost-benefit analysis of projects would clarify the need for public funding, and, in some cases, attract PSP and generate finance from a commercial basis, thus saving on public funds.

Tariff Policy

Generating revenues from service provision for water supply and sanitation, and for solid waste management, is the necessary condition to build and environmental infrastructure in a market-oriented perspective.

The legal context for tariff policy in the WSS sector was established at the turn of the century. Granted by the State Council, on June 4, 1997, the Ministry of Finance, the State Committee of Planning, the Ministry of Construction and the State Administration of Environment Protection jointly issued Notice of Concerning Questions for Cities along with Huaihe River Basin Trial Implementation of Sewage Treatment Charges, specifically regulating the collection, management and usage of the sewage treatment charges of cities along with Huaihe River Basin. On May, 1999, the State Committee of Planning, the Ministry of Construction and the State Administration of Environment Protection jointly issued Notice of Strengthening Collection of Sewage Treatment Charges, Setting up Sound Operation Mechanism of Urban Sewage Discharge and Centralized Treatment, regulating the approving principle and jurisdiction of sewage treatment charging criteria.

Since 2000, the relevant departments, such as the State Council and the State Committee of Planning issued Notice of the State Council for Strengthening Urban Water Supply, Saving and Pollution Control（[2000]No.36）, Notice of Further Promoting Price Reform of Urban Water Supply（[2002]No.515）and Opinion of Promoting Industrialization of Urban Sewage and Garbage Treatment successfully. In these documents, it is stated that "All the cities with county level cities should charge sewage treatment fees as soon as possible adhering to relative regulations, when cities adjust the prices of urban water supply and sewage treatment fees, the charging standards of sewage treatment fees should be given priority to adjust to the levels of break even and slight profit to meet the needs of sewage treatment construction and operation".

Tariff policies for garbage were more recently formulated. On June 7, 2002, the State Committee of Planning, the Ministry of Finance, the Ministry of Construction and the State Administration of Environment Protection jointly issued Notice of Implementation of Charging System for Urban

Living Garbage Treatment and Promotion of Industrialization of Garbage. Treatment fees and service fees, and the price standards should be carried out on the basis of the cost recovery principle, compensating for garbage collection, transportion and treatment costs, and allowing for a reasonable profit. Opinion of Promoting Industrialization of Urban Sewage and Garbage Treatment([2002]No. 1591) further defines that "The cities that have built sewage and garbage treatment facilities should start to charge at once, the other cities should begin to charge at the end of 2003." "The charging standards should be carried out according to the principle of achieving break even and slight profit, and be implemented step by step. The business firms and the households, including those using self-supply water resource, which discharge sewage and produce garbage in the range of cities, should pay the fees of sewage and garbage treatment."

The tables below compare tariffs and collection rates in wastewater and solid waste management in various regions.

Table 15. Situation of wastewater charge collection in 2002

Collection rate	<30%	30%-50%	50%-70%	70%-90%	>90%
Number of cities	8	16	56	69	40
Percentage	7.5%	14.6%	26.4%	32.6%	18.9%
Number of province	1		15	12	2
Percentage	3.3%		50%	40%	6.7%

Source: Tsinghua University 2003.

Table 16. Standard of urban wastewater charge in 2002

Standard	<0.3 Yuan / ton	0.30-0.50 Yuan / ton	0.50-0.70 Yuan / ton	>0.70 Yuan / ton
Number of cities	112	80	17	10
Percentage	51.1%	36.5%	7.8%	4.6%

Source: Tsinghua University 2003.

Table 17. Situation of garbage charge collection in 2002

The rate of collection	<10%	10%-30%	30%-50%	50%-70%	70%-90%	>90%
Number of cities	8	16	35	32	33	2
Percentage	6.3%	12.7%	27.7%	25.4%	26.2%	1.6%
The rate of collection	<30%		30%-60%		70%-90%	>90%
Number of province	9		9		1	1
Percentage	45%		45%		0.5%	0.5%

Source: Tsinghua University 2003.

Re-structuring Municipal Asset Ownership

Urban Development Investment Corporations can own assets, borrow for infrastructure financing, or guarantee the borrowing of other parties. In China, several cities like Shenzhen, Shenyang are in the process of re-structuring municipal asset ownership.

Box 5. Cooperation between SZWG[14] and Changxing County

In September 2003, the contract about the cooperation of Changxing County water supply and sewage treatment plant was signed between SZWG and Changxing County government, Zhejiang Province. It was the first integrated urban water supply and waste water project with social capital. The total investment of this cooperation project was RMB 160 million. A new water supply and drainage joint venture corporation was set up, to provide urban water supply and waste water treatment for Changxing County. SZWG possesses 70% ownership of this new corporation with cash, and Changxing Qingyuan Investment Assets Management Center owns a 30% share with assets. The joint venture corporation got the concession contract for urban water supply and waste water treatment for 50 years. This ownership structure is more appropriate than the first one, where SZWG owned 45% of shares.

The cooperation project with Changxing County will follow the cooperation model between SZWG and Jiaozuo City, Henan Province. SZWG possesses 70% of shares of the joint venture corporation which is managed by Changxing. It is an integrated collaboration with Urban Tap Water General Corporation.

The integrated transferring share ownership model is also applied in other cities. The recent cooperation between Beijing Urban Drainage Group and Lianyungang also adopted the integrated transferring share ownership approach. It is reported that the process of cooperation between Thames Water Group and Shanghai Water Bureau has resumed rapidly after the two parties have signed a memo about the integrated joint venture of Shanghai North Tap Water Ltd.: it was agreed that 50% ownership of Shanghai North Tap Water Ltd. would be transferred in 2004.

The integrated transferring share ownership model will become mainstream for financing and developing water industry in medium cities. But in megapolis, such as Beijing, Shanghai, the integrated transferring approach would restrict the market to a few big water corporations, which are the only ones to afford the tremendous capital needs.

Source : H2O China 2004.

[14] Shenzhen Water Group.

Box 6. Shares of Shenyang Tap Water General Company for sale

Shenyang Tap Water General Company, the biggest urban water supply enterprise in Northeast China, was established in 1915. It includes 8 regional operation corporations, a large-scale engineering corporation, and 21 sub-units. 9 underlying water supply corporations are serving most of Shenyang.

Shenyang Tap Water General Company plans to utilize its total asset as cooperation base after assessment. The Chinese party will become a shareholder with 50% of the assets and the counterpart will buy the remaining 50% with cash. The investors possess the following rights and interests:

- assets and concession management right of water resource,
- water plant and the whole water production system,
- assets and concession serving management right of pipe networks, secondary pumped water supply instruments and sales serving system; and
- assets and concession production management right of North Waste Water Treatment Plant.

Shengyang Tap Water General Company will process institutional reform for 11 underlying corporations in terms of requirement of Shengyang Economic and Trade Committee.

Source : H2O China 2004.

References

CCICED (The China Council for International Cooperation on Environment and Development). 2003. Summary report for Task Force on Financial Mechanisms for Environmental Protection in China. October 2003. Beijing.

Chang, M., Memon, M.A., and Imura, H. 2004. Financial Strategies for Urban Environmental Infrastructure in Asia – Public – Private Partnerships Development. Japan: Urban Environmental Management Project, Institute for Global Environmental Strategies.

China Development Bank. Web page of China Development Bank http://www.cdb.com.cn/cdb_e/index.html 20 February 2004.

Construction Industry Publisher of China 2002. The Study on Urban Infrastructure Investment and Finance in China. 2002. Beijing.

H2O China .2004. Investment Weekly of Water Industry. 2004. Beijing

JBIC 2004. Web page of Japan Bank for International Cooperation http://www.jbic.go.jp/english/environ/support/overseas/index.php 19 January 2004.

National Bureau of Statistics of China. 1987-2002. China Statistical Yearbook 1986-2001 (in Chinese). Beijing. China Statistics Press.

Pan, WT. 2004. Presentation for Strategic Forum of Water Industry organized by Tsinghua University and China Water Network: 3rd Meeting of Financing and Investment for Water Industry. February 20. 2004. Beijing.

Pei, X.F, Ren, Y., and Zhou, X. 2003. Study on Market-based Approach for Construction and Operation of Urban Environmental Infrastructure and Relevant Policies in China. Paper for Proceeding of the First Task Force Meeting for "Financial Mechanisms for Environmental Protection", China Council for International Cooperation on Environment an Development. November 6 2003. Bejing.

Song,XT. 2003. Analysis on Financing for Urban Environmental Construction and Development in China. Paper for Proceeding of the First Task Force Meeting for “Financial Mechanisms for Environmental Protection”, China Council for International Cooperation on Environment an Development. November 6 2003. Bejing.

Tsinghua University 2003. Report for Ministry of Construction: Industrialization and Marketization Process for Urban Sewerage Treatment and MSW Disposal. Beijing.

Wang,W. 2000. Presentation at the 1st Pre-symposium for Ministerial Conference on Environment and Development for Asia and the Pacific (in Japanese). Kitakyushu: Institute for Global Environmental Strategies.

Wang,YX, Fang,Z, Ji, M, Huang ,JL, and Tan L. 2003. A Study on the Multi-Channel Investment in China: Urban Environmental Infrastructure Construction in China. Paper for Proceeding of the First Task Force Meeting for “Financial Mechanisms for Environmental Protection”, China Council for International Cooperation on Environment an Development. November 6 2003. Bejing.

World Bank. 1994. World Development Report: Infrastructure for Development: World Development Indicators. Washington,D.C: Oxford University Press.

Kazakhstan[15]

Overall Development of the Municipal Credit Market

Municipal Level Credit Market Overview

Administrative Features

According to the Constitution, the Republic of Kazakhstan is a unitary state, a principle that determines its organizational structure. The existing system of local government is a part of unified state administration system. Local public administrations include local executive bodies (akimats and akims) and local representative bodies (maslikhats). Kazakhstan is divided into the following level of local government:

- Oblast level, which includes the local state administration of fourteen oblasts and two cities (Almaty and Astana);
- Raion level, which includes the local state administration of 160 raions and 79 cities;
- Rural level, which includes local administration of towns, villages (auls) and rural counties.

The Constitution officially recognizes the rights of local self-government (article 89) as well as local government (article 85). But for the last 9 years, the Law on Local Self-government has not been adopted. The akims of the administrative-territorial units head the local executive authorities and present the president and government of the Republic. They are appointed in a top-down process.

The budget system of Kazakhstan corresponds to the governance structure. The budget of central government is a republican budget. The local budgets are oblast and raion budgets. The rural level jurisdictions do not have a separate budget.

---

[15] The country case study was written by Mrs. Meruert Makmutova, international expert on environmental finance, based in Almaty, Kazakhstan.

The complex structure of intergovernmental transfers deserves a particular attention.

Structure of sub national governments budgets and intergovernmental transfers

The revenue of local budgets at oblast, raion and city level is low. Local taxes, which feed the local budgets (property tax on legal and physical entities, land tax, transport tax) account for 14% of local governments revenues; fees are insignificant, accounting for some 1.5% of local budget revenues.

Local jurisdictions have no right to set tax rates or to determine the tax base, with the exception of the land tax. Depending on the location, water supply and production conditions of a given territory, local governments can amend tax rates within a range of fifty % (see the Law on Taxes and Other Payments to Budget). In addition, the city of Almaty has the special right to charge firms which use Almaty symbols in their company names, service signs and trademarks. A part from these exceptions, local governments possess almost no control over taxation on their territories.

The mechanisms for inter-governmental budget regulation were reformed in 1999. Budget surpluses are deducted from the revenues of oblasts which perform well, and allocated in the form of subventions to oblasts which cannot cover their needs through legally assigned revenues.

The methodology to determine the amount of resources to be withdrawn from an oblast budget in 1999-2003 was approved by the Resolution No. 529 of the government of Kazakhstan (4 May 1999). The resolution defines a normative amount of expenditures, which is subtracted from the estimated revenues of the oblast. Unfortunately, revenues tend to be overestimated and expenditures underestimated; thus, the anticipated amount to be withdrawn is often inflated.

Both contributing and recipient oblasts have criticized the existing system of withdrawals from local budgets and subventions from the republic budget. The critics insist that the methodology neither draws on economically sound norms, nor stimulates efficient local spending. The sheer size of local transfers curtails incentive for local governments to enlarge budget revenues or increase collection of taxes or other payments. The size of subventions depends on the accrual of budget withdrawals; and budget withdrawals are approved in absolute figures and are looked as directive plans.

The table below shows that contributing and recipient oblasts are the same every year. Contributing oblasts include Aktiubinsk, Atyrau, Karaganda, Mangistau, Pavlodar, and the city of Almaty. Recipient oblasts include Akmola, Almaty, Zhambyl, West Kazakhstan, Kzylorda, South-Kazakhstan. The city of Astana has not participated in these transactions since it was defined as a Free Economic Zone.

Table 18. Budget subventions and withdrawals 1999-2003 (mln. tenge)

	1999	2000	2001	2002	2003
Budget withdrawal	*37,259*	*50,251*	*84,155*	*49,065*	*57,630*
Aktubinskaya oblast	1,646	1,830	3,626	569	429
Atyrauskaya oblast	6,766	13,227	28,790	19,601	20,115
Vostochno–Kazakhstanskaya obl.		1,279	2,460		
Zapadno-Kazakhstanskaya obl.			887		497
Karagandinskaya obl.	3,939	5,820	9,856	81	
Kostanaiskaya obl.	363	377			
Mangistauskaya obl.	4,844	4,262	10,629	9,000	10,651
Pavlodarskaya obl.	3,539	1,590	2,106	1,896	974
Almaty city	16,162	21,867	25,801	17,915	24,637
Subvention	*24,814*	*27,118*	*35,504*	*59,763*	*80,513*
Akmilinskaya oblast	3,928	4,153	4,391	7,192	9,353
Alamatinskaya obl.	5,891	6,055	8,298	10,289	10,125
Vostochno–Kazakhstanskaya obl.	275			5,190	9,348
Zhambylskaya obl.	2,286	3,158	4,866	6,877	10,470
Zapadno-Kazakhstanskaya obl.	335	254		1,286	
Karagandinskaya obl.					1,835
Kyzylordinskaya obl.	3,169	2,403	1,262	6,645	8,972
Kostanaiskaya obl.			841	4,182	5,191
Severo-Kazakhstanskaya obl.	2,971	3,192	3,732	5,202	6,206
Uzhno–Kazakhstanskaya obl.	5,959	7,902	12,115	12,901	19,072
for info: Astana city	*5,103*	*2,200*	*4,646*	*5,435*	*12,974*

Source: Ministry of Finance.

General Overview of Local Financial and Capital Market Development

According to Article 18 of the Law on Budget system, only local administration of oblast level (including Almaty and Astana cities) have a right to borrow. They have the right to borrow from higher level of government for the implementation of local investment projects. Analysis of local expenditure shows that capital investment is not a major share of local budgets.

Table 19. **Capital investment at oblast level (billion Tenge)**

	1999	2000	2001	2002	2003
Local budget expenditure	215,0	303,8	393,8	394,5	479,1
Capital investment on local level	21,8	38,1	41,7	54,5	59,5
As a part of local expenditure, %	10,0	12,5	10,6	13,8	12,4

Source: Ministry of Finance, Statistic Agency.

Thanks to government policy, capital investment at local level is rising every year, but on average only 12 % of local budget expenditure is spent on local (oblast, city) investment.

Local administrations at oblast level (Almaty city, Astana city) have a right to borrow from:

- Republican budget in the frame of financial year's limit;
- Companies and natural persons for the implementation of local investment program;
- Republican budget on financing investment program that was approved by the Law on Republican budget.

Local administration of raion and city level can receive a special investment grant from oblast budget. The Government sets the rules to consider investment projects.

The development of the local (municipal) credit market over the last ten years can be divided into three stages:

- During the first stage (1991-1998) investments were not sufficient at central and local levels, and only international financial institutions implemented some projects;

- During the second stage (1998-2001), a legal basis was developed for the local loan programs. Some regions started issuing municipal bonds;

- The third stage began in 2002, when the Public Investment Program was developed. All budget programs were divided in two types: current and development budgets.

Yet, the local credit market for water and environmental infrastructure remains underdeveloped.

Legal Framework for Local Borrowing

In Kazakhstan, the legislative basis for borrowing at local (municipal) level is the Law on Local Public Administration[16], Law on the Budget system[17], the Law "On State and state – Guaranteed Borrowing and Debt"[18].

The general framework is very restrictive, as the central government has strived to mitigate the macro and microeconomic risks related to the debt of local jurisdictions. Loans can only be used by local executive bodies to finance regional investment programs. In addition, the Government of Kazakhstan is not liable to service and does not guarantee the repayment of the debt made by a local executive body.

The Law "On State and State-Guaranteed Borrowing and Debt" identifies the basic regulations for loans made by local executive bodies, and sets limits for loans size. The nexus of thresholds is defined as follows:

- local governments cannot borrow more than 10% of their local budget revenues for a given fiscal year; local budget revenue are defined as total revenue of local government, excluding transfers to republic budget;

[16] Law on Local Public Administration (adopted 23 January 2001).

[17] Law on the Budget System in Kazakhstan (adopted 1 April 1999).

[18] Law on State and State-guaranteed Borrowing and Debt (adopted in 1999).

- local jurisdictions cannot incur debt for more than 25% of their revenues for the corresponding year;
- the spending to repay and to service the debt made by a sub-national government should not exceed 10% of budgetary revenues.

These limits apply to all kinds of borrowing of local governments: municipal bonds, and debt from republican budget.

It should be noted that such thresholds for borrowing and debt are applicable to local governments only. They do not apply to the vodokanals. If a vodokanal (as every legal entity) is interested to borrow from a commercial bank (or from other financial institutions), the financial institution will assess the creditworthiness of the utility.

In 2003, the Law "On State and State-Guaranteed Borrowing and Debt" was revised and amended. In particular, local governments were forbidden to borrow from external sources (article 9). Moreover, local governments can not use state guarantees to secure debt (article 18).

Principal Vehicles for Lending to Municipalities

The following sources of finance can be considered for water related projects at the local level:

1. Current revenue of republican or local budget;
2. Special grants from republican budget;
3. Investment from international financial organizations contracting with the Government; indeed, some projects of capital investment in water and wastewater sector were implemented thanks to International Finance Institutions (the World Bank, the Asian Development Bank);
4. Commercial banks; bank borrowing has failed to develop to finance long term investments in water-related infrastructure, as tariff policy restrains the capacity to pay back financial costs.

5. Municipal bonds issuance, although it will be clear that local administrations have limited opportunities to issue municipal bonds;

6. Own funds of enterprises, although enterprises face hard constrains to finance investment from their own funds;

The first two vehicles have become available to finance investment only in the last three years, when Kazakh economy demonstrated rapid growth.

State Lending

In 2000, the Government of Kazakhstan endorsed the Public Investment program. The State contributes to the finance of the Public Investment program, in two ways:

- Direct financing from the republican budget;
- Projects financed by external loans and grants, including co-financing from republican budget.

Various programs financed by the republican budget include projects for the reconstruction of the WSS:

- State Agriculture program on 2003-2005;
- Drinking water program;
- State program of rural territory development on 2004-2010;
- Extra-program project.

In the context of such national programs, the central state provides long term loans for infrastructure financing in the water and wastewater sector. The government has signed financing arrangements with international financial institutions and is entitled to on-lend these resources to local governments, as in the case of the "Atyrau pilot water supply project" (see the box below).

In the case of this pilot project, the central government has signed a contract with the World Bank, for a loan dedicated to «The Atyrau Pilot

Water Supply and Sanitation Project». Then, the project was passed to the local level, via an additional agreement with Atyrau oblast akim. The local government at the oblast level has become responsible for the implementation of this project; it should also provide 20% of Kazakh side's co financing.

The Ministry of Finance has agreed that the local government incur debt in that context. According to this agreement, Akimat pays the interest on the principal sum of debt; the maturity of the loan is 20 years, with a 5 year grace period.

The opportunity to devolve this loan to the local vodocanal has not been considered. The party responsible for the implementation of the project is the local authority. The future of tariff policy is unclear, as it should allow paying back the debt.

Box 7. Atyrau pilot project

The Atyrau Pilot Water Supply and Sanitation Project aims to strengthen the capacity of the Vodocanal (the water and wastewater enterprise) in the City of Atyrau to provide reliable and safe drinking water and to dispose of sewage in an environmentally responsible, financially, operationally, and institutionally efficient and sustainable manner. There are five project components:

1) Rehabilitation of the water supply and sewerage systems will cover the rehabilitation of mains, replacement of pipe work, leak detection works, construction of a new booster pumping station, replacement of selected sections of sewers and renovation of pumping station in both Privokzalny District and City Center District;

2) Emergency repair is for smaller civil works repairs/rehabilitation and urgent replacement of meters, pumps, and other materials identified by Vodocanal during project implementation;

3) Institutional strengthening and project management will provide technical assistance a) to strengthen operational and financial management of Vodocanal, b) to strengthen the institutional capacity and administration of the city of Atyrau, and c) to the implementation and supervision of the project;

4) Incremental operating cost will finance administrative support, office equipment, and other operational cost for Committee for Water Resources and Atyrau Oblast Akimat;

5) Refinancing of project preparation facility will finance detailed design and preparation of bid documents for the project.

FDI of Municipalities

In Kazakhstan, there is no experience of direct lending by banks or international financial institutions to municipalities. This is a consequence of the national policy, that forbids municipalities to incur debt. All external loans must be included into the state budget.

The local administrations of Almaty and Atyrau cities made an attempt to attract foreign direct investment from EBRD and other sources of finance for WSS. Unfortunately they weren't successful:

- In 2000, the local administration of Almaty announced that a French company, with the support of the French Government was invited to work on the reconstruction of the water and wastewater infrastructure. EBRD was considered as one of the possible donor.

There was a plan to establish a new joint stock company "Almaty Suy", with Almaty vodocanal and the French company as co-founders. The French side was interested to receive a central government guarantee in the form of future tariffs rising. However, the Kazakh government has refused to commit such a tariff policy, and the project was abandoned.

- In a subsequent attempt to attract foreign investment, Almaty has forged the "Almaty solid waste management rehabilitation" project. This project has been abandoned as well, because the government and the donor could not find an agreement on future tariff policy and the capacity to pay off the debt.
- "Atyrau municipal infrastructure development" has been another EBRD project but the government has refused to adopt it, as it was a case of direct foreign investment at the municipal level.

Bank Lending

Kazakhstan has a well developed and highly concentrated bank system. Banks lending to the economy has increased as a part of GDP over the last three years.

Table 20. Commercial banks' credit to economy (in %)

	Total credit /GDP	Structure by currency		Structure by maturity		Structure by sector	
		Tenge	Foreign Currency	Short tern	Medium and long term	Non-bank legal entities	Households
1999	7	46	54	51	49	94	6
2000	11	49	51	52	48	95	5
2001	15	29	71	49	51	94	6
2002	18	32	68	43	57	91	9

Source: IMF Country Report n°03/211 *"Republic of Kazakhstan: Selected Issues and Statistical Appendix".*

According the data of National Bank, commercial banks are lending to the different entities, which are involved n the WSS sector. However, banks have no experience of direct lending to municipalities.

Table 21. Bank credits in water supply and sewerage, in Kazakh regions
thousand tenge, on the end of period

Date	Region	Short term		Long term		Total	
		Collecting, water purification and distribution	Sewer, waste disposal	Collecting, water purification and distribution	Sewer, waste disposal	Collecting, water purification and distribution	Sewer, waste disposal
01.01.2001	Aktubinskaya		5,832				5,83
	Almatinskaya			249		249	
	Almaty city				32,203		32,20
	Vostochno-Kazakhstanskaya	3,000				3,000	
	Karagandinskaya		506				50
	Mangystauskaya		315		7,291		7,60
	Pavlodarskaya	6,000				6,000	
	Severo-Kazakhstanskaya		11,715				11,71
	Akmolinskaya				2,714		2,71
	Astana city				4,063		4,06
	Uzhno-Kazakhstanskaya		2,000		183		2,18
	Total	9,000	20,368	249	46,454	9,249	66,82

Table 21. Bank credits in water supply and sewerage, in Kazakh regions (continued)

thousand tenge, on the end of period

Date	Region	Short term		Long term		Total	
		Collecting, water purification and distribution	Sewer, waste disposal	Collecting, water purification and distribution	Sewer, waste disposal	Collecting, water purification and distribution	Sewer, waste disposal
01.01.2002	Almaty city				10,859,176		10,859,176
	Karagandinskaya	25,070	602			25,070	602
	Kyzylordinskaya				562		562
	Mangystauskaya		202,308				202,308
	Severo-Kazakhstanskaya				10,000		10,000
	Akmolinskaya		21,204		273,812		295,016
	Astana city				3,970		3,970
	Uzhno-Kazakhstanskaya		6,000				6,000
	Total	25,070	230,114		11,147,520	25,070	11,377,634
01.01.2003	Aktubinskaya		13,010				13,010
	Almaty city			178,088	25,400	178,088	25,400
	Vostochno-Kazakhstanskaya				10,074		10,074
	Karagandinskaya	23,350				23,350	
	Kyzylordinskaya	88,800			170	88,800	170
	Mangystauskaya	32,000				32,000	
	Pavlodarskaya			14,462	43,640	14,462	43,640
	Severo-Kazakhstanskaya				3,400		3,400
	Zapadno-Kazakhstanskaya	760				760	
	Akmolinskaya		29,400		299,276		328,676
	Astana city				8,548		8,548
	Uzhno-Kazakhstanskaya	8,000				8,000	
	Total	152,910	42,410	192,550	390,508	345,460	432,918

Table 21. Bank credits in water supply and sewerage, in Kazakh regions (continued)

thousand tenge, on the end of period

Date	Region	Short term	Long term	Total			
		Collecting, water purification and distribution	Sewer, waste disposal	Collecting, water purification and distribution	Sewer, waste disposal	Collecting, water purification and distribution	Sewer, waste disposa
01.01.2004	Aktubinskaya			75,000		75,000	
	Almaty city	70,932			2,614	70,932	2,61
	Vostochno-Kazakhstanskaya		2,666		28,718		31,38
	Atyrauskaya	120,042				120,042	
	Karagandinskaya		1,000				1,00
	Kyzylordinskaya	84,000		12,400	606	96,400	60
	Kostanaiskaya	50,666			6,376	50,666	6,37
	Mangystauskaya	5,000	208,442		6,750	5,000	215,19
	Severo-Kazakhstanskaya	40,036	6,000			40,036	6,00
	Zapadno-Kazakhstanskaya		51,516				51,51
	Akmolinskaya		39,818		299,278		339,09
	Astana city	49,812	754	16,772	1,238	66,584	1,99
	Total	**420,488**	**310,196**	**104,172**	**345,580**	**524,660**	**655,77**

Source: National Bank.

Table 22. Interest rates on loans to real sector (%; end of period average weighted)

	2000	2001	2002
Domestic currency loans			
Legal entities	18.8	15.3	14.1
Households	27.0	24.5	21.5
Foreign currency loans			
Legal entities	14.7	13.1	12.1
Households	19.5	19.6	17.1
Loans to SME			
Domestic currency loans	18	16.9	16.4
Foreign currency loans	14.3	15.0	14.3
Loans to SME as share of total loans	26.9	24.9	21.8

Source: *IMF country report No 03/211 "Republic of Kazakhstan: Selected Issues and Statistical Appendix.*

Municipal Bonds

The legal base for municipal securities was established in 1999. Under this context, two oblasts administrations (Mangistau, Atyrau) and two cities (Almaty, Astana) have been allowed to issue bonds to implement several regional investment projects.

Table 23. Municipal bond issues

Issuer and number of issue	Date of Issue	Date of maturity	Maturity of bond, year	Value of retirement of bonds, USD	fee rate, % year	Nomination
Mangistauskaya oblast -1	30.07.99	28.07.00	1	3,468,100	14,71	100 USD
Almaty City–1	28.12.99	25.12.00	1	3,270,600	13,00	100 USD
Astana City- 1	28.12.99	26.12.00	1	1,085,300	13,00	100 USD
Atyrauskaya oblast –1	11.07.00	10.07.01	1	4,555,000	10,99	100 USD
Vostochno-Kazakhstanskaya oblast – 1	20.06.01	18.06.04	3	7,190,500	8,58	100 USD
Astana City - 2	22.09.01	20.09.02	1	6,203,100	8,50	100 USD
Atyrauskaya oblast –2	26.09.01	25.09.03	2	12,727,600	8,62	100 USD
Atyrauskaya oblast –3	26.09.01	24.09.06	5	8,887,100	8,85	100 USD
Astana City - 3	27.12.01	25.12.04	3	6,657,700	9,80	100 USD
Vostochno-Kazakhstanskaya oblast – 2	10.08.02	08.08.05	3	4,511,600	8,50	100 USD
Vostochno-Kazakhstanskaya oblast – 3	16.08.02	14.08.09	5	Bonds were not distributed		100 USD
Astana City - 4	11.10.02	09.10.05	3	10,565,579	8,31	100 tenge
Astana City - 5	11.10.02	09.10.06	4	6,258,900	8,50	100 tenge
Atyrauskya oblast - 4	15.05.03	13.05.08	5	22,419,832	8,50	100 tenge
Astana city -6	26.06.03	26.06.07	4	8,757,000	9,80	100 tenge

Source: *Information Agency of financial market IRBIS.*

According to the texts that regulate the implementation of loans made by local executive bodies[19], the Ministry of Finance and the Ministry of Justice

[19] The Resolution of Government " The Regulations of implementing the Government loan and loans made by local executive bodies" (adopted 8 June, 2000, # 874).

should conduct a financial and legal expertise of projects. Financial expertise means conducting an audit to determine whether the conditions of a loan are corresponding to the limits set by the Regulations[20]. At the time the Draft Law "On State Budget" is considered, an administrative body evaluates the economic and financial sustainability of the regional investment draft program; this involves a risk analysis. This is done within the framework of loan limits that have been established for each region according to the regulation[21].

The decision on municipal lending is made by the maslikhat (local executive body) upon presentation by akim, but it should be approved by the Ministry of finance and be mentioned in the Law on republican budget. The purpose of the transaction, and its cost should also be approved by the Ministry of Finance.

The Government has passed special resolutions on bond issuance, on a case-by-case basis. This is illustrated by the "Temporary order for issuing bonds of local executive body of Almaty City", and by similar texts for Astana and other cities. These decrees regulate the procedure for issuance, circulation and redemption of the bonds.

The improvement of the macroeconomic situation and the decrease of the National bank refinancing rate have favourable consequences on the extensions of maturity of bonds. However, the aggregated value of municipal bonds offer remains small in the comparison with GDP.

[20] The Resolution of Government " The Regulations for determining of limit of size for a bonus and limit of loan" (adopted 6 June, 2000 , # 863).

[21] The Resolution of Government "Regulations on concordance procedure with the Government of the Republic of Kazakhstan of regional investment programs that are financed at the expense of local public loans" (adopted 17 June, 2000, # 1082).

Table 24. Value of municipal bond

	1999	2000	2001	2002	2003
Value of municipal bond, M USD	7.8	4.6	38.7	21.3	31.2
GDP, M USD	16,854	18,290	22,150	24,640	29,745

Source: *Ministry of Finance and Information Agency of financial market IRBIS.*

In 1999 and 2002, banks and pension funds were the main holders of municipal bonds (see the box below). In 2002, the Ministry of Finance announced that Government would restrain municipal bonds issuances. That was before the 5% threshold applies to pension funds, after the new regime was established in 2003.

In this new context, the prospects for the development of municipal bonds are blurred. The government considers it should not to allow local authorities to incur additional debt. Rather, the government tends to centralize fiscal revenues into the central budget; this is illustrated by a corporate income tax which was incorporated into the republican budget in 2002. At the same time, it expands its financial contribution to regional (oblast) budgets. Such contributions are discussed each year, in the context of the budgetary decision making process. As a result, the number of oblasts which receive subventions from central budget has risen from 6 in 1999 to 12 in 2004.

In the history of local governments bonds, only Atyrau and Astana have issued bonds to finance investment in water supply and wastewater.

Box 8. Pension funds and local financial and capital markets

Prior to 1997, a uniform solidarity pension system existed in Kazakhstan. Since then it was reformed and replaced by a "accumulative pension system", in which individuals accumulate contributions (10 % from salary) throughout their working life. This new system applies for the people who start working after 1 January, 1998, while those with six month or longer working experience at the beginning of 1998 receive, or will receive, a blend of benefits from both schemes. Currently, the government is responsible for pensions paid under the former system.

Employees can choose the Pension Fund in which their contribution will transferred, to a personal account. In February 2005, there were 15 private and one state accumulation funds. They have a wide network of branches (72) and representative offices (73) across the country. The government is going to privatize the State Accumulative pension fund.

Ten organizations compete for the management of pension assets. This includes two Accumulation Pension Funds (State APF and APF of Halyk bank), which have a right to manage their own assets.

Until 2003, the Kazakh National bank was responsible for the regulation and the supervision of both pension funds and asset management companies. In 2003, the Agency for Financial Supervision was established to take this responsibility.

The pension system has a fundamental problem in the allocation of pension assets across different groups of financial products. According the "The Regulation of investment management of pension assets"[22], pension funds can invest their assets in local government bonds. However, the share of sub national governments bonds should not represent more than 5% of the fund's asset (see annex 2 for details).

[22] "The Regulation of investment management of pension assets". Attachment 1 of National Bank of the RK decree (adopted 29 July, 2003).

Rating of Sub National Governments

International Rating Agencies have issued financial ratings of Kazakh regions in 2000-2002.

Table 25. Kazakh region's ratings by international rating agencies

Rating Agency	State/Oblast/city	Date	Long term foreign currency	Short term foreign currency	Long term local currency	Long term rating alert
Fitch	Mangistauskaya	December, 2000	BB-		BB-	
Fitch	Almaty city	2001	B+			Outlook stable
Moody's Investors Service	Atyrauskaya	8.06.01	B1		B1	Outlook positive
Moody's Investors Service	Astana city	October,01	Ba3			Outlook stable
Fitch	Mangistauskaya	March, 02	BB-	B	BB-	Outlook stable
Fitch	Almaty	August,02	B+	B	B+	Outlook stable
Fitch	Mangistauskaya	October, 2002	BB-	B	BB-	Outlook positive
Fitch	Almaty	October, 2002	B+	B	B+	Outlook positive
Moody's Investors Service	Atyrauskaya	February, 2003	Ba2		Ba2	Outlook positive
Fitch	Almaty	June, 2003	BB	B	BB	Outlook positive
Fitch	Mangistauskaya	November, 2002	BB-	B	BB-	Outlook stable
Standard &Poor's	Republic of Kazakhstan	May, 2003	BBB-	A-3	BB+	Outlook stable

Source: Information Agency of financial market IRBIS, www.moodys.com, www.standardandpoors.ru.

Only Vostochno-Kazakhstanskaya oblast was not rated by International Rating Agencies. This is due to the oblast's high dependence on the activity of Kazzink, which contributes to 70% of the oblast's budget revenue.

Water Supply and Sanitation Sector

56% of Kazakh population lives in urban areas, 93 % of which are connected to centralized water supply systems; the connection rate is much lower in rural areas: 26%.

Kazakhstan's location and climate determine that water and its management are of great importance to the country's economy. About half of water consumed is derived from transboundary water inflows from Kyrgyzstan, Tajikistan and China. Agriculture traditionally uses four fifths of all water consumed. Inefficient irrigation practices, lack of drainage, and deterioration of infrastructure have contributed to water waste, water logging, and the salinization of many lands. Limited investment has been made in municipal water and wastewater treatment during 1990s; it has been revived only recently.

The Ministry of Agriculture has the overall responsibility for the implementation of new important projects: Agricultural program, Drinking water program, etc. The Water Resources Committee (WRC) of the Ministry of Agriculture is responsible for water resources management of the eight water basins of Kazakhstan.

The Government defines main principles of national strategy for the water supply and sanitation sector. It is well aware of the urgent need to improve water services through policy and institutional reforms. This requires repair and upgrading of existing infrastructure. In this perspective, Kazakhstan has adopted a number of reference documents:

- a revised version of the Water Code. It defines the principles and types of water use. According to it, citizens have a right to general water use which cannot be withdrawn, under any circumstances. General water use is free of charge. Special water use is chargeable and can be accessed if a license is obtained. It should be noted that such license is granted only to primary water users, taking water directly from water sources to satisfy their own needs or to service secondary water users. Water bodies can be designated by legal authorities for permanent or temporary use. Temporary designation may be short term (up to 5 years) or long term (5-49 years).

- Conception of Water Economy Development and Water policies until 2010,

- Drinking Water Program for 2002-2010. This program provides an assessment of water supply and estimates future needs and priorities to resolve drinking water problems.

These documents do not specify particular targets, action plans, and the medium-term investment program in the sector.

The infrastructure for WSS can be owned by national, municipal or private entities:

- trans-boundary, inter-basin and inter oblast waterworks, as well as those of strategic significance, are all owned by the central government; the republican (central) budget is responsible for their maintenance

- inter-rayon, inter-sector waterworks and urban water supply networks belong to municipalities; they should be financed by local budgets. These enterprises can generate income through the delivery of water supply services

- other waterworks are private property.

According to the law, nationally or municipally owned water-related infrastructures can be rented, privatized or transferred to trust management structures.

The majority of water pipelines were brought into operation or repaired 25-30 years ago. Since then, the physical condition of the infrastructure has deteriorated.

Future prospects include:

- improving the capacity of water user associations and local governments in administration, financial management;
- integrating water supply development with the improvement of sanitation facilities;
- developing a community management approach for the delivery of rural water and sanitation services to ensure their sustainability.

ADB is going to assist the Government in this prospect. This will include

- assisting in the formulation and implementation of the national sector strategy for water supply and sanitation,
- building the institutional capacity for sustainable management of WSS facilities,
- improving the quality and efficiency of safe water and sanitation services, and
- rehabilitating and developing rural water supply and sanitation facilities.

Private sector

There is no information on private investors investing their own financial resources in WSS in Kazakhstan.

Tariff policy

Tariff policy in the water supply and sanitation sector is defined by the Government of Kazakhstan. The Anti Monopoly Agency (AMA, or Agency for Regulation of Natural Monopolies and promotion of competition) checks the activities of natural monopolies, such as vodokanals, and regulates user charges. Municipal level institutions have a very limited autonomy to increase tariffs.

Due to the very limited ability-to-pay of the population, tariffs for water supply are below the cost recovery threshold. User charges cover only operational expenditure of WSS sector enterprises, although the tariff collection rates range between 67 % and 75 % (which is a satisfactory level in the region).

A number of features inhibit the required changes in water use patterns:

- low tariffs serve as hidden subsidies for industries with large water consumption,
- water consumption by private individuals is often paid by other legal entities (such as apartments cooperatives).

As a result of systematic under funding many water suppliers are on the verge of bankruptcy.

In 2002, the Government adopted a program to reform the tariff policies of natural monopolists[23]. The program main objectives are:

- To develop flexible mid term tariff policies that balance the interests of the state, natural monopolists and service users;
- To create a favourable investment environment in the sectors;
- To improve the methodology for setting tariffs;
- To strengthen consumer protection.

The Anty Monopoly Agency began to apply the new methodology for tariffs in WSS in 2003. It has engaged technical due diligence of companies to determine the total cost basis (operation and investment) on which tariffs should be based, under the new price cap methodology.

Principles of tariff calculation for water supply and wastewater[24] state that all justified costs related to the provision of the service should be

[23] The Resolution of Government " Program for enhancing tariff policies of natural monopolists for 2002-2004". (adopted 15, October, 2002, # 1126).

covered by user charges, including the capacity to generate profit. Tariffs will be approved by the authorized body for each utility separately, on the basis of justified costs and benefits.

Tariffs can be revised on a quarterly basis, at the request of utilities. Revised tariffs are approved by the Anti Monopoly Agency, not the local governments (maslikhats).

The next step towards the implementation of the new principles for tariff policy is the analysis of household's revenue, and of the affordability of new tariffs. Until this is done, the poorest part of the population receives a small compensation from the local budgets to pay for the service.

Future Development of WSS Sector Credit Markets

The current economics of water in Kazakhstan is not favourable to the development of local credit markets to finance investment in the water supply and sanitation sector:

- The government has implemented strict restrictions on local borrowing;

- Local governments' creditworthiness is very low, as they have little capacity to raise tariffs to an economically relevant level, and as their revenue depend largely upon intergovernmental transfer mechanisms which generate unpredictable financial flows.

In that sense, the system is safe, as the macroeconomic consequences of excessive local debt are under control. Now, the current scheme appears unsustainable:

- On the one hand, utilities are facing bankruptcy, and the financial resources allocated in the sector cannot finance the maintenance of the infrastructure;

- On the other hand, water economics rely in part on intergovernmental transfer mechanisms which are suboptimal, and

[24] Approval by the order of the Chair of AMA on August 15, 2003.

which fail to generate the incentives of virtuous budgetary behaviour.

In that context, local financial and capital markets have been limited to some bond issuance by municipalities and to recourse to commercial banks to finance short term treasury. They can only develop in Kazakhstan if some radical changes are considered:

- To restore the capacity of local governments to incur debt;
- To restore the creditworthiness of local governments which requires, in particular, that some responsibility for tariff policy is devoted to them, and that intergovernmental transfers mechanisms are reformed.

Such reforms would be in line with the Government's policy towards a decentralized community management approach.

The prospects are probably higher as regards borrowing from utilities. Still, their creditworthiness would be significantly enhanced, if they were able to demonstrate stable revenue streams which could be used to service debt and as collaterals. This, again, looms back to the tariff issue and to the ability of the institutions in charge of the tariff policy to set and to implement principles which are consistent with market needs.

References

Constitution of Kazakhstan (adopted 30 August 1995, amended 7 October 1998).

Law on Local Public Administration (adopted 23 January 2001).

Law on the Budget system in Kazakhstan (adopted 1 April 1999).

Law on State and State-guaranteed Borrowing and Debt (adopted in 1999).

EBRD site: www.ebrd.com.

"The Regulation of investment management of pension assets". Attachment 1 of National Bank of the RK decree (adopted 29 July, 2003).

IMF country report No 03/211 "Republic of Kazakhstan: Selected Issues and Statistical Appendix.

The Resolution of Government " The Regulations of implementing the Government loan and loans made by local executive bodies" (adopted 8 June, 2000, # 874).

The Resolution of Government " The Regulations for determining of limit of size for a bonus and limit of loan" (adopted 6 June, 2000 , # 863).

The Resolution of Government "Regulations on concordance procedure with the Government of the Republic of Kazakhstan of the regional investment programs that are financed at the expense of local public loans" (adopted 17 June, 2000, # 1082).

WB presentation "WB assistance in water sector."

The Resolution of Government " Program for enhancing tariff policies of natural monopolists for 2002-2004". (adopted 15, October, 2002, # 1126).

Convention of the UN European Economic Commission on Access to Information, Justice and Decision-Making on Environmental Issues

Principles of tariff calculation on water supply and wastewater. Approval by the order of the Chair of AMA on August 15, 2003.

Law on Status of the Capital City of Kazakhstan (adopted 20 May 1998), and Law on Special Status of Almaty City (adopted 01 July 1998).

Annex. Assets accumulated by pension funds

Table 26. Aggregate pension assets allocation(February 2004, million Tenge)

Accumulating Pension Fund (APF)	Pension assets	in %
ABN AMRO Asset Management	29,668	8.04
JSC "Corporate APF Philip Morris Kazakhstan"	840	0.23
JSC "APF Capital"	2,519	0.68
JSC "ABN AMRO CaspiMunaiGaz APF"	26,309	7.13
Jetysu	63,455	17.19
Close corporation "APF Ular Umit"	63,455	17.19
Ak niet	0	0.00
Bank Turan Alem Asset Management	32,045	8.68
JSC "APF Kazakhstan"	10,555	2.86
JSC "APF Kurmet"	15,496	4.20
JSC "OTAN"	5,994	1.62
Aktiv-Invest	13,911	3.77
Close corporation "Valut-Transit Fund"	13,911	3.77
BESTINVEST	41,843	11.34
Close corporation "APF Senim"	16,348	4.43
JSC "APF Korgau"	5,495	1.49
JSC "APF Kazakhmys"	10,646	2.88
Close corporation "APF NefteGaz-DEM"	9,354	2.53
NURTRAST	8,926	2.42
JSC "Narodny Pesionny Fund"	7,905	2.14
Close corporation "APF named Kunayev"	1,021	0.28
JSC "APF Halyk bank Kazakhstan"	89,135	24.15
Close corporation "State APF"	90,079	24.41
Total	369,062	100.00
Investigated Pension Fund assets	**Pension assets**	**in %**
RK Government paper, including	182,784.4	50.33
RK Eurobond	24,079.9	6.63
Securities of the Ministry of Finance	69,394.4	19.11
Bonds of National Bank	88,580.9	24.39
Bonds of local government	729.1	0.20
Deposits in second level's banks	27,134.1	7.47
Securities of IFI	9,308.2	2.56
State securities of foreign issuer	16,290.3	4.49
Non-state securities of RK issuer, including	115,427.6	31.78
Stock	15,473.0	4.26
Loan securities including	99,954.6	27.52
Foreign currency in USD	34,978.9	9.63
Domestic currency in KZT	64,975.7	17.89
Non-state securities of foreign issuer	12,227.4	3.37
Stock	10,571.8	2.91
Loan securities	1,655.5	0.46
Total	363,171.9	100.00

The Russian Federation[25]

Overall Development of Municipal Credit Market

Municipal Credit Market Development Overview

Institutional Arrangements for Federal, Sub-Federal and Municipal Borrowing

The Constitution of Russian Federation sets three levels of governance in the Russian Federation: federal, subject level (regional) and municipal. Each level consists of legislative and executive branches. On the federal level, legislative branch is represented by State Duma and executive branch – by the government. Each sub-national level also has its own Duma and executive branch is headed by governor (in case of regions) or by mayor (municipalities). The Russian Federation consists of 11 republics, 6 territories (Krai), 59 regions (oblast), cities of federal significance – Moscow and St. Petersburg, 10 autonomous districts, Jewish autonomous region – a total of 89 subjects of Russian Federation[26]. In the Soviet Union, autonomous districts and autonomous region were included in krai administrations. Today, all subjects of Russian Federation have equal rights. Republics have their own Constitutions and legislation. Krai, oblast, federal significance cities, autonomous region and autonomous districts have their own statutes and legislation.

The budget system in Russia, set by the Budget Code, corresponds to the governance structure set by the Constitution. The Budget Code sets three budget levels:

- federal budget and budgets of state off-budgetary funds;
- subject of federation budgets and territorial off-budgetary funds;

[25] The country case study was written by Mr. Emin Askerov, Institute for Urban Economics, Moscow, Russian Federation.

[26] Hence, Moscow and St. Petersburg are not considered municipalities with respect to the Budget Code, but rather subjects of the Federation.

- local budgets (budgets of municipalities)[27]

Each budget level is considered independent from the others, with its own sources of revenues and expenditures.

The Budget Code regulates issues of state and municipal finance and borrowing. All budgets' expenditures consist of current expenditure and capital expenditure. According to the Budget Code, current budget expenditure cannot exceed budget revenues (Article 92). Budget revenues consist of tax revenues and non-tax revenues. Non-tax revenues do not include credit finance of any sort. Article 113 states that all credit finance is reflected in the budgets as sources of budget deficit finance. Article 92 states that the size of the federal budget deficit cannot exceed the sum of federal budget investments and state debt service expenditure in current financial year. The size of budget deficit of subject of federation cannot exceed 15% of budget revenues, excluding financial help from federal budget. The size of local budget deficit cannot exceed 10% of local budget revenues, excluding financial help from federal and subject of federation budgets. Also, in case a subject of federation and municipal sales some property, the budget deficit is allowed to exceed the thresholds, but only by the amount of sales revenues.

Articles 94, 95, and 96 identify the sources of finance for state, subject of federation, and local budget deficits respectively.

[27] Article 10 of the Budget Code of Russian Federation from 31.07.1998 N 145-FZ.

Table 27. Sources of finance for budget deficits as definied by the Budget Code

Level of budget	Sources of finance to bridge budget deficit
State budget deficit	credits from financial institutions in local currency and credits from foreign governments, banks and firms, international financial organizations in foreign currency; state debt in the form of securities issued by the Russian Federation on domestic market, denominated in local currency, and state securities, denominated in foreign currencies, on foreign markets; budget credits and budget loans from other budgets of Russian Federation; proceeds from state property sales; excess of revenues over expenditures on state reserves; changes in demand balance of accounts of budget of federation
subject of federation budget deficit	state debt in the form of securities, issued by the subject of federation; budget credits and budget loans from other budgets of Russian Federation; credits form financial institutions; proceeds from the sale of subject's property; changes in demand balance of accounts of budget of subject of federation.
Local budget deficit	municipal borrowing in the form of securities, denominated in local currency, issued by municipality; budget credits and budget loans from other budgets of Russian Federation; credits form financial institutions; proceeds from the sale of municipal property; changes in demand balance of accounts of local budget.

It is important to draw a distinction between budget credits and budget loans. According to the Budget Code, budget credit is a form of budget expenditure finance that is provided to other budgets and legal entities on a reimbursable basis. A budget loan is provided only to other budgets on reimbursable or non-reimbursable basis for no more than six months.

State debt can be issued by the Russian Federation or by the subject of federation (article 98-99). State debt includes credit agreements, securities issues (denominated in local or foreign currency) by federation or subject of federation, budget credits and loans received by federation or subject of federation, guarantee agreements provided by federation or subject of federation. State debt of the subject of federation is secured by all property of the subject unless debt agreement states otherwise. Maturity of state debt issued by the subject of federation cannot exceed 30 years. Costs of debt service cannot exceed 15% of budget expenditure of the subject or municipality. The maximum amount of debt of subject of federation or municipality is limited to the total budget revenues excluding financial help from other budgets.

Municipal debt includes credit agreements, securities issues by municipalities (denominated in local currency), budget credits and loans received by municipality, guarantee agreements provided by municipality. Municipal debt is secured by all municipal property unless debt agreement states otherwise. Maturity of municipal debt cannot exceed 10 years. Russian Federation carries no responsibility for local or subject of federation debt, unless such responsibility is specifically stated.

The Budget Code states that any authority that incurs debt must keep a "debt book". Each act of borrowing has to be recorded in this book. The minimum amount of information recorded must include the volume of debt, date of issue, debt security, information on debt service. The information in this book is available to a limited list of authorities and is not available to potential investors.

Issue of securities by the subject of federation or by municipality has to be registered with Ministry of Finance. The purpose of issue is usually stated as "budget deficit finance". There are no requirements to provide more specific targets of securities issue.

Budgets of subjects of federation and local budgets also receive financial help from the upper budgets in the form of grants, subventions and subsidies. Budget grants are provided by the higher level budget to the lower level budget for current expenditure financing. Subventions are provided by the higher level budget to the lower level budget on a free, non-returnable basis and are earmarked. Subsidies are provided to lower level budgets, legal entities or persons as co-financing of specified expenditures.

Budgets of all levels can also issue credit to legal entities and state and municipal enterprises (article 76-77). Credit to legal entities is issued in accordance with the Civil Code of Russian Federation. Credit to state and municipal unitary enterprises can be interest-free.

Credit Market Development

After the collapse of the Soviet Union, the banking system was reformed, and today there is no state-owned bank that specializes in provision of credit for municipal infrastructure development.

There is also no municipal bond or credit market as such. Municipalities borrow directly form commercial or state-owned banks that do not specialize in providing credit to municipalities. Bonds that are issued by municipalities are usually issued on the regional or federal bond markets. Thus, municipalities are forced to compete directly with regions and corporations for credit.

During the 90's the sub-national credit market grew, but its resources were seldom used in municipal infrastructure development. Municipalities were considered risky borrowers and regional bonds could not withstand the competitive pressure of federal government bonds (GKO). Municipal utility companies preferred (and many still prefer) to raise funds through tariff increase, increase in collection rates, budget finance but not credit financing.

Today, however, the federal government aims at introducing private sector participation in municipal infrastructure development, development of long-term financial instruments and this may provide the much needed incentive for municipal and regional credit market growth.

Currently, the Russian sub-federal bond market is on a rise. As of May 2003, the Russian sub-federal bond market was valued approximately at 40 billion rubles (1.3 billion US dollars), which is 11% of national bond market. Most active players on sub-federal bond market are the regional administrations. In 2004, 15 regions and three municipalities have their bonds circulating on the market and 17 more regions and 3 municipalities have voiced their intentions to issue bonds in 2003[28]. Whether the proceeds of any of these issues will go to financing water and wastewater sector is unclear as bonds issues by municipalities and subjects of federation are not usually ear-marked[29].

[28] "Russian regional and local powers" Standard and Poor's, 13.03.2003.

[29] See "Institutional arrangements for federal, sub-federal and municipal borrowing".

Russian commercial bank loans have also been used to finance municipal and regional expenditure. The data on bank borrowing by regions and municipalities is scarce, as most of these loans are used to finance operating expenses of municipality or region and have maturity of less than one year. Available data shows that about 2/3 of all debt finance of regions and municipalities comes from bank loans. Loans are considered less expensive than an IPO of bonds in terms of time and transaction costs and loans can be issued for smaller amounts than bonds. Hence, commercial bank loans play a larger part in financing budget deficits and temporary cash-flow gaps – the main aim of most borrowing done by Russian sub-federal governments[30]. Commercial bank loans are also used in financing operating expenditures of water and wastewater companies. Long term borrowing for development of WSS sector by either Subject of Federation Governments (SFGs) or WSS companies is very rare. Most of long-term finance is provided through ear-marked federal subsidies and subventions or through credits by international financial institutions such as European Bank for Reconstruction and Development (here and after - EBRD) and the World Bank (here and after - WB).

Loans from international financial institutions (here and after - IFI's) are sometimes used for financing projects in infrastructure. However, such loans usually place high costs on SFGs as they require use of international expertise, sub-contractors etc. The terms of such loans are strict and may considerably limit the flexibility of SFG to operate its financial resources which already face stringent legal constraints. Still, there are several cases where municipalities and subjects of federation borrowed from IFI's such as EBRD loan to the Yaroslavl Vodokanal. The passing of new law "On general principles of local self-governance"[31] will considerably reduce the fiscal autonomy of municipalities and at the same time charge them with responsibility for financing of additional federal mandates[32]. Hence, SFGs will have much more responsibility but fewer resources. This leads SFGs to refrain from borrowing from IFIs.

[30] Sub-federal governments – subject of federation here and after – SFG.

[31] Federal Law from 06.10.2003 N 131-FZ "On general principles of local self-governance in Russian Federation".

[32] Federal mandates include, but not limited to, financing of federal privileges for social groups such as veterans, disabled, etc.

The adoption of new law "On general principles of local self-governance" will increase the importance of local credit market for financing additional obligations of SFGs. However, currently most investment projects in WSS sector are financed through a combination of budget subsidies from multiple levels (local, regional and federal), tariff increases and short-term commercial bank loans to cover gaps in cash flow and operating expenditures.

Credit Sources

Russian municipalities have access to several sources to finance their activities:

- local budgets,
- upper budget credits, loans and transfers,
- commercial bank loans,
- environmental funds,
- municipal bonds.

The balance between these sources of finance is greatly skewed towards the use of federal and subjects of federation credits, loans and transfers. As an example, each autumn, the Russian Federal government begins what is called "preparation of utilities sector for winter" which involves transfer of funds from the federal budget to regional administrations to use for purchases of fuel for boilers and investments in rehabilitation and modernization of heating infrastructure. So far bonds were issued by very few municipalities because of the high transaction costs involved and perceived high risks. On the other hand, commercial bank loans are widely used, but mostly for financing current operations. They are used much more often than bonds or other sources of finance, except federal and subject of federation credits, loans and transfers. Grants and loans from IFIs and environmental funds are rarely used, but when a municipality obtains such a grant or loan, its use is strictly ear-marked. The analysis below details each principle vehicle for lending to municipalities and explains their differences.

Local Budgets

Local budgets are used in capital investment finance either through provision of budget credit to enterprises or through direct budgetary transfer. According to the Budget Code of Russian Federation, local governments can provide credit to legal entities and municipal enterprises. These credits are often used by municipalities to finance municipal infrastructure projects. Most of the time, they are preferred by enterprises to commercial credit as local authorities can be persuaded to provide better credit terms than commercial banks.

In fact, most of infrastructure investments that are not financed by enterprises own resources, comes from municipal credit, or is financed directly out of the local budget. According to the research by the Institute for Urban Economics[33], about 88% of total capital investments carried out by municipalities is financed out of the local budget income. This constitutes a violation of the Budget Code. However, as other sources of finance are scarce, officials turn a blind eye to such practices.

Federal and Subject of Federation Credits, Loans and Transfers

In 2002, the total amount of federal credits to SFGs amounted to 0.47% of GDP[34]. The share of federal credit and transfers in municipal borrowing was 56.5%[35] compared to 20.5% in regional borrowing[36]. Municipalities rely on federal credits and transfers more heavily than regional governments. This source of finance is appealing to municipalities for several reasons. First, it's the legacy of soviet system of finance, and that means that municipal officials, most of whom are former soviet "apparatchiks", feel more comfortable dealing with upper levels of government structure than with commercial banks. Second, most of federal credits carry zero interest rate. Third, the level of control and transparency of implementation of federal

[33] Analytical report "Local government borrowing. Regulations and practice", The Institute for Urban Economics, Moscow, 2003.

[34] Ministry of Finance (Minfin) data.

[35] Minfin data, A. Shadrin "Municipal and regional credit market in 2002", RCB, N 5 (236) 2003.

[36] For more data on SFG debt structure see Annex 2.

credits is low. Fourth, federal credits may have greater maturity than commercial bank loans and lower costs than municipal bonds, which allows financing long-term projects.

Budget loans from the federal and subject of federation budgets usually have maturity of six months, however, they are often extended to the next financial year. In this case, they are reflected in the municipal budget as deficit financing.

Most of the transfers (especially federal and regional grants) go into financing obligations for privileges for housing and communal services, and other federal mandates. The new law "On general principles of local self-governance" is not likely to make federal and regional funds more available for financing projects in municipal infrastructure development. Transfers form federal and regional budgets to local budgets amounted to 6% of total local budget income in 2002[37] while in 2001 it was only 4,3%. There is a tendency towards greater share of transfers in local budget income, which might be a result of reduction in fiscal autonomy of municipalities.

Subsidies and subventions are usually considered the principle vehicles for transfer of funds to municipalities as a part of federal or regional targeted investment programs. Unfortunately, available data does not break down transfers to grants, subsidies and subventions. As subsidies and subventions are earmarked, such information would clarify what share of these transfers go into financing municipal infrastructure projects.

Over time, the role of federal budget credits and loans in municipal budgets grew. As of 2002, federal credits have comprised 43.1% of total municipal debt in Russia. The prevalence of federal budget credits and transfers over other sources of finance is likely to remain for some time as fiscal autonomy of municipalities is decreasing and federal budget credits and transfers become more important for financing of federal mandates. So, despite being the largest source of borrowing, federal and subject of federation budget credits, loans and transfers do not provide necessary funds for investment in municipal utility infrastructure.

---

[37] Analytical report "Analysis of municipal finance development in Russia in 1992-2002", The Institute for Urban Economics, Moscow, 2003.

Municipal Bonds

So far, the Russian sub-national credit market has seen rise, peek, fall and rebirth. The market for municipal and regional bonds has started to develop from early 1992[38]. The first region to issue regional bonds was Khabarovski Krai. In 1992-1993 bonds and other securities issues were rare and mostly experimental. Regional bond markets were isolated and underdeveloped. Slow bond market development was largely due to hyperinflation and absence of strong legislative base. In 1992 the Ministry of Finance registered 5 issues of sub-federal and municipal bonds for total value of 5.6 million rubles (denominated) and in 1993 – 8 issues with a value of 9.3 million rubles.

Starting from 1994, SFG's and municipalities started to use bonds as an alternative to commercial bank credit. In 1994, there were 28 registered sub-federal and municipal bond issues for the total value of 2701 mln. Rub., in 1995 – 73 issues for the total value of 6516 mln. rub. and in 1996 – 39 issues for 10789 mln. rub. In some regions the share of bonds issued by the subject of federation and municipalities in budget deficit financing has amounted to 50% in 1995-1996.

However, the bulk of credit financing still came through the federal budget credits and commercial bank credits. The absence of borrowing limits and absence of aims for credit finance for regions and municipalities has often led to over-borrowing by regions and municipalities[39]. No credit-risk assessment took place, the terms and conditions for bond issues were lousy structured and most of regions and municipalities did not have financial plans for coupon and principle repayments.

The regional and municipal credit market grew rapidly in 1995-1997. Most of the bond issues by regions and some municipalities have appeared during this period[40]. Unfortunately, practically none of these bond issues

[38] T. Bondar "History and perspectives of Russian regional and municipal bonds", RCB (The Securities Market) N 5 (236) 2003.

[39] Analytical report "Analysis of municipal finance development in Russia in 1992-2002", The Institute for Urban Economics, Moscow, 2003.

[40] See Annex 2.

were used to finance capital investments. Most of them were directed at financing regional budget deficit. The competitiveness of municipal bonds during this time was low due to the availability of high return and, as it was perceived at that time, riskless federal government bonds – the GKO's.

Despite the crowding-out effect of GKO's, the number of registered bond issues by subjects of federation and municipalities in 1997 grew to 313 and the total value of issued bonds grew to 29488 mln. rub. As of 1st of January 1998, the Ministry of Finance has registered a total 466 regional and municipal bond issues from 1992.

In 1997, several major Russian regions (Moscow, Saint Petersburg, Nizhny Novgorod Region) issued Eurobonds. Before undertaking these obligations they were at the focus of Standard & Poor's and Moody's credit evaluations resulted in assignment of credit ratings similar to those assigned to the federal government. The key advantage of these projects was an opened opportunity to raise a substantial - compared to the domestic finance market - amount of funds for a rather modest price. The years of 1997-1998 became a good evidence of a success of these projects: Eurobonds were in good demand among investors, and their liquidity on the market was also very good.

The 1998 financial crisis had an adverse impact on the emerging market for regional and municipal bonds. The general credibility gap resulted in a sharp fall of bond quotations, rapidly increasing rates of return and a sequence of defaults declared by subjects of federation (most notably – Nizhny Novgorod Region). The failure of sub-federal and municipal governments to fulfill their obligations was caused by their inability to refinance their debts on the market, declining budget revenues, investment of their reserves into GKO/OFZ that were on default, delays in obtaining regional transfers from the federal budget. Only the St. Petersburg bond market managed to survive after the 1998 crisis, while the majority of Russian regions had to restructure their debts in an effort to postpone the retirement.

After 1998, experts evidenced a sharp fall in the number of registered debt issues: in 1999, the Ministry of Finance registered 8 regional issues, which was three times less than in 1998, and 6 municipal issues, which was

1.5 times less than in 1998. In 2000, 9 regional governments (Moscow, St. Petersburg, Tomsk Region, Volgograd Region, Chuvash Republic, Komy Republic, Mary El Republic, Kabardino-Balkaria Republic and Primorsky Kray) and 3 municipalities (Volgograd, Kostroma and Yekaterinburg) registered their debt issues.

At present, municipal bond market still comprises relatively low share in total municipal debt. At present, only four major municipalities (excluding Moscow and St. Petersburg) have issued bonds for the total value of approximately 800 million rub. One of the main reasons for that is high transaction costs of first placement of the bonds and limits on municipal borrowing[41]. With cancellation of tax on registration of municipal bond issue, that is 0.8% of nominal value of issued bonds, the attractiveness of bond financing for municipalities may increase. However, even the reduction in direct costs of bond issue is not likely to significantly increase competitiveness of municipal bonds compared to commercial bank loans.

[41] See part "Authority to borrow" for details.

Figure 4. Municipal Bond Market (Million RUB)

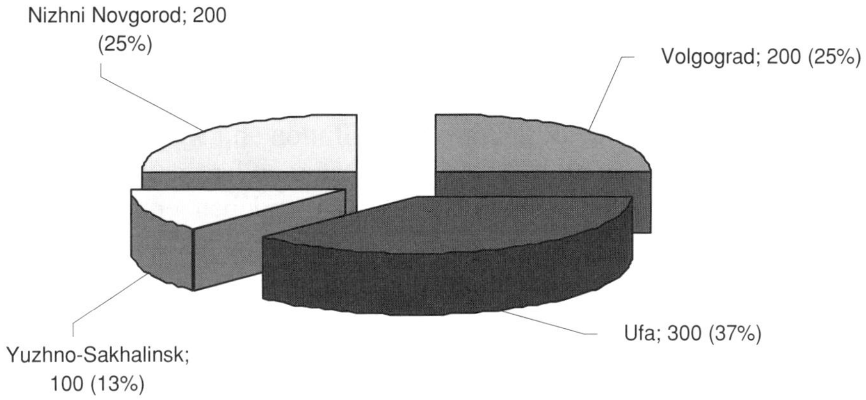

Commercial Bank Loans

Commercial bank loans are more readily available source of credit finance for municipalities than bonds. Loans from commercial banks are less expensive, easy to arrange than a bond issue and it takes less time to get a loan than to issue bonds. The reduction in total bond debt of municipalities and regions during 2001 was financed partly through commercial bank loans.

The purpose of most of bank loans to municipalities is unclear. Municipalities do not have to state the exact purpose of the loan in the agreement with the bank. The inside transactions of municipal budgets with regards to use of borrowed funds is opaque at best. Although commercial bank loans were and still are in great demand by municipalities, there is no data available on loans to municipalities during the period from 1992 to 2000. After that, the amount of borrowing by municipalities from commercial banks has been slowly increasing, but still does not get anywhere near of the share of state credits[42].

Environmental Funds

The process of formation of environmental funds across Russia started in the late 80-ies as an attempt to create one more self-sustaining public source of environmental finance. Funds were initially established as off-budget public institutions at federal, republican, regional or local levels, capitalized by ear-marked revenue of charges for pollution and fines for non-compliance with environmental regulations. Their status and revenue sources had very ambiguous legal basis. Some of them were independent legal persons (e.g. the Federal Fund and some regional funds), while others could not be distinguished from the environmental departments of the Oblast administration.

Environmental Funds in Russia have been established without clear spending programs. In the law their objectives and mandates were ambiguous.

The Federal Environmental Fund of Russia was abolished on 1 July 2002. The status of the regional and local funds is still not very clear. Most local funds have been abolished too while most of the Oblast funds the funds of the autonomous republics of Russia have survived. Those which did, have been fully consolidated into the regional budgets and are now earmarked budgetary funds.

The inadequate legislation ruling the performance of environmental funds failed to define who and what types of projects were eligible for financing, or how to coordinate activities of funds at different levels of government.

Environmental funds have never become significant players in financing environmental expenditure in Russia. The volume of resources available to these Funds were typically very small. The Funds have often provided important financial support to environmental administrations affected by

[42] See Annex 2.

frequent budget cuts, but their role in financing environmental investments remained negligible. The total revenue of environmental funds at all levels of government was equal to 6% or 17% of the value of environmental investments implemented in the country in 1997 (depending on the source of data) (OECD 1999; Goskomekologia 1997). In fact, the share of the funds in financing these investments was much smaller because typically most of the Russian funds revenue (up to 75%) consisted of money surrogates, barter and pollution charge offsets. Only Federal Fund was prohibited from using non-monetary transactions and was receiving up to 20 Million USD annual revenues in the peak years.

Environmental funds at all levels suffered seriously from the lack of accountability, transparency and managerial efficiency. Most regional and local Funds were not financing institutions as they are mainly focused on revenue collection from pollution charges/fines and direct public procurement on behalf of the government, instead of project appraisal and financing.

For the first time the extra-budgetary status of environmental funds became the focus of attention in 1995, when resources of the Federal Environmental Fund (hereinafter FEF) were commingled with the federal budget resources in accordance with the applicable federal budget law. Sub-federal governments were recommended to do the same with their environmental funds. In 2001, the federal budget law called for entire liquidation of targeted budgetary funds including the FEF. It was suggested that now all money flows accountable to the federal government will be just treated as national income controlled by the Finance Ministry's Federal Treasury and subject to further apportionment according to the federal budget of expenditures.

The FEF was liquidated in 2001, however, sub-federal environmental funds, and those whose activities were financed from local budgets, remained. Their main operations include ecological monitoring, pollution control and educational programs. However, at the moment there are several private ecological funds that not only carry out the same functions as their budgetary counterparts, but also involve themselves in financing ecological investment projects such as construction of wastewater plants[43]. Budgetary ecological funds usually have legal status of an Municipal Unitary Enterprise. Their activities in water and wastewater sector usually financed through collection of water tax from the water companies. Private ecological funds rely on dividends, interest on deposits including bank deposits, share in the profit earned in the result of use of the fund's property by manufacturing companies or other businesses currency proceeds from foreign legal entities and grants from private companies.

Russian environmental funds, both public and private, have been financing environmental infrastructure projects for the last decade. However, their share remained small, and they usually provide expert advice, consultancy and oversight, rather than investing their own resources.

Russian environmental funds support their targeted investment activities through grants (most often – public environmental funds) and/or through loans (private). However most of the time, environmental funds provide their expert advise and consultations, rather than direct investments.

In case of public environmental funds, municipalities usually have the ability to request finance from them, but they spend it only on environmental projects. Environmental funds always participate in the project in which their funds were invested.

Though, conceptually, environmental funds were designed to become an autonomous source of environmental finance in addition to budgetary and producer's own environmental investments, today, due to the scarcity of budgetary resources and legal constraints, they became actually the only source of environmental finance for municipalities, which also use them to support municipal nature protection services. Local environmental funds were mostly used for making grants to public manufacturing companies and utilities.

[43] For example of private environmental fund see Water Eurasia on www.we.ur.ru for example of public environmental fund, see MUE "Volgograd ecologic fund" on http://volg.ecoinfo.ru/htmls/Efv/efv0.htm.

Debt Security

Debt security arrangements vary depending on who is the borrower. In Russia necessary finance for investement in municipal utility infrastructure can be obtained either by municipality or by municipal unitary enterprise, that is in charge of provision utility service. In each case, lenders may expect different debt protection measures and covenants imposed on the borrower.

Municipal Debt Security

In lending to municipalities, lenders very rarely know the final aim of the borrowing. At best, municipality can state a very broad objective like "investments in water utilities". This of course does nothing to improve the chances of repayment of the debt. However, the Budget Code of Russia specifies that current budget expenditure cannot exceed current budget revenues. This means that a budget deficit can result only if municipality has some capital expenditures. The Budget Code also states that borrowing can be used to finance budget deficits and to finance corresponding budget expenditures within the limits of meeting obligations on government and municipal debt. Hence, when lending to a municipality, lenders know that their credit will be used either to finance capital expenditure or to finance the repayment of another debt.

This situation creates a lot of uncertainty in lending to municipalities and increases the risk of lending. One type of security that can be provided for municipal debt is a gurantee of debt repayment (full or partial) by an upper-level budget. For example, a loan for municipality may be guaranteed by the regional budget. On the one hand, this helps to reduce risks of non-payment. On the other hand, the upper budget may also fail on its guarantee or manage a significant delay in meeting its obligations which might erode most of the credit value.

Another type of security commonly provided by municipalities to lenders is providing the assets of municipality as a collateral for the loan. Usually, it is implied in the agreement that municipal assets may serve as a collateral in case of municipality defaulting on its obligations. Exact specifications of collateral are rare.

Debt security for municipal borrowing is also provided on the federal level. The law states that government fiscal departments must exert control over execution of sub-national budgets and must take actions to prevent default. If a municipality has violated one of the limits on budget borrowing set by the Budget code, then this municipality will be allowed to incur new debt only after it adjusts its own budget to meet all the set criteria[44], even though it is capable of servicing its debts. The only exception is made for borrowing, which is aimed at restructuring existing debt and/or repayment of existing debt principle amount. If a municipality is not able to service its debts and repay the principle amount, then a fiscal body of Russian government may:

- Order a check on budget discipline;
- Transfer the responsibilities for execution of the budget under the control of a regional governing body; note that some interpretation suggests that such an action violates the Constitution of Russian Federation;
- Take other actions that are in accordance with Russian Federation law.

Municipal Unitary Enterprises

Most of the municipal services are provided by municipal unitary enterprises (MUE) – a legacy of the Soviet era. These MUEs act as independent commercial entities and may freely borrow and issue bonds. MUEs are not subject to the same limits on debt issuance and ceilings as municipalities as they are considered separate legal entities. They cannot however issue shares as their status is not that of a private or public limited company or a joint-stock company.

The MUE status is regulated by the Civil Code articles 294 and 295. It states that an owner of municipal assets may create MUE, appoint its director, set targets for MUE, reorganize and terminate MUE, exert control over the use of municipal property, and has the right to a share of MUE profit

[44] See part "Authority to borrow".

(the latter is not specified). The MUE has no rights to sell or lease municipal property, register it as a part of its own capital or use it as collateral. MUE is never a legal owner of municipal assets. The special status of MUE also means that Municipality doesn't own any equity in MUE because MUE status does not allow for equity issue.

The most common form of security that is provided by MUE to commercial lenders is their assets. Lenders generally view the assets of MUE (especially those in utilities sector such as heating and water companies) as a good collateral. Despite that most of the time the lenders would not be able to liquidate a collateral such as pipelines or boilers, they are happy to accept them instead of the debt repayment because it transfers them some monopoly power of MUEs.

In recent years, a lot of MUEs in utility sector went bankrupt and most of those that did not were close to bankruptcy. As MUEs are working on municipal property, municipalities have devised a way to avoid giving up their property as a collateral in case of MUE bankruptcy. They would transfer all property rights to a newly created MUE, leaving the old MUE burdened with debt and without assets. This practice is now gradually becoming obsolete after a series of court decisions in favor of lenders that allowed them to oblige newly created MUE to meet the obligations of its predecessor.

In lending to municipal utility companies the practice of using future payments for utility services as a collateral for the loan is very scarce. One such example is EBRD loans to MUE's of Surgut and Yaroslavl. However, the exact terms of these arrangements are considered confidential information, so it is not possible to detail the mechanisms used. In any case, provision of this kind of security requires is rarely used as it requires complex legal analysis, for which most of the MUEs do not have a capability, in an environment of complete legal and regulatory vacuum.

Authority to Borrow

The Budget Code regulates municipal borrowing in Russian Federation. It was first adopted on the 31 of July 1998 and was enacted in 2000. Before that, the Russian legislation that regulated municipal borrowing has went through several stages of development. In the first half of 90's the laws that regulated municipal borrowing were quite liberal. Two main laws regulated municipal borrowing at that time: the law "On fundamentals of budget rights and rights of formation of outside budgetary funds…" (1993) and the law N 154-FZ "On fundamental principles of organization of local self-governance in Russian Federation" adopted on 28 August 1995. The former law is now redundant and the latter will be largely made redundant this year (2004) with the new law "On fundamental principles of local self-governance" that will replace it in 2006. The current law, adopted in 1995 "On fundamental principles of organization of local self-governance" allowed municipalities to issue bonds and other securities, lotteries, issue loans and take loans, create municipal banks and other credit institutions. The law did not specify the upper limit of borrowing, nor did it specify the aims of borrowing[45].

Federal law "On securities market", adopted in 1996 provided that any issue of securities by municipalities must be registered with the registration body – Federal commission on securities. The federal law "On financial fundamentals of local governance" (1997) has set up a limit of municipal borrowing at 15% of the total budget income. It also stated the aims of municipal borrowing. The law states that municipalities can issue bonds only for the purposes of program realization and projects of municipal development. This statement is quite opaque and the law did not state any aims for commercial bank borrowing by municipalities. These limits, including the mandatory registration of municipal and sub-federal securities issues, were stipulated again by the Budget Code in 1998[46].

Municipal veksels have been widely used in the first half of 90's. However, terms of their issue, circulation and maturity were not specified by than current legislation. This has led to adoption in 1997 of a Federal law "On veksels and bills of exchange" that has prohibited municipalities to issue veksels and bills of exchange.

The financial crisis of 1998 has resulted in chain of defaults on municipal and regional bonds and loans. The adoption of the Budget Code was aimed at reducing the risks of SNG borrowing and providing a legal structure for SNG borrowing. The Budget Code has solved some of the

[45] Analytical report "Analysis of municipal finance development in Russia in 1992-2002", The Institute for Urban Economics, Moscow, 2003.

[46] See part "Overall development of municipal credit market".

uncertainties associated with SNG borrowing; however, it has left some unresolved issues, and has its own flaws.

The Budget Code defines municipal debt as a combination of all debt obligations of a municipality:

- Nominal value of debt on issued municipal securities,
- Principal value of commercial loans,
- Principal value of budget loans,
- Values of municipal guarantees provided by municipality.

It states that municipal debt is secured by all municipal property that constitutes a municipal treasury. According to the Budget Code, the maximum maturity of municipal debt cannot exceed ten years. Management of municipal debt is carried out by an authorized municipal governance body.

A municipality is allowed to borrow in forms of:

- Loan agreements
- Municipal securities issue
- State credit agreements

Any other form of borrowing by municipalities is prohibited.

The Budget Code sets limits to the level of municipal debt. Borrowing in any form and provision of guarantees may take place only after approval by the municipal Duma. By decree, the Duma may set any of the following parameters for a given fiscal year:

- The amount of funds for budget deficit financing, from each of the sources made available by law;
- Maximum value of municipal debt, together with specification of municipal guarantee level;

- The amount of funds directed to municipal debt service.

These parameters cannot exceed the limits stated by the Budget Code. The maximum amount of funds devoted to servicing municipal debt cannot exceed 15% of total municipal expenditure. The maximum value of outstanding municipal debt cannot exceed total revenues of municipal budget excluding financial help from other budgets.

The limit on the level of municipal borrowing however is not clearly defined by the Budget Code. The size of debt in itself does not necessarily increases the probability of default, because default mainly depends on debt structure and debt service cost. Also, it is not clear from the Budget Code what should be counted as budget income (especially income in what year). Finally, this restriction may prohibit municipality from borrowing on realization of major, capital-intensive projects.

According to the Budget Code, current budget expenditure must be financed completely from the budget revenues. This limitation is often violated, as municipalities are limited in their fiscal autonomy and are charged with financing of federal mandates and/or actions of federal government (such as a decision to raise wages of municipal employees). This situation urges municipalities to cut their capital expenditure and direct financial flows to fulfilling obligations placed on them by the federal government.

There also exists a wide range of negative aspects of municipal borrowing that are not caused by the Budget Code. Most municipalities lack a comprehensive borrowing strategy. They are not engaged in preparation of strategic financial plans, and have no borrowing plan for the medium term. Another negative aspect of municipal borrowing is that the debt structure of municipalities is mainly short-term. The maturity of municipal borrowing does not match municipal capital investment programs, and this situation increases lending risks. Finally, there are no criteria for assessment of effectiveness of usage of borrowed funds.

Credit Rating

As it was noted above, municipalities or lenders rarely conduct any kind of credit risk assessment. The credit risk assessment or a credit rating is not required for municipal borrowing. However, the situation has being changing and some municipalities that are issuing debt now have a credit rating from Standard and Poor's branch in Moscow or from other national credit rating agencies such as Expert-RA[47] or Interfax[48].

The ratings of Standard and Poors reflect the general ability to meet obligations of the sub-federal and local budgets. Credit rating reports do not provide any information on how the proceeds from bond issues are used (www.standardandpoors.ru). This may be due to the fact that all municipal bond issues are secured by the whole budget and credit rating agencies are thus concerned with an overall ability of municipalities to meet their obligations rather than with perspectives of a particular investment project. Examination of recent bond issues of Moscow and Volgograd[49] shows that no statement is made on how these funds will be used except that they will finance budget deficit. The issue prospectus of Volgograd however states that in 2003, the city planned to spend 526 546 thousands rubles on its utility sector[50].

Credit ratings form S&P and Interfax for regions and municipalities are provided in the Annex 1.

Water supply and Wastewater Overview

The WSS sector is fairly well-developed in Russian Federation. The water supply and wastewater services however do not cover 100% of

47 Rating Agency Expert-RA has not yet issued a credit rating to municipality, however, it has issued credit ratings to all regions.

48 Interfax is a strategic partner of Moody's Investment Services in Russia.

49 Volgograd has issued municipal bonds of nominal value 200 million rub. On 14 May 2003 with maturity period of three years. The issue prospectus does not state any aims of the issue other than budget deficit financing.

50 The Volgograd report is available on http://www.cbonds.ru/emissions/emission.phtml?id=571 but only in Russian.

population of Russian Federation. The table below provides data on water and wastewater service coverage.

Table 28. Percentage of population connected to service

	1995		1997		1999		2001	
	Urban area	Rural area	Urban area	Rural area	Urban area	Rural area	Urban area	Rural area
Centralized water supply	84	35	85	37	86	38,5	86	39
Centralized wastewater service	82	24	83	26	83,8	28,3	84	30

Source: Goskomstat of Russia, Gosstroi of Russia.

In 2001 88% of total population of RF had 24-hours access to water services. On average in Russia, the water is supplied for 23.41 hours per day. However, the main concern is the low quality of water and low level of wastewater filtering. Approximately 50% of the population receive water services that are below sanitary standards[51]. The table below provides data on water supply and wastewater collection and treatment in 2001. The table also shows the cost of these services.

Table 29. Volume and costs of service provided, by consumer group

	Volume of services provided million. M3		Cost of services provided millions of rub	
	Water supply	Wastewater	Water supply	Wastewater
Households	9 783	9 211	3 199	2 340
Budgetary enterprises	2 668	1 456	N/A	N/A
Other consumers	3 368	2 950	2 226	1 554
Total	15 819	13 617	5 424	3 894

Source: Goskomstat of Russia, Gosstroi of Russia, "Indicative survey of water and wastewater companies" The Institute for Urban Economics, Moscow 2002.

Institutional Arrangements for WSS

The Federal law "On general principles of local self-governance" states, that municipalities are responsible for provision of water and wastewater services to their residents. Article 6 of this law also states that municipalities

[51] Estimates of the Institute for urban economics.

are responsible for organization, maintenance and development of water and wastewater systems.

Municipalities are not directly involved in provision of water and wastewater services. Instead, they delegate this authority to municipal unitary enterprises (MUEs) and only carry out regulatory functions. So far, MUEs have proved their inefficiency in managing water and wastewater enterprises. MUEs in water sector have no economic incentives for cost reduction or quality of service improvement[52]. They operate water and wastewater systems on the basis of agreement of "Economic management". This type of agreement is again a legacy of the Soviet Union. According to it, MUE conducts all operations and capital investments but has little legal responsibility. Two main courses exist for regulation of MUE: tariff regulation and administrative regulation. The latter form of regulation involves applying direct administrative pressure to the management of MUE. The former is explained in the next point.

Tariff Regulation

Under the Soviet system, municipal enterprises providing communal services operated on a cost-reimbursable basis, a variation of a "rate-of-return" regulation[53]. Investments were funded separately. They were not estimated according to investment plans, but as a rate of return on operating expenses. In addition, certain types of expenses, such as extra contributions to the employee funds for vacations or training, were covered by investments. The rate of return is set by municipal officials as a percentage of operating expenses.

These Soviet accounting rules are still in force and have a profound impact on the operations of utilities. Utilities are forced to include most investment spending in amortization and maintenance expenditures, as the share of profits that can be used for investment is strictly limited at is the maximum profit rate.

[52] See part "Tariff regulation".

[53] The following analysis is the summary of findings of analytical report "Practice of housing and communal sector reforms" The Institute for urban economics, Moscow, 2003.

It is important to distinguish between two possible expenditure bases that could be used for regulatory purposes. Under one, the regulations determine tariffs for monopoly communal service firms, particularly water companies, as the cost of goods (or services) produced (or sold) by these enterprises. Thus, for a water utility it is the cost of a unit of water delivered to the boundary of the customer property (e.g., connection to the internal pipe network of a multifamily dwelling). The regulation of tariffs for communal services for Russian households is based on an alternative approach. It differs from the standard western tariff regulation of utility monopolies in three important ways:

- The tariff may include not only the tariff for the services of the utility, but also the cost of works and services of other organizations engaged in the service delivery (in case of water supply, the cost of maintaining internal building nets, water meters in buildings or apartments, etc.).

- The tariff for services to the households may cover only a portion of the cost of service delivery, with the remainder covered by other sources: the public budget (subsidies for the difference between full costs and the tariffs) and/or higher tariffs for other consumers (cross-subsidies).

- Tariffs for the households typically regulate not just the cost of the service, but also a normative volume of service consumption when metering equipment is unavailable; thus the payment for the service equals the value of the regulated tariff multiplied by the regulated normative consumption rate. Metering for residential use of water and district heating, even at the building level, is extremely rare.

In the first days of the transition, the federal government transferred to municipalities the ownership of state housing (mostly of state enterprises), municipal housing, and utility assets associated with them. In practice this meant that municipalities became the owners of the great majority of district heating and WSS enterprises. The main regulatory document issued in September 1993 on reforming the prices of housing and communal services empowered local administrations to establish tariffs for housing and communal services. It also called for the development of a methodology for the determination of "economically justified" rates and tariffs.[54] A 1996 Government Resolution confirmed that households should pay the full costs of these services by 2003 but again failed to address the methodology for setting tariffs.

It wasn't until 2001 that a regulation was issued which actually addressed tariff setting at the municipal level[55]. For the first time, it declared the need for developing procedures linking tariff regulation at the municipal and regional levels, and established that the tariff structure should correspond to the system of contractual relations in the housing and communal service sector.

At the end of 2002, the determination of tariffs for municipal communal services was influenced by the federal, regional, and municipal levels of government, because the production of these services involves inputs that have prices regulated by the federal and regional authorities. The effective legislation assigns each level its own regulatory powers. More specifically, the distribution of responsibilities is as follows.

At the federal level

- approving the federal standards of the cost of housing and communal services that are used in computing the federal contribution to locally paid housing allowances that subsidize communal service payments;
- establishing tariffs for the electricity and gas delivered to the wholesale market by all participants in this market; and
- establishing limits for fuel and energy consumption by organizations financed by the federal budget.

---

[54] Resolution of the RF Council of Ministers, *On Transition to a New System of Payments for Housing and Communal Services, and Procedures for Granting Compensations (Subsidies) to Citizens for Housing and Communal Services Payments.* (N. 935 September 22, 1993).

[55] RF Government Resolution No. 797 of November 17, 2001, *On the Subprogram "Reform and Modernization of the Housing and Communal Service Complex in the Russian Federation" of the Federal Targeted Program "Zhilishche" for 2002–2010.*

At the regional (Subject of the Federation) level

- regulating tariffs for the electricity, gas, and heat procured on the wholesale market from enterprises of the fuel and energy complex (FEC), for all consumer groups;
- establishing regional prices and tariffs for the electricity and heat produced by large cogeneration plants operating in the region and sold on the retail market;
- establishing tariffs for the electricity and heat, as well as water supply and wastewater collection, for private enterprises producing these goods and services for sale in the retail market; and
- exercising control over compliance with the regulatory legal acts of local governments.

At the municipal level

- regulating prices and tariffs for water and heat for municipal enterprises;
- establishing normative rates for the consumption of housing and communal services; and
- establishing rates for households' payments for communal services.

The above list reveals multiple overlapping authorities. Prominent among these is that the competent regulatory agency in the area of water supply depends on the legal form of the operating company. Private entities are regulated at the regional level even if they provide services only within a municipality. This creates serious, sometimes irresolvable, problems in attracting private businesses for management of municipal communal infrastructure.

It is important to note that the existing legislation does give some direction to the tariff-setting process by stating that municipalities should establish rates and tariffs for the housing and communal services (except tariffs for electricity and gas) *and* implement cost-reduction measures based on expert examination of the tariffs for goods, works, and services. The decision to review the rates and tariffs for the housing and communal services should be preceded by such an expert examination[56].

This statement and the assignment of tariff-setting authority to local governments constitute the entire legislative base.

In addition to these laws and regulations, three methodological documents have been issued by the national government:

- Methods for planning, counting and calculating the self-cost of the housing and communal services (hereinafter – Methods)
- Guidelines for forming economically justified tariffs for the housing and communal services (hereinafter – Guidelines)
- Methodological recommendations on the financial substantiation of the prices for water and sewerage (hereinafter – Methodological Recommendations for Water).

The first two comprehensive documents are based on the concept of an economically justified tariff for a housing or communal service (hereinafter EJT), which is understood as a fee charged for maintenance or repairs of housing (including capital repairs), or to cover the costs of the provision of a sustainable service in compliance with the service quality standards. The EJT entails the identification of the production cost, and the profit required for normal reproduction of the service. It is recommended to calculate expenditures based on normative indicators that adjust current costs to make them more realistic, rather than on the actual data for the preceding period.

The Methodological Recommendations for Water pursue similar goals, defining cost based on the adopted production and investment programs, effective norms and standards for material, labour, and financial costs, with regard to the data reported by the organization for the preceding period. The price of a unit of service is defined as a fraction of the sum of costs and the planned production volume.

[56] RF Government Resolution No. 707 as of June 18, 1996, *On Reorganizing the System of Payments for Housing and Communal Services.*

According to the Methods, the cost of services is projected based on data characterizing efficient use of fixed assets, materials, energy and labor resources subject to compliance with the minimum state standards for the service quality.

Despite that all the above documents state that an enterprise's production and investment programs should be based on available finance, the calculation of the EJT is usually reduced to calculation of costs and profits, based on profitability standards. The main attention is given to item-by-item calculation of the cost function, each item being budgeted according to standards.

Stated otherwise, these methods presume normative cost-accounting. On the one hand, this approach is appropriate for production processes involving similar or recurring operations, such as water supply, wastewater collection. On the other hand, this approach imposes very high requirements to the definition of standards which should take into account the current state of fixed assets, technologies, organizational arrangements and qualification of staff. Moreover, the standards-setting process is not just a determination of values, but an instrument of motivation. In other words, the standards are designed as incentives for cost reduction, labor efficiency and product quality, etc. However, experience proves that the existing standards fail to meet these targets.

The mechanism for calculating planned profit required for the implementation of the production and investment programs is described ambiguously in both the Methods and the Guidelines.

Overall, one can say that practically all methodological recommendations reduce tariff calculation to a cost function, paying lip service to the development goals of the regulated enterprises.

These recommendations say nothing about a system of tariff regulation at the municipal level, tariff regulation procedures, etc. While they are not binding for local governments, they have gained broad acceptance because of the opportunity they offer to fill the regulatory vacuum.

This weak legislative and methodological basis for municipalities results in poor tariff policies. Indeed, tariff regulation practices in Russian municipalities suffer from the following problems[57]:

1. Almost universally, decisions by regulators are a belated response to changes in the environment of service provision, such as general inflation or increased power tariffs.

2. Tariffs are, as a rule, determined as "costs plus profitability." This system is not an incentive to reduce costs.

3. Tariffs are set without taking into account investment needs of utilities. Several vital expenditure items (e.g., extension or modernization of fixed assets) may be financed from "profit" only. Since profit is determined as a specified percentage of self-cost, it often turns out to be insufficient to finance investment, and sustainable operation.

4. The majority of municipalities lack formal tariff regulation procedures. There is no formal definition of the reasons for which a tariff may be reviewed. Tariff review processes are opaque; they do not provide for the participation of all interested parties; they are not designed to reconcile the needs of the enterprise and the capacity-to-pay of consumers.

5. Tariffs tend to be used to serve the political objectives of the local administrations. As a result of populist decisions, municipal utilities are deprived of the financial resources they need for normal

[57] This list was prepared by experts at the Institute for Urban Economics in Analytical report "Practice of housing and communal sector reforms" The Institute for urban economics, Moscow, 2003. It is highly consistent with World Bank observations. See in particular, World Bank. 2000. "Project Appraisal Document: Russian Federation, Municipal Heating Project." Report 21153–RU. Washington, D.C.: World Bank; World Bank. 2001. "Project Appraisal Document: Russian Federation, Municipal Water and Wastewater Project." Report 21416–RU. Washington, D.C.: World Bank; and Frienkman, L. 1998. "Russian Federation: Housing and Utility Services—Policy Priorities for the Next Stage of Reform." Report 17483-RU. Washington, D.C.: World Bank.

operations, which leads to depreciated fixed assets and reduced service quality.

6. In practically all municipalities, the tariff review and approval procedure is not connected to budgetary decision making. As a result, the budget is based on tariff effective when the budget is formulated. If tariffs are reviewed during the fiscal year, this is not reflected in the charges paid by public organizations.

The adoption of the new law "On general principles of local self-governance in Russian Federation" will devolve tariff regulation for MUEs in WSS sector to local Dumas. This will generate additional political risks, as Duma delegates are prone to take political, rather than economic, decisions.

Blending Grants and Subsidies

There are no strict rules for blending grants or subsidies with market-rate credit. Sometimes, a grant or a subsidy may have specific purposes and implicitly state the terms and conditions of blending with market-rate credit.

The WSS sector is subsidized both directly and indirectly. Direct subsidies usually take the form of a lump-sum transfer form the budget (municipal, regional or federal). Other kinds of direct subsidies include grants for environmental projects (see "Credit sources"), and in-kind transfers of equipment or technical know-how from other countries water companies.

One common practice is cross-subsidized tariff for water and wastewater. The table below shows tariffs for different consumer groups in WSS sector in 2003.

Table 30. Tariff for one cubic meter (rub, including VAT)

Consumer category	Water supply	Wastewater
Households	4.06	3.30
Budgetary enterprises	4.06	3.30
Other consumers	10.30	8.75

Source: Goskomstat 2003.

The tariff for other consumers is significantly higher than the tariff for households and budgetary enterprises. The tariff for households and budgetary units is usually set below the cost-recovery level, hence other consumers effectively subsidize households and budgetary enterprises. The situation is changing now. The government proposed to eliminate cross-subsidization in 2004, however, the date has later been moved to 2005[58].

Use of Credit in Water Supply and Wastewater Sector

The Russian enterprises of the WSS sector have been using credit from commercial banks and municipalities to finance their infrastructure investments. However, these credits were short-term and aimed for financing current expenditure of projects. Long term finance is scarce on the Russian credit market, and lenders usually consider investments in WSS projects to be high risk investments. Thus, credit resources for WSS investment projects have been scarce so far.

The risks of long-term investments in WSS sector are very high. One major source of risk is the current tariff regulation system[59]. Another one is the unstable political environment of municipalities. A new mayor and/or Duma may cut tariffs and thus hinder repayment capacity, if they consider the purpose of the loan is not a priority, or the impact on tariffs is too high. Political risks of investment may exceed those of tariff regulation.

Due to high risks, infrastructure investment is usually carried out in the following manner. A vodokanal (an MUE that is responsible for water supply

58 Federal government Resolution N 609 of 21/07/2001 "On actions for elimination of system of cross subsidization of consumers of water, wastewater, heating, solid waste collection and utilization services"

59 See part "Tariff regulation" for more information on the rate setting.

and wastewater) sets up a special purpose company (SPC) for carrying out a particular investment, jointly with investors, usually commercial banks. Having a stake in the project somewhat reduces investors' risks, as they can easily claim whatever infrastructure has been built, as their own in the event of default. Then, investors issue short-term credits to finance current expenditure of the new company.

Special purpose companies are created when it is necessary to finance significant amounts of investments and when a collateral for the loan can be identified and isolated (in financial terms) from the rest of the infrastructure. Thus, reconstruction of pipelines is not usually carried out by SPCs: this would fragment the network and increase transaction costs associated with regulation. However, construction of wastewater treatment plants or water pumping stations can be financed through SPC.

One such example is the construction of new wastewater treatment plant in Ekaterinburg.

Box 9. Illustration of WSS investment financed by and SPC

The city of Ekaterinburg is planning to build a new residential area in a northern part of the city. The building site does not possess any water and wastewater infrastructure and it is estimated that existing wastewater treatment plants will not have the capacity to process wastewaters from this area.

Thus, a decision was made to build a new wastewater treatment plant, using the resources of municipal unitary enterprise "Vodokanal" and private sector investments. MUE "Vodokanal", jointly with Ecological Foundation "Water Eurasia" and commercial bank "Interregional investment bank" have founded a SPC named "Direction of wastewater treatment facilities". The SPC is in charge of all construction work. The total amount of investment is estimated around 590 millions rub.

Project financing is carried out on the following basis. The "Interregional investment bank" provides short-term (one year) credit (with interest rate equal to current Central Bank interest rate plus 2%[60]) to SPC, which is used to finance current operations. "Vodokanal" has an investment agreement with SPC by which all expenses of the project are included in the wastewater tariff and "Vodokanal" transfers these funds to SPC[61]. The credit is repaid when SPC receives the funds from "Vodokanal". In case of default by SPC to pay the principle of the loan, the "Interregional investment bank" has the right to seize assets already in place. This includes rather expensive technology which can be separated from the plant and sold.

Long-term investment is still not an issue as tariff regulation risks remain high. Unfortunately, there is no data on the level of such investments in WSS.

Private Sector Participation

The government has stated that private sector participation was one of the key elements of housing and communal sector reform in the Russian Federation[62]. The main aim of private sector participation is provision of funds to invest in the housing and utility sectors. However, events seem to

60 At the moment, the Central Bank interest rate is 14%.

61 The exact contents of this agreement is unknown as relationships between the "Vodokanal" and SPC are opaque.

62 Government Resolution N 797 from 17/11/01 "On sub-program "Reform and modernization of housing and communal complex of Russian Federation" of targeted Federal program "Zhilische" for years 2002-2010".

overtake government plans. In 2004, there were at least five private companies in Russia that are already engaged in provision of water and wastewater services at municipal level. Four of these companies are Russian and one is a German private operator.

The creation of Russian Utilities Systems (RKS), a first national scale private operator, as a part of RAO UES was a clear signal of the trend towards private sector participation in WSS sector. Approximately at the same time[63], a private company "Modern City", a subsidiary of Interros holding, announced that it would operate Perm vodokanal (a regional center with population over a million people) on a 49 years lease contract. Already in Zelenograd, WTE Wassertechnik GmbH, a German company, has built a wastewater treatment plant, under a BOOT[64] contract.

Despite increasing activities of private sector in WSS, very limited investment activity is underway. At the moment, only WTE Wassertechnik GmbH and a JSC "Syzranvodokanal" have undertaken direct investments, using their own resources. Other private operators, including RKS, have not yet made any investments in WSS sector. Most of other private operators are not yet concerned with fund-raising and concentrate on improving management efficiency.

At the moment, Russia is at the crossroads of choosing a form of private sector participation in WSS sector. The choice is between full privatization of WSS sector and development of concession-based mechanisms. No law exists that provides institutional arrangements for concession-type contracts, and only two forms are available for private sector participation: lease or privatization of utility infrastructure. However, the Draft Law on concessions in utility sector was supposed to be adopted by the end of 2004.

This year (2004), the Ministry of Gosstroi has announced that it will propose a legislative initiative to the Federal government in the form of draft of 30 legislative documents (government resolutions, laws, methodologies) aimed at improving the situation in housing and utilities sector and greater private sector participation in municipal housing and infrastructure projects.

[63] May 2002.

[64] BOOT – acronym for Built-Own-Operate-Transfer.

Private investments are included in the possible sources of finance of the Targeted Federal Program "Providing population of Russia with drinking water" drafted by Gosstroi.

Credit Market Development in WSS

As stated in Government Resolution N 797 from 17/11/01 "On sub-program "Reform and modernization of housing and communal complex of Russian Federation" of targeted Federal program "Zhilische" for years 2002-2010" government expects that the main bulk of investments in WSS sector will be carried out by the private sector. Whether that will be commercial banks, or private operating companies is unclear. It is also unclear whether commercial credit will go to the existing MUEs, or whether private operators of WSS sector will operate and invest their own funds. The share of municipal budget and other budget resources is planned to be small and mostly directed towards provision of guarantees for private investments. Hence, municipal bonds are not likely to be the source of finance for municipal infrastructure projects.

Currently, a ministry of Gosstroi of Russia is considering a possibility of creating a special guarantee fund that will provide expertise for private investors in terms of risk assessment, and provide guarantees to their investments. The start-up capital of the "Guarantee Agency" will be provided by the federal budget; however, the Agency will operate on a competitive basis.

International multi-lateral organizations have recently started to actively support development of Russian water and wastewater sector through provision of credit, grants and consultancy services. At present, several investment projects in WWS sector are funded by the World Bank, EBRD, Danish government and DFID. Most of the projects are still in their early stages and it is difficult to draw conclusions from them.

The largest project so far has been the World Bank Municipal Water and Wastewater project. The total value of the project is 168.9 million US dollars and the project is implemented in 14 Russian municipalities. The main objectives of the project are:

- providing support for improvement in the operations in water and wastewater systems,

- implementing a specific set of institutional and commercial reforms aimed at improving physical system operations and financial performance of vodokanals.

The project focuses not only on providing funds for investments, but also on provision of technical assistance, training, project management and implementation support.

The project was initiated by Russian Federal authorities, and Russian Federation provides guarantees for the World Bank loan. This is a common situation with most of the municipal water and wastewater projects that receive financing from multi-lateral organizations. A Federal Government guarantee is usually required, even for less expensive projects (see Table below). Other loans usually have a guarantee from regional authority and/or municipality.

Project financing by multi-lateral organizations is done either through on-lending from federal or regional level, or through direct landing to a Vodokanal. The former mechanism was implemented in the World Bank Municipal Water and Wastewater project and in EBRD project in Komi Republic. The latter mechanism was used in the EBRD project with Yaroslavl Vodokanal. In any case, multi-lateral organisations provide only a portion of finance, while the rest is provided by the federal, regional and municipal budgets, and vodokanal's own resources.

Most projects that involve multi-lateral organisations usually involve not only direct investments in particular projects, but also provision of technical assistance, encouragement of reforms in utility sector and provision of support in project management. The level of such assistance varies with each project. However, this kind of assistance is necessary as current management practices of vodokanals and regulatory practices of municipalities may seriously endanger successful project realization.

Table 31. Examples of WSS projects financed by IFIs

Period	Lender/Borrower	Loan amount	Guarantee	Purpose
21.12.2000/ 30.06.2006	World Bank/Russian Federation	168.9 M USD	Sovereign	Access to WWS services for the poor, pollution management in 14 Russian municipalities
15.01.2003/ 15.01.2006	EBRD/Yaroslavl Vodokanal	490.6 M RUR (16 M USD)	Not specified	Reduction in operating costs involving emergency rehabilitation and general upgrading of the municipal water system in Yaroslavl
27.04.1999	EBRD/Russian Federation	18 M USD	Sovereign	Improvement of the water supply and waste-water services in the city of Kaliningrad
01.07.2003	EBRD/Komi Republic (RF)	10 M EUR – Syktyvkar 5 M EUR -Vorkuta	Komi Republic	Rehabilitation of water and waste-water infrastructure and services in the municipalities of Syktyvkar and Vorkuta
19.12.1997	EBRD/City of Novgorod	35 M USD	Sovereign	Improvement of performance of Novgorod's utilities, particularly water services and district heating, improving the city's ability to manage its utilities, and enhancing its creditworthiness.
18.04.1997	EBRD/Vodokanal of St. Petersburg	35 M DEM	St. Petersburg	Improvement of water supply and water demand management as well as waste-water collection services in the city of St Petersburg.
16.09.2002	EBRD/Vodokanal of St. Petersburg	23.8 M EUR	St. Petersburg	Construction of sludge incinerator at the Northern Waste Water Treatment Plant in St Petersburg
04.09.2002	EBRD/Vodokanal of St. Petersburg	42 M EUR	St. Petersburg	Completion of the South West Waste Water Treatment Plant to reduce the discharge of untreated waste water in the Gulf of Finland
30.03.2001	EBRD/Surgut	1,350 M RUR		Municipal water and district heating infrastructure in the city of Surgut

Source: World Bank, EBRD.

Obstacles to the Development of Credit Market in WSS Sector

The main obstacle to greater and more efficient use of credit in WSS sector is underdevelopment of institutional arrangements that help to reduce risks of such investments. On the demand side, municipalities find it hard to attract long-term finance due to its scarcity and high costs. Municipalities are also cautious to borrow, as they may loose their assets in case of default. Ceilings placed on municipal borrowing by the Budget Code also restrict the use of borrowing by municipalities.

Borrowing by MUEs is also severely restricted. One of the main reasons is that most of municipally-owned vodokanals operate with net losses and have high outstanding debt to energy companies. Management of MUEs is another risk factor: managers usually refer to a technical approach, and tend to ignore the economic and financial dimensions of service provision. Most of managers at MUEs have held their positions since the times of the Soviet Union and they are managing their enterprises with methods that are long outdated in a transition economy. Creating a special purpose company to carry out investments is one of the ways of reducing management risks, as it allows investors to hire trusted professional managers.

On the supply side, provision of credit to municipalities is a risky undertaking. Loan repayment is done by inclusion of interest and principal repayment in the tariff, but current tariff regulation systems provides no guarantees that the tariff will be high enough to repay the loan. A high share of vodokanal's revenue consists of budget compensation for privileges, tariff differences[65] and subsidies. These compensations are almost never paid in full. This generates cuts and uncertainty on vodokanals' revenues and may hinder loan repayment. Finally, the Russian credit market is mainly short-term, and availability of long-term resources is limited. Municipalities find it hard to compete for long term finance with oil, gas and energy companies which are commonly viewed as relatively low-risk investment compared with municipal WSS sector.

[65] Russian municipalities set tariffs for households, but frequently they adopt what is called "the level of payment by households". It means that citizens do not pay the full tariff, but only a portion of it, as set by municipality. The difference between the actual tariff and the level of payment is supposed to be financed out of municipal budget but frequently, the budget does not have necessary funds.

Main Conclusions

The development of credit market for WSS sector in Russia is closely tied to increasing private sector participation in this sector. Commercial lenders view private companies in WSS sector as more reliable borrowers than municipalities. However, before private sector can fully enter the market for water and wastewater services, several steps have to be taken.

First, there is a need to clarify the legal and institutional framework for private sector participation in WSS sector. This will facilitate the development of credit market for financing investment projects in WSS sector. The adoption of the law on concessions in utility infrastructure, planned for the end of 2004, will set the framework for long-term contractual relationships between private companies and municipalities. Private sector participation through concession agreements will reduce contractual risks of investments and thus lower the cost of capital for private operators.

Another important step is devising an efficient tariff regulation system for water utilities. Tariff setting procedures have to allow for recovery of invested funds, and the tariffs should be so stable that investments can be planned. Tariff regulation system also has to reduce political risks to minimum, by establishing rigid regulation procedures and methodologies for tariff calculation. Tariff regulation procedure has to account for budget debts, increases in prices of inputs and has to set profit rates, not as normatively defined rates of return but as a result of planned investments. The regulatory level also has to be consistent with the scale of water and wastewater enterprise. In other words, if vodokanal provides WSS services to a municipality, it has to be regulated by the municipality. The legal status of an enterprise should not be the factor defining regulatory level. All these issues are addressed in a law on tariff regulation in utilities sector that is also currently being developed by the Ministry of Gosstroi.

Development of municipal credit market will have little impact on WSS sector financing as it will be the concern of private utility companies. However, financing of social improvement programs of municipalities can, and should be done through municipal credit market. The development of pension funds and insurance companies in Russia will increase the demand for long-term, low-risk financial securities that can be provided by municipalities.

The provision of institutional and legal framework for WSS credit market development however will not solve the problems of inefficient use of funds for WSS investment projects, poor management quality and will not in itself help to create effectively functioning credit market. There exists a great scope for provision of technical assistance and training for municipal officials, managers of MUE and private companies management.

Training

It is necessary to create resource centers for information dissemination and provision of training. Such resource centers will train municipal officials and utility managers in the areas of municipal finance, strategic planning, budgeting, tariff regulation, contract preparation, utility financial and investment management, public sector awareness, public relations and so on. Resource centers will also disseminate information on best local and international practices in public-private partnerships and other issues through holding conferences, seminars, issuing practical guides and handbooks.

Technical Assistance

There is demand for technical assistance at federal and municipal levels. At federal level, this includes provision of legal support with drafting legislation for concessions, tariff regulation and strategic development of national WWS sector; technical support may come in the form of:

- Provision of financial support to foundation of Guarantee Agencies,
- Provision of financial support to Environmental Agencies,
- Provision of expertise in risk assessment in WWS sector investments,
- Encouraging competition among consultancy firms in WWS sector,
- Development of methodology and a database of technical and financial performance indicators of WWS companies.

At the local level, technical assistance is required for the development of local credit markets, assistance to potential borrowers and potential lenders in loan terms negotiations, assistance to municipalities in various areas that will help to strengthen local governments capacity to efficiently allocate budget resources and develop solid contractual relationships with private operators of WWS infrastructure. Such areas include:

- Preparation of tenders for WWS management,
- Contract preparation,
- Financial and fiscal management,
- Capital investment planning, including preparations of business-plans, optimal allocation of funds, increasing energy efficiency, reducing water leaks etc.
- Strategic budget planning,
- Complex strategic city development planning.

Technical assistance can be delivered in a variety of ways, including the provision of expert advice and consultancy services, research of potential opportunities in developing credit market for WWS sector, monitoring indicators and development of the sector, or providing guarantees for private investments and financing consultancy and technical assistance services for potential borrowers.

Annex 1. Rating of Government Agencies

Table 32. Standard and Poor's ratings. International scale

Issuer name	Date assigned (last changed)	FC/Outlook	LC/Outlook
Sovereign rating			
Russian Federation	27.01.2004	BB+/Stable	BBB-/Stable
Public Ratings			
Balashika Rayon	03.11.2003	B-/Stable	--/--
City of Moscow	02.02.2004	BB+/Stable	--/--
City of St. Petersburg	02.02.2004	BB/Positive	BB/Positive
City of Surgut	21.01.2004	B/Stable	B/Stable
Irkutsk Region	01.10.2003	B/Stable	--/--
Khanty-Mansiysk Autonomous Okrug	06.02.2004	BB-/CreditWatch Negative	--/CreditWatch --
Klin Rayon	02.09.2003	B-/Stable	--/--
Moscow Region	18.08.2003	B+/Stable	--/--
Rep. of Bashkortostan	25.04.2003	B+/Stable	--/--
Rep. of Tatarstan	22.09.2003	B-/Stable	--/--
Samara Region	25.04.2003	B+/Positive	--/--
Sverdlovsk Region	06.01.2004	B/Positive	B/Positive
Vologda Region	04.02.2003	B/Stable	--/--
Yamalo-Nenets Autonomus Okrug	06.02.2004	B/Stable	--/--

Source: Standard and Poor's.

Table 33. Standard and Poor's ratings. National scale

Issuer name	Issuer rating (Date assigned (last changed))	Debt rating	
		State registration number (repayment date)	Rating (Date assigned (last changed))
Sovereign rating			
Russian Federation	ruAA+ (22.02.2002)		
Public Finance Ratings			
Balashika Rayon	ruBBB (03.11.2003)		
Vologda Region	ruA- (04.02.2003)		
Vologda Region		Bonds VLG25001(23.12.2004)	ruA- (10.12.2003)
Karelia	ruBBB+ (12.11.2003)		
Karelia		Bonds RU25005KAR(19.04.2004)	ruBBB+ (19.11.2003)
Klin Rayon	ruBBB- (02.09.2003)		
Moscow Region	ruA+ (18.08.2003)		
Moscow Region		Bonds RU25001MOO(19.04.2004)	ruA+ (18.08.2003)
Moscow Region		Bonds RU25002MOO(10.06.2005)	ruA+ (18.08.2003)
Moscow Region		Bonds RU25003MOO(19.08.2007)	ruA+ (18.08.2003)
Samara Region	ruAA- (25.04.2003)		
Samara Region		Bonds RU25001SAM(04.07.2006)	ruAA- (01.07.2003)
Tomsk Region	ruA- (14.08.2003)		
Tomsk Region		Bonds RU25011TMS0 (19.11.2005)	ruA- (10.11.2003)

Table 33. Standard and Poor's ratings. National scale (continued)

Issuer name	Issuer rating (Date assigned (last changed))	Debt rating	
		State registration number (repayment date)	Rating (Date assigned (last changed))
Tomsk Region		Bonds RU25012TMS0 (11.06.2005)	ruA- (05.12.2003)
Tomsk Region		Bonds RU25016TMS0 (27.07.2006)	ruA- (21.01.2004)
City of Surgut	ruA- (21.01.2004)		
Khanty-Mansiysk Autonomous Okrug	ruAA (07.03.2002)		
Khanty-Mansiysk Autonomous Okrug		Bonds RU24004HMN (08.12.2005)	ruAA (20.12.2002)
Khanty-Mansiysk Autonomous Okrug		Bonds RU25005HMN (27.05.2008)	ruAA (27.05.2003)
Yamalo-Nenetskii Autonomous Okrug	ruA (06.02.2004)		
Yamalo-Nenetskii Autonomous Okrug		Bonds RU24001YML (03.08.2008)	ruA (06.02.2004)
City of Cherepovets	Rating withdrawn (02.07.2003)		

Source: Standard and Poor's.

Annex 2. Financial instruments for sub national budgets

Table 34. Structure of internal borrowing of subnational budgets, 2001-2002 (%)

Indicator	2001		2002	
	Regional budgets	Municipal budgets	Regional budgets	Municipal budgets
Total, mln. Rub.	77 432.0	54 113.2	154 077.4	101 206.3
Bonds	18.4	1.7	18.3	1.0
State credit	20.5	56.5	16.7	43.1
Other borrowing	61.1	41.8	65.0	56.0

Source: Ministry of Finance.

Table 35. Municipal bonds issues (2003)

Issuer	Date of issue	Type of security/purpose	Nominal value (rub)	Tenure of bonds (months)	Interest (coupon or discount)
Ufa city administration	UFA-002/00137 19.03.2003	Municipal bonds - meeting debt obligations	1000	from 1 to 3 years	discount + coupon
Volgograd city administration	VGG-009/145 от 16.04.2003 г.	Municipal bonds - budget deficit financing	1000	from 1 to 5 years	variable coupon
Volgograd city administration	VGG-010/146 от 16.04.2003 г.	Municipal bonds - budget deficit financing	500	from 90 days to 1 year	coupon
Ekaterinburg	EKB-004/00151 от 04.06.2003 г.	Municipal bonds - budget deficit financing and debt repayment	Every 25 rub., from 1000 to 1800	from 1 to 5 years	1%of par value
Krasnoyarsk city administration	KRN-001/00153 от 21.06.2003 г.	Municipal bonds - budget deficit financing and debt repayment	1000	from 1 to 2 years	coupon
Yuzhno-Sakhalinsk city administration	USH-002/0163 от 28.08.2003 г.	Municipal bonds - budget deficit financing and debt repayment	500	2 years	coupon
Novosibirsk city administration	NSB-001/00180 от 08.12.2003 г.	Municipal bonds - budget deficit financing and debt repayment	1000	from 1.5 to 5 years	coupon

St. Petersburg Financial department	GSP-031/00126 27.02.2003г.	Municipal bonds - budget deficit financing and debt repayment	100	up to 1 year	discount
St. Petersburg Financial department	GSP-032/00127 27.02.2003г.	Municipal bonds - budget deficit financing and debt repayment	100	from 1 to 5 years	discount + coupon
St. Petersburg Financial department	GSP-033/00128 27.02.2003г.	Municipal bonds - budget deficit financing and debt repayment	100	from 1 to 5 years	discount + coupon
St. Petersburg Financial department	GSP-034/00129 27.02.2003г.	Municipal bonds - budget deficit financing and debt repayment	100	from 1 to 5 years	discount + variable coupon
St. Petersburg Financial department	GSP-035/00130 27.02.2003г.	Municipal bonds - budget deficit financing and debt repayment	100	from 5 to 30 years	discount + coupon
St. Petersburg Financial department	GSP-036/00131 27.02.2003г.	Municipal bonds - budget deficit financing and debt repayment	100	from 5 to 30 years	discount + coupon
St. Petersburg Financial department	GSP-037/00132 27.02.2003г.	Municipal bonds - budget deficit financing and debt repayment	100	from 5 to 30 years	discount + coupon
St. Petersburg Financial department	GSP-038/00133 27.02.2003г.	Municipal bonds - budget deficit financing and debt repayment	100	from 5 to 30 years	discount + variable coupon
St. Petersburg Financial department	GSP-039/00134 27.02.2003г.	Municipal bonds - budget deficit financing and debt repayment	100	from 1 to 5 years	variable coupon
Moscow city administration	MOS-010/0138 28.03.2003г.	Municipal bonds - budget deficit financing and debt repayment	1000	from 1 to 5 years	variable coupon
Moscow city administration	MOS-011/0139 28.03.2003г.	Municipal bonds - budget deficit financing and debt repayment	sum that can be divided by 100 rub.	from 1 to 5 years	variable coupon
Moscow city administration	MOS-012/0140 28.03.2003г.	Municipal bonds - budget deficit financing and debt repayment	1000	from 1 to 5 years	coupon

Moscow city administration	MOS-013/0141 28.03.2003г.	Municipal bonds - budget deficit financing and debt repayment	sum that can be divided by 100 rub.	from 1 to 5 years	coupon
Moscow city administration	MOS-014/00164 от 06.10.2003 г.	Municipal bonds - budget deficit financing and debt repayment	1000	from 5 to 10 years	coupon
Moscow city administration	MOS-015/00165 от 06.10.2003 г.	Municipal bonds - budget deficit financing and debt repayment	1000	from 5 to 10 years	coupon

Source: Country case study

Ukraine[66]

Overall Development of the Municipal Credit Market

Municipal Credit Market Development Overview

Ukrainian sub-national credit system for infrastructure development historically constituted a minor portion of the overall Ukrainian capital market. Except for a short-term financing, little borrowing is underway at the local level. Limited amount of available capital investment financing does not address capital needs of sub national governments (SNG[67]) and communal service enterprises (CSEs)[68]. The amount of municipal bonds issues constituted less than 1% of the overall securities issues, registered by the Securities and Stock Market State Commission (SSMSC) since 1995 until the end of 2002. Only limited examples of commercial bank lending to SNG are known. Two corporate bond issues by CSEs have been used to attract financing for capital improvement in municipal services sector. As a result, essential municipal infrastructure and provision of services, such as water supply and treatment, wastewater collection and treatment, district heating, highways, education and health have been under financed.

---

[66] The country case study was written by Alyona Babak, Price Setting and Municipal Finance Specialist, PADCO, Inc., Kyiv, Ukraine. Inna Lunina, Financial and Budgetary Projections Department Head, Institute of Economic Projections, National Academy of Sciences of Ukraine, prepared a section on intergovernmental finance in Ukraine; Ministry of Finance of Ukraine, Securities and Stock Market State Commission and the State Committee of Housing and Communal Services have provided statistics, presented in the Attachments.

[67] In this chapter, SNGs include executive and legislative bodies of autonomous Republic of Crimea, oblasts, rayons, cities, rayons (districts) in the city, villages, and residential settlements. *Local Self-Governments* (LSG) are governments of municipalities, villages, and residential settlements. The rayon and oblast councils are LSGs, which represent joint interests of territorial communities of the villages, residential settlements and cities. Executive powers in oblasts, rayons, rayons of the Autonomous Republic of Crimea, rayons in the cities of Kyiv and Sebastopol are executed by oblasts, rayon, Kyiv and Sebastopol Local State Administrations (LSA).

[68] Communal service enterprises are businesses, responsible for provision of specific municipal services, among which are water supply and wastewater, district heating, solid waste disposal, housing, public transport etc.

Budgetary subsidies or tariff increases for the services provided to current system users cannot cover costs of complying with European Union standards for municipal service delivery, a requirement that comes from the tasks, set by the President of Ukraine in his address to the Supreme Council of Ukraine.[69] To meet such needs, the total capital investment requirements for the water supply and wastewater sector only have been estimated at EUR 22-26 billion[70] over the next 20 years[71], of which EUR 4-6 billion correspond to urgent investments[72]. About 20% of water supply networks and 25% of wastewater collection networks require replacement. Approximately 40% of water treatment plants and water and wastewater pumping stations require rehabilitation and replacement of equipment[73].

SNG borrowing in Ukraine is considerably lagging behind general development trends of the overall financial markets due to the following factors:

- decentralization of central government powers[74] resulting in autonomy and strengthening of material and financial base of local self-governments[75],
- reforms in the system of intergovernmental finance[76],

---

[69] Address of the President of Ukraine to Supreme Council of Ukraine "European Choice. Conceptual Basis of Economic and Social Development of Ukraine for 2002-2011".

[70] Exchange rate 1 EURO = 6.66 UAH (on January 30, 2004).

[71] State Budget of Ukraine revenues for 2004 are estimated at EUR 9.2 billion.

[72] COWI/DANCEE, Ukraine National Water Sector Strategy and Action Plan, Strategic Issues Report, September 2002. No similar sector studies have been recently carried out for district heating.

[73] COWI/DANCEE, Ukraine National Water Sector Strategy and Action Plan, Interim Report, June 2002.

[74] Constitution of Ukraine, Article 140. Chapter XI.

[75] Law of Ukraine„On Local Self Governments" No.280/97 –VR of May 21,1997 (with amendments).

[76] The Budget Code of Ukraine No. 2542 – III of June 21, 2001.

- separation and definition of responsibilities of the central government and local self-governments for execution of economic functions, including organisation of local public service delivery, regulation, human resource management and control.

Substantial legal and regulatory uncertainties regarding sub-national credit market operation that followed the changes that have been mentioned earlier became an impediment to the development of self-sustaining SNG borrowing. In the past, studies of capital market access strategies for SNGs and CSEs, conducted in Ukraine by IBRD, had revealed other key constraints to sub national access to long-term credit market on both the supply and demand side, some of which have been removed after the approval of the Budget Code of Ukraine in 2001 and other regulatory acts that followed it.

The latest research[77] of the SNG debt market development, conducted by the Ministry of Finance of Ukraine in support of the World Bank financed Municipal Development Loan Fund project (MDLF), indicated that Ukraine is currently in the process of setting essential elements of legal framework for a development of a particular loan program under the MDLF and a municipal credit market in general. These include not only drafting of new legislation and setting of regulatory framework but also amending the conflicting laws that currently affect SNGs capacity to incur debt. The Urban Institute experts, who prepared a report on legal and regulatory framework for sub-national borrowing in Ukraine, envisage the success of further SNG credit market development by building at a national level a legal and policy framework, supporting credit market operations, and accumulating practical experience at the local level that allows smoothing implementation of newly approved legislation.

The importance of the local (municipal) credit market in the total picture of overall economic development of Ukraine has currently been determined as a way to further investments that allow the implementation of strategic economic and social goals of Ukraine over the next decade. In October 2003, the Inter-Agency Working Group representing Government of Ukraine,

[77] "Ukrainian Municipal Development Loan Fund Project. Legal and Regulatory Framework for Sub -National Borrowing", prepared by the Urban Institute/M. DeAngelis, E. Korniychuk, Y. Gregirchak/ for Ukrainian Municipal Development Fund Projects, The Ministry of Finance of Ukraine (June 2002).

International Donor Agencies, International Finance Institutions, and municipalities was created to assist in the development and implementation of financing mechanisms of local development projects, which are expected to be carried out by local self-governments without provision of sovereign guarantees[78]. Prudent borrowing through commercial bank intermediaries is viewed to augment investment capacity of local self-governments and CSEs, enhance efficient use of energy and material resources in provision of public services in a market economy [79].

Principle Vehicles for Lending to Municipalities

In the past, three principal vehicles for lending to SNGs or CSEs have been available:

1. lending from higher levels of government;
2. lending by commercial banks;
3. municipal and corporate bond issuing.

Historically, both bank loans and bonds have been competing with each other on cost basis. Until approval of the Budget Code of Ukraine in 2001, borrowing from higher levels of government have not been built on the principles of hard credit culture and effectively resulted in subsidization of local budgets by the state. The Budget Code set new rules regarding this type of borrowing and prohibited short-term lending from one budget to another[80].

Currently, sub national borrowing market features several kinds of debt instruments:

[78] Decree of the Cabinet of Ministers of Ukraine "On Creation of the Inter-Agency Working Group on the Issues of Financing Mechanisms for Local Development Projects Without Provision of Sovereign Guarantees" No. 1608, October 20, 2003.

[79] "The National Program of Reforming and Developing Housing and Communal Economy for 2004-2010", Draft Law of Ukraine, in review by the Supreme Council of Ukraine since October 2003.

[80] Article 73.

1. State credits, borrowed from international development organizations or International Financial Institutions;

2. commercial bank loans;

3. municipal and corporate bonds;

These debt instruments are offered on a competitive basis by respective intermediaries to sub national governments, which are principal administrative and territorial units where *local self-government* and the *powers of Autonomous Republic of Crimea* are exercised. Pursuant to the Budget Code of Ukraine (2001) only Verkhovna Rada of Autonomous Republic of Crimea and city councils have the right to borrow. Utilities (CSEs) that provide municipal services also have direct access to the local debt market.

On-lending to Municipalities Through State Credits

State credits, borrowed from International Financial Institutions, such as IBRD and European Bank for Reconstruction and Development (EBRD), have recently become the source of long-term financing for municipalities and their respective CSEs, providing project financing in the area of water supply, wastewater and district heating. Pursuant to the Decree of the Cabinet of Ministers, in 2003, the Ukrainian Municipal Development Fund[81] was established as a result of an agreement between the Government of Ukraine and IBRD that was reached under MDLF project to support socially important projects of local self governments in the cities.

Four long-term loan agreements have been concluded by IBRD and EBRD with the Government of Ukraine and one with the city of Zaporizhzhya for infrastructure finance purposes. IFIs' loan funds are providing project financing in the area of water supply, wastewater and district heating in the cities of Zaporizhzhya, Lviv and Kyiv. A credit line for municipalities of Donetsk, Luhansk, Lviv and Volyn oblasts have been provided with IBRD funding to soften social impacts of reforms in coal industry where coal mines are shutting down and infrastructure ownership is

[81] Decree of the Cabinet of Ministers of Ukraine "On Creation of Ukrainian Municipal Development Fund" No. 1101, July 2003.

transferred from state to municipalities (for details, see Attachment 1). EBRD is negotiating three loan agreements with the cities of Kherson, Dnipropetrovsk and Luhansk for implementation of projects in water and wastewater sector.

Standard terms for IBRD and EBRD loans so far have included a requirement for provision of sovereign guarantee and co-financing on the part of the borrower. At the same time, EBRD would prefer direct lending to municipalities; however, perceived absence of reliable security for large amount loans at municipal level (excluding Kyiv) is viewed as an obstacle for direct lending to the SNGs at this stage of local credit market development.

In addition, EBRD has required private sector participation and availability of financing that is provided either by the borrower or the owner of the utility, the latter might be reaching 30% of the overall project-financing requirement. EBRD promotes private sector participation (PSP) in any form, which can be realistically applied: either participation of a corporate partner (performing consulting services), or conclusion of a management or concession contract. In addition, EBRD requires that tariffs be set at full cost recovery level, including debt service. If the tariffs do not cover full cost of service, a plan should be developed, to increase tariffs accordingly.

Given the above, a very limited number of municipalities and CSEs can get access to IFIs funding, due to the large scale of projects that can be financed from these sources, and the limitations generated by current requirements of World Bank and EBRD to provide sovereign guarantees for thc loans.

Commercial Bank Loans to SNGs and CSEs

Although various kinds of debt instruments have been available on the market since early 90s, practically no long-term credit resources have been attracted for financing of capital projects, while short-term credits have been continuously providing a source of short-term liquidity to SNGs and CSEs.

At the same time, ten-year development of the overall commercial bank credit market reveals shifts in banks' credit portfolio structure from short-term to long-term lending. National Bank of Ukraine classifies short-term loans as one-year loans. Since 1993, the share of overall long-term bank lending was steadily growing. From 3% of total loans, in 1993, to 28% of total UAH 42.035 billion of loans extended by commercial banks into Ukrainian economy by the end of 2002 (For details, see Attachment 1).

These tendencies in the banking sector are reflecting growth of Ukrainian economy over the last three years, stable currency of Ukraine, decreasing interest rates and improved banking regulation.[82] Most banks report that the quality of the loan portfolio has been steadily improving during 2002 and 2003, with average share of bad loans for the 10 largest banks dropping from 13% at the end of 2002 to an average 6% in August 2003[83].

Despite the steady strengthening of the banking sector since 2000, the loosening of reserve requirements, the drop of interest rates and the respective increase in lending to the real sector of the economy, the level of banking sector involvement in the real economy remains low. Deloitte's assessment of the ratio of loans to GDP for 2003 has been expected to reach only 23% or USD 13.4 billion[84].

Municipal Bonds

Sub-national governments' experience with municipal bond issues, occurring between 1995 and 1998, is considered an exception specific to the Ukrainian SNG mid- to long-term debt market development in the 90s. It is characterized by the surge of municipal bond issuance activity in 1995-1998, and by an abrupt ending after the Odessa city UAH 61 million[85] bond default in 1998. Presidential Decree[86] that followed the default introduced legal restrictions for municipal long-term borrowing and effectively stopped

[82] "Financial Condition of Ukrainian Banks in the First Half of 2002 and Ways to Improve Their Performance", by V. Krotiuk, O. Kireev, G. Karcheva, National Bank of Ukraine.

[83] "Ukrainian Banking Study", Deloitte, 2003.

[84] "Ukrainian Banking Study", Deloitte, 2003.

[85] Nominal value of the bond issue.

[86] Presidential Decree "On Procedure for External and Internal Borrowings Performed by Local Self-Government" No. 655/98 of June 1998.

municipal bond market development, causing municipalities to give preference to borrowing from the banks, which had become less restrictive.

Municipal bond market has been inactive until November 2003, when for the first time since 1998, the Securities and Stock Market State Commission (SSMSC) registered a new municipal bond issue of the city of Kyiv. As of January 2002, the amount of municipal bond issues constituted less than 1% of overall securities issues, registered by the SSMSC since 1995 (for details, see Attachments 1 and 2), reflecting a very low level of debt securities by the municipalities.

Corporate Bonds

During the overall period of corporate bond market development, only two projects in municipal services sector have been financed through corporate bond issues. In 2002, as reported by the SSMSC, one State-owned solid waste collection and disposal company "Ukrecocomresurs" placed two bond issues with 10-year and 20-year maturities for total nominal value of UAH 100 million. One municipally owned CSE had issued corporate bonds for rehabilitation of the district heating system[87]. No other corporate bond issues for infrastructure development purposes has been registered with the SSMSC so far, representing very low level of activity of the CSEs in the corporate debt securities market.

At the same time, during 2002 alone, SSMSC registered 108 corporate bond issues for the amount of UAH 4.3 billion, which exceeded the amount of total corporate bond issues for 1996 - 2001 by more than 4 times[88]. This statistics is indicative of the sharp increase in the development of the corporate bond market, a trend that is expected to be maintained with the development of the market of institutional investors, such as mutual funds and non-state pension funds, and the improved legislation on corporate bond issuance, which was enacted by the Decision of SSMSC No.322 "On

[87] In 2003- Jan. 2004, Kherson Telplokomunenergo (Kherson Heat Supply Company) issued four series of corporate bonds for total value of UAH 10 million.

[88] For 1996-2001 total amount of registered corporate bond issues was UAH 1.03 billion (SSMSC. http://www.ssmsc.gov.ua/4/2002/2.2.2.1.shtml).

Approving Regulation on the Procedure of Corporate Bond Issues" (July 17, 2003).

Sources of Credit: Interest Rates, Tenor of Loans, Institutional Arrangements

Bank lending and municipal bond issuing have been major lending instruments available to municipalities and their CSEs over the last decade. Until 1998, both forms of debt have been utilized by the SNGs, showing that from the legal and economic point of view, Ukraine had no reason to favor one form of lending over the other. The Odessa bond default on the first payment date for the bonds and the risks related to borrowing by SNGs, which became clear after the default, revealed the need to improve the legal framework, as a prerequisite for credit market development at the level of sub-national governments, especially with respect to issuing debt securities. Potential investor's distrust to Ukrainian legislation related to the SNG borrowing has created obstacles for further development of the municipal bond market, and has slowed down its development until Budget Code approval in 2001.

In the current context, bonds and bank loans have some distinctions in terms of cost, interest rates, tenor of loans, institutional arrangements, and other important considerations, such as partnership relationship, going beyond lending to include technical assistance in project preparation.

SNG Bonds

Some experts believe that bond issuance may have some benefits to SNG because it is not mandatory to secure debt with liquid assets, and municipality still has an ability to diversify sources of debt financing by obtaining loans.

However, procedure for municipal bond issuance is more complicated than with the commercial bank loan: it requires extensive legal support, mandatory engagement of the financial intermediary to organize the issue; it may also require higher interest rate payment as compared to the terms offered by the banks, which until 2004 could maintain SNGs operating accounts (see the next section).

Publicly offered bonds were favored by the SNGs during 1995-1998 due to the lack of defined legal provisions on key positions and absence of formal registration of the issues with the SSMSC. This has become a strong precondition for growth in the volume of issues by the SNGs as compared to commercial mid- and long-term lending. In 1996 interest rates on commercial loans were reaching 80% per annum (see Table 2) vs 65% on bonds. However, at present, it is hard to find significant differences between the two instruments with respect to interest rates or tenor of loans (Table 1).

The latest municipal bond issue of the City of Kiev had the following features: Kyiv City municipal bond is a term bond with principal amount due at maturity, while interest payment is made every three months. There are 20 interest payment periods, with determined interest rates: 1st – 4th interest period – 14% p.a.; 5 - 8 th th – 13% p.a.; 9 -12 th th – 12% p.a.; 13 - 20 th th –1.5 of the National Bank of Ukraine discount rate but no less than 10% and no more than 14% p.a.

Table 36. Municipal bond maturities and terms of compensation

Period	Tenure of Bond (in months)	Compensation, interest p.a.
1996	3 – 66	Up to 64,8% annual interest on face value
1997	12 – 13.5	50%
1998	12	25-30%
1999	-	-
2000	-	-
2001	-	-
2002	-	-
2003 (September)	60	14%- 12%

Source: SSMSC.

Bank Lending to SNGs

Bank lending to SNGs is realized within the framework of standard commercial banking. There are no special municipal banks in Ukraine. This means that municipalities and their utilities are exposed to savings and lending horizons, offered at the overall commercial debt market on a competitive basis and no subsidized lending program is available. Table 2 represents data on the weighted average annual interest rates, offered by the commercial banks over the 1996-2003 period on credits and deposits in national currency.

Table 37. Commercial bank annual interest rates on loans and deposits in national currency

Period	Loans	Deposits
1996	77.0	34.3
1997	49.1	18.2
1998	54.5	22.3
1999	53.4	20.7
2000	40.3	13.5
2001	31.9	11.2
2002	24.8	7.8
2003 (September)	17.2	6.7

Source: National Bank of Ukraine (For details, see Attachment 1, Table3).

Historically, borrowing from commercial banks has been utilized by oblasts and medium-sized cities. Cash deficit financing was the primary reason of borrowing by the SNGs. Banks, which were holding current accounts of the respective governments, were lending short-term funds to their sub national clients without performing any kind of creditworthiness analysis. The banks used to manage municipality's financial accounts and maintain the municipality's deposits. These allowed the banks to become familiar with the financial affairs, needs of their SNGs clients and set basis for mutually beneficial relationship. As a result, some commercial banks were building their relationship with the clients on the principles of municipal bank philosophy, e.g Bank "Khreschatyk" that offers all spectrum of financial services to the City of Kyiv Administration, among which are financial consultation services, underwriting, municipal bond issue organization services and many other.

Pursuant to the Budget Code[89], since 2002 the State Treasury has started executing both the revenue and expenditure (since 2004) side of the local budgets. Some experts and SNG financial managers envisage that this restriction of the Budget Code will become an impediment in the

[89] Article 72-14.

development of the local debt market by inhibiting the willingness of the banks to lend to SNGs.

Bank Lending to CSEs

Until 1990, CSEs were obtaining state funding for capital investment. Although the situation have changed due to the lack of State budgetary financing, CSEs have continued looking to the State and the municipality for financing and have seldom sought to borrow from commercial banks, which resulted in the relative absence of demand and lending activity to the CSEs.

Now, demand on the part of CSEs for bank loans has started to increase. Many CSEs realize that no funds will be transferred from the State, unless it is a case of emergency, and little financing can be expected from the municipalities. They understand that the best way to mobilize financing for capital investment is to borrow it from banks.

PADCO, Inc., implementing US AID financed "Tariff Reform and Communal Services Enterprises Restructuring Program in Ukraine" project, observed that while two or three years ago CSEs routinely expressed lack of interest in borrowing at 27- 30% interest from commercial banks, chief economists and directors are increasingly likely to compare those interest rates to the financial internal rates of return of energy-saving capital investment projects, which are often higher than 30%. Enterprises understand better and better the potential value of commercial loans for the financial performance of their enterprises. Selected data on CSE borrowing in 25 oblast centers (Table below) indicate that only 20% of oblast center utilities have been utilizing commercial loans for financing their operating or investment activity. Available data also shows a shift in borrowing from short-term to longer-term loans attracted for capital investment since 2002 (for details, see Attachment 1).

Table 38. Bank lending to CSEs in the oblast centers of Ukraine, 1996-2003

Period	City	Short - term loans, annual interest rate	Long - term loans, annual interest rate	Long - term loan term, years
1996				
1997	Cherkasy	no interest		
	Ivano-Frankivsk	60%		
1998 -1999	Ivano - Frankivsk		75%	3
2000	Mykolaiv	30%		
	Donetsk	35%		
	Zaporizhzhya	36-35%	Libor +1%*	15
	Lviv	28%		
2001	Mykolaiv	27%		
	Donetsk	24-30%		
	Ivano - Frankivsk		33%	1.5
	Kherson		18%	2
	Khmelnytsky	29 - 20%		
	Zaporizhzhya	36 – 7%	Libor +1%	15
	Lviv	30%		
2002	Mykolaiv	18%	18%	3
	Donetsk	20-25%		
	Ivano - Frankivsk		28%	3
	Khmelnytsky	20-18%		
	Lviv	28 -20%		
	Zaporizhzhya	36 – 7%	Libor +1%	15
2003 (September)	Mykolaiv		17%	5
	Chernivtsy		23%	3
	Zaporizhzhya	14,6 - 11%	Libor +1%	15

* Interest rates for Zaporizhzhya indicate terms of the long-term loan in foreign currency with EBRD for water wastewater project.

Source: State Committee on Housing and Communal Services of Ukraine, January 2004.

Corporate Bonds

Corporate bond market in the public sector has not been developed at all. No corporate bonds have been issued by the communal utilities until 2002 for the purposes of municipal infrastructure development. The first corporate bond issue for this purposes occurred in 2002, when State-owned solid waste collection and disposal company “Ukrecocomresurs” placed two bond issues (see above).

The second corporate bond issue took place in July of 2003, when municipally owned Kherson Heat Supply utility placed the first series of one-year bonds at 14% annual interest rate. Nominal value of four consecutive series of bond issues is UAH 10 million. Interest payment comes due at maturity of each series.

Kyiv based investment company became a lead manager for the issuer. The city of Kherson showed preference to the short-term bond issue over commercial lending due to absence of a mandatory requirement to pledge physical property as collateral. In the legislation, the provision for issuance of an asset-backed bond is an optional one. Backed bonds are called “additionally backed bonds” and assume that issuer liabilities are partially or fully backed by the insurance company or the guarantor.

The managers of Kherson Heat Supply utility preferred issuance of corporate bonds to bank lending because they can place an issue with big employers in the city, employees of which are customers of heating supply utility. One of such employers has outstanding accounts payable on salaries to its employees; consequently, the employees cannot pay for communal services. Heat supply utility believes that by placing the corporate bond with this corporate client, it will solve a problem with non-payment of communal services by the employees of the corporation, who will be able to offset debts for heating services through corporate bonds initially purchased by their employer. This example shows one of the ways in which Ukrainian CSEs are trying to find solutions to investment financing problems.

In order to issue corporate bond, the Kherson Heat Supply utility had to undergo financial and technical audit, which had not to be performed under standard commercial bank lending, and paid for the services of the lead manager. The city preferred not to be debt issuer because it had to obtain approval for debt issuance from the Ministry of Finance and obtain credit rating. In this respect, corporate bond issue by the CSE allowed the city to obtain financing for capital investment in shorter period of time as compared to financing through municipal bond (for comparison of corporate and municipal bond features, see the comparative table in the synthesis section).

Security for SNG Debt

Ukrainian legislation distinguishes several types of security that can be offered to lenders by the SNGs:

1. collateral: pledges of physical assets, general obligation, pledges of future revenues;

2. guarantees.

SNG Collateral

Collateralized lending, secured by municipally owned physical assets, is the most common type of security. Banks are mostly familiar with this type of collateral and have established procedures for documenting this type of security. Current experience with loan collaterals indicates that the ratio of collateral value to the loan amount varies from 2 to 5, depending on the negotiations with the lender and borrower's risk assessment[90]. As regards debt market development, reliance on physical asset collateral distracts attention from a project underlying performance, and holds up SNGs from gaining experience with project costs and benefits analysis and development of SNG finances.

General obligation borrowing, secured by general obligation of the municipality to pay from the SNGs budget funds, is less common, because lenders are concerned whether the subsequent SNG administrations will honor commitments made by a prior council. So, this type of security is mostly used for short-term borrowing. However, lender's concern appears to be more of market perception rather than legal imperfection, since the Budget Code requires municipalities to include both interest and principal obligations

[90] Resolution of the Board of the National Bank of Ukraine "On Approval of the Regulation on the Order of Setting and Using Reserve for Recovery of Potential Losses on Banks' Credit Operations" No.279, July 6, 2000, sets forth regulatory preferences for collateral, which is taken into account for determining amount of reserve to compensate for credit risk of a particular borrower.

in the budgets. When longer term lending becomes common practice, this issue may not be a concern anymore.

Until 2004, lenders could require that municipal borrowers maintain their operating accounts with the bank so that they could automatically withdraw any loan payments due. However, such form of guarantee will no longer be utilized and available to the lenders, because State Treasury started execution of revenues and expenditure side of the budget and municipalities now keep all the accounts with the Treasury.

Since borrowing authority is restricted to the cities and Council of Autonomous Republic of Crimea only, local state administrations are not allowed to use state property or property of local self-governments, which is operated by the local state administrations, as collateral[91].

SNG Guarantee

The Budget Code provides that an SNG may act as a guarantor with respect to the loans of legal entities owned by the community. Local council has the right to authorize inclusion of guarantees within permitted limits in the respective local budget, and executive bodies are authorized to issue guarantee within such limits. Such provision gives more power to the executive bodies than with the authorization of debt, since only local councils have the right to authorize debt issuance. Nevertheless, the Law on the State Budget for 2003 and the State Budget for 2004 do not allow the implementation of this provision, thus disallowing SNGs from issuing guarantees. Additionally, pursuant to the newly enacted Civil Code of Ukraine (2004), only financial institutions or insurance companies may issue guarantees[92] and, pursuant to the Budget Code, a guarantee may be issued subject to a counter-guarantee, the meaning of which is not yet clearly defined.

Concerns regarding lack of clarity in the provisions of the Codes with respect to issuance of guarantees have not yet developed (exception is

[91] Law of Ukraine "On Local State Administrations" No.586-XIV, April 9, 1999. Article 15. Chapter III

[92] Civil Code, Article 560.

lending by IFIs) since there has been little lending and mostly for short maturities. However, it is expected that existing legal framework for guarantees will have to be amended to incorporate necessary elements. Government of Ukraine currently acts as a guarantor with respect to the loans granted to the government of Ukraine and to individual municipalities by the International Financial Institutions for the purposes of financing municipal infrastructure development projects (see Attachment 1).

Transfer Intercepts

Transfer Intercepts of State Budget Transfer Funds are not legally authorized in Ukraine due to the absence of the relevant provisions in the legislation. The issue of establishing intercept form of security for SNG debt has been discussed by various expert groups, which believe that such mechanism can be effectively utilized in Ukraine by the cities that receive State Transfer Funds. However, proper intercept provisions should be drafted carefully allowing credit market development and not becoming subject for abuse by the local governments.

CSEs Debt Securing

Pursuant to the National Bank's requirements, bank loans granted to the CSEs or any other borrower have to be secured. Loan collateral in the form of municipally owned property or assets owned by municipal enterprise is the most typical type of security accepted by the banks. Since most CSEs in Ukraine are fully owned by their respective municipalities, they are not able to use their fixed assets as collateral on bank loans without approval of the city council. Bank collateral requirements can be up to five times the value of a loan.

Securing loan with physical assets is a challenging issue for Ukrainian CSEs, since present legal framework on privatization[93] prohibits alienation of property rights for communal services infrastructure. At the same time, such laws as the Law "On Local Self-government" and the Budget Code, support the municipality's right to use its property as loan collateral. Assets, which

[93] Law of Ukraine "On Privatization of State Property" No. 2163-XII of March 4, 1992 (as amended), Article 5.

can easily be transferred to the third parties, such as municipally owned buildings, are commonly used as loan security. As a result, the legal framework is quite controversial, and some understand current legislative provisions in the way that, with the city's support, the CSE can put up selected facilities (such as pumping equipment or boiler houses) as collateral for loans, should the commercial bank accepts this as collateral.

The procedure for documenting the CSE's ownership of these facilities is quite complicated, and includes several steps that the CSE has to take. This process includes the following key steps:

- obtaining the permission of the City council to pledge specific property as collateral,
- attesting the "commercial management rights" to said property, and
- obtaining the "Certificate of Ownership" for said property.

Latest statistics from the oblast center-cities that was gathered by the SCHCS of Ukraine in January of 2004, indicated that some utilities pledged revenues as repayment of one-year loans, or accounts receivable. Such utilities had 3 to 5-year positive credit history, which allowed them to obtain such loan terms. In addition, loans were short-term, which allowed lenders to make projections of the cash flows of the utilities and conduct risk assessment with great degree of certainty.

This confirms that CSEs have problems with securing debt, both with physical assets (which are mostly infrastructure objects that can not be alienated), or with revenue pledge for longer than one year term (due to absence of revenue predictability).

SNG Authority to Borrow. Restrictions on the Issuance of Debt

In Ukraine, numerous legal provisions govern SNG borrowing. The Budget Code of Ukraine[94], The Law of Ukraine "On Local Self-

[94] The Budget Code of Ukraine, No. 2542-III of June 21, 2001.

government"[95], The Law "On Securities and Stock Market"[96], Presidential Decree "On Procedure for External and Internal Borrowings Performed by Local Self-government" [97], the Resolution of the Cabinet of Ministers "On Approval of Procedure for Borrowing to Local Budgets"[98], Regulation of the Securities and Stock Market State Commission " On Procedure for Internal Municipal Bond Issues" [99], are legal documents which can be viewed as key building blocks in the process of creating an improved system of intergovernmental finance and implementation of intergovernmental decentralization.

The Budget Code is a primary document, setting principle provisions regarding SNG authority to borrow and restrictions on debt issuance:

- Supreme Council of the Autonomous Republic of Crimea and the city councils are allowed to borrow internally. Only city councils of the cities with a population over 800,000 people are authorized to borrow externally (Article16).
- The maximum amount of debt and guarantees shall be set fourth in the SNG budget for the budget year (Article 18).
- All SNGs may secure short-term loans for a term up to three months but within the limits of a current budget year (Article 73).
- Debt service cannot exceed 10 percent of the current general budget fund expenditures *in any budget period in which the debt is to be serviced* (Article 74).

---

95 Law of Ukraine "On Local Self-Government", No. 280/97-VR of May 21, 1997 (as amended).

96 Law of Ukraine "On Securities and Stock Market" No. 1201- XII of June 18, 1991 (as amended).

97 Decree of the President of Ukraine "On Procedure for External and Internal Borrowings Performed by Local Self-government" No. 655/98 of June 18, 1998.

98 Decree of the Cabinet of Ministers No. 207 of February 24, 2003.

99 SSMSC Decision No. 414, October 7, 2003 (cancels Resolution "On the Procedure of Issuance and Circulation of Local Bonds", brought into force by Resolution No.48 of the Securities and Stock Market State Commission on October 13, 1997.

- The failure to pay principle and interest of the debt contract on time shall prohibit the borrower from new borrowing for five years (Article 74).

The Budget Code of Ukraine determines that the Cabinet of Ministers of Ukraine defines rules for local borrowing. Pursuant to this provision of the Budget Code, in 2003, the Cabinet of Ministers of Ukraine approved the procedure for borrowing for local budgets[100] that set further requirements regarding SNG borrowing, among which are:

- requirement to obtain municipal credit rating of a rating agency;
- requirement to submit documentation on borrowing to obtain an approval of the Ministry of Finance of Ukraine, summarizing that decision of the SNG on borrowing meets the requirements of the budget legislation.

Authorization requirement on central government approval is consistent with the Presidential Decree No. 655/98 of June 18, 1998, which have set such condition in respond to unsuccessful experience with Odessa municipal bond issue. The Ministry of Finance must approve each SNG borrowing without providing sovereign guarantees or assuming responsibility for SNG debt.

The Resolution of the SSMSC followed Cabinet of Ministers Decree and specified rules on Internal Municipal Bond Issues[101]. Such resolution eliminated conflicting provisions, which existed in the legislation until 2003, and introduced new rules on municipal bond issuance as compared to the legislation on corporate bonds.

SNG Debt Credit Rating

Prior to approval of SNG borrowing by the Ministry of Finance of Ukraine, municipalities or Government of Autonomous Republic of Crimea

[100] "On Approval of Procedure for Borrowing for Local Budgets", Cabinet of Ministers Decree No. 20, February 24, 2003.

[101] Resolution "On Procedure for Internal Municipal Bond Issues", SSMSC Decision No. 414, October 7, 2003.

should obtain rating from a credit agency on the ability of the relevant SNG to service debt. The agency may be a domestic or foreign legal entity, which is exclusively specializing on provision of rating services. The ability of a rating agency to perform the required tasks should be proved by an expert summary of IBRD, IMF, or EBRD[102].

Only one Ukrainian rating company has performed rating of a municipal debt issue so far, which has been accepted by the Ministry of Finance for approval of a municipal borrowing in 2003. The city of Yuzhne (Odessa oblast) obtained short-term credit rating of uaK3 (not speculative) under the National Credit Rating Scale of a Ukrainian-rating Agency "Credit – Rating."[103] This city obtained a one-year loan of UAH 2.4 million with interest of 22% p.a., which is in the higher spectrum of credit interest rate horizon (for details see Attachment 1).

As of January 2004, two more cities are in the process of obtaining credit ratings, as reported by "Credit- Rating" Agency. No other precedents of municipal debt issue ratings or issuer ratings are reported, other than International rating, which has been assigned to the city of Kyiv in 2003 (see table below)

Table 39. Selected ratings of long term debt by international rating agencies, 2003

Rating Agency	Standard & Poor's	Moody's Investors Service	Fitch Ratings
Sovereign rating	B/Positive (1)	B1/Stable (2)	B+/Stable (3)
Municipal rating City of Kiev (4)	B/Stable	B2/Stable	

(1) Rating assigning date November 10, 2003.

(2) Rating assigning date October 28, 2003.

(3) Rating assigning date June 25, 2003.

(4) City of Kiev has been assigned credit rating for the purpose of obtaining a fiduciary loan from Dresdener Bank for USD 150 million at 8.67% p.a. in 2003 and for the municipal internal bond issue in November 2003.

Since there is not enough statistics on assignment of ratings to the municipalities, it is too early to make conclusions regarding the effect of

[102] Cabinet of Ministers Decree No. 20, February 24, 2003.

[103] http://www.credit-rating.com.ua/ru/ratings/list.html

credit ratings on the interest rates; however, availability of such rating is a mandatory precondition for municipal borrowing.

About ten municipalities, which have participated in PADCO/USAID "Tariff Reform and Communal Services Enterprises Restructuring Program in Ukraine" and IBRD/MDLF project during summer of 2002, view availability of a credit rating requirement as overly restraining and unjustified. It is not clear yet that this is the case, since two cities showed their ability to meet the requirement; however, it is obvious that credit rating generates obstacles in practice. One is the cost of assigning and updating the rating by the national credit agency, which may amount to 3% of loan amount (as in the case Yuzhne city)[104]. Financial cost of rating service might become an intolerable burden for quite considerable number of cities.

Preliminary Synthesis

Since there is a difference in some features of municipal and corporate bonds, a comparative table will allow defining pros and cons of both instruments.

[104] http://www.pension.kiev.ua/Ukr/Analit/Review/ see PADCO, Inc. Analytical reports, prepared by PADCO's Ukraine Pension Reform Implementation Project sponsored by USAID.

Table 40. Comparative features of municipal and corporate bonds in Ukraine, 2003

Characteristic	Municipal Bond	Corporate Bond
Debt amount limit	Total debt should not exceed 10% of the expenditure side of the general fund of the budget during period of debt service	No. Except for Stock Holding Companies – bond issue amount should not exceed 25% of the charter capital.
Type of borrowing	Cabinet of Ministers Decree No. 207: No direct external debt issuance. Budget Code: External borrowing is allowed for the cities, with the population of 800 000 people*	Internal and External.
Security	No	No. Optional: "additionally backed"
Intermediary	Issue organizer is required. Underwriting is not mandatory.	Underwriting is mandatory.
Central Government approval	Required	Not required
Credit rating	Required	Not required
Registration process tenure	20 working days (approval with the Ministry of Finance of Ukraine) 30 calendar days (registration with SSSMC)	30 working days (registration with SSSMC)
Duties	No state duties.	State duty: 0.1% of the nominal value of the issue.
Profit Taxes of the Holder (except Institutional investors)	General taxation rules. Institutional investors do not pay taxes on investment income.	General taxation rules

* There are six cities in Ukraine with population that is not less than 800 000 people – Kyiv, Dnipropetrovsk, Donetsk, Kharkiv, Odessa and Zaporizhzhya.

In this context, corporate bonds may be viewed as a better instrument to finance municipal infrastructure investment. Unless the loan is large, the process of municipal bond issuance seems to be overly complicated and financially burdening for municipalities. Issuance of corporate bonds allows municipalities and utilities to take advantage of the less complicated issuance process by avoiding credit rating, Ministry of Finance approval, and restrictions on the amount of lending.

Current legal provisions are still quite conflicting and pose a lot of confusion to lenders and borrowers. These relates to:

- setting limits on the maturity of short-term loans and not setting limitation on the amount of such borrowing relative to the budget;

- basing a debt test as a function of expenditures rather than revenues;
- setting penalties that prohibit borrowing for defaulting borrowers, which hampers the ability of such borrowers to refinance the loan;
- difference in requirements for testing debt and guarantees;
- absence of a reliable methodology to determine debt limitation;
- absence of clear SNG bankruptcy provisions.

The pending Draft Law "On Local Borrowing" is meant to solve these inconsistencies.

Water Supply and Wastewater Sector

Water Supply and Wastewater Sector Overview

Total water and wastewater services charges without VAT for all customer groups in 2002 were in the range of UAH 1.5 billion,[105] including UAH 678 million (USD 283 million[106]) for piped water supply and UAH 821 million (USD 155 million) for wastewater services. In 2003 these services were provided by 379 water supply and wastewater utilities (Vodokanals) and about 800 non-specialized housing-municipal production enterprises.

[105] Estimated on the basis of statistical data from the State Committee of Housing and Communal Services of Ukraine.

[106] Exchange rate 1 USD = 5.33 UAH (on December 30, 2003)

Table 41. Structure of the Water Supply and Sanitation industry

Indicator	2002	2003
Total number of entities, which provide WSS services:	339	379
Private	28	36
State	24	25
Owned by Communities	287	318

Source: State Committee of Housing and Communal Services (SCHCS) (Indicators on the Status of Reforms in the Housing and Communal Services Economy, January 2004).

The National Water Sector Strategy Study, carried out by the Danish Government in 2001-2002, indicated that 83% of the urban population and 23% of the rural population are connected to centralized water supply. This means that the national coverage rate for Ukraine was 78% in 2002.

More than 70% of the population in urban areas is connected to wastewater systems providing treatment as against only 9% in rural areas. About 26 million people in total, or approximately half of the national population, benefit from wastewater services.

Eight national programs are currently approved and affect the development of initiatives in the WWS sector in Ukraine:

- Water and Wastewater Development Program (Decree of CMU No.1269, November 17, 1997, as amended);
- Program of National Production of New Highly Efficient Coagulant and Flocculants Technologies (Decree of CMU No. 2232, December 9, 1999);
- National Program of Water Sector Development (Law of Ukraine No. 2988-III, January 17, 2002);
- National Program of Protection and Renewal of the Azov and the Black Sea Environment (Law of Ukraine No. 2333-III, March 22, 2001)

- Plan of Primary Measures on Improving Water Supply of Residential Areas in Luhansk Oblast for 2002-2005 (Decree of CMU No. 280, March 13, 2003);
- On Improving Reliability and Efficiency of Kharkiv City and other Residential Areas of Kharkiv Oblast Water Supply Systems Functioning (Decree of CMU No. 1844, December 20, 2000);
- National Program on Ecological Recreation of the Dnepr River Basin and Improvement of Drinking water Quality (Supreme Council Decree No. 123/97, February 27, 1997).

Currently, the draft Law of Ukraine "On National Program "Drinking water of Ukraine" is being reviewed by the Ministers of the Cabinet of Ministers of Ukraine before submission to the Supreme Council for approval.

Institutional Arrangements for Provision of Water Supply and Wastewater Services

Responsibility for provision of housing and municipal services, which includes water supply and wastewater, rests with the local self-governments, which in most cases are the owners of municipal infrastructure. As of 2003, communities own 84% of water supply and wastewater utilities. In accordance with the legislation on local self-governments, the latter are responsible for the provision of water and wastewater services that are provided by the utilities owned by the community. Such provision implicitly sets requirements for the local governments to ensure that sufficient financing is available for service supply on the territorial units where their power is exercised. This means that the local government body may choose to provide budget financing to the CSE for capital investment, or incur debt for this purpose.

Execution of communal property management functions by executive bodies of local governments means making decisions in regard to

- creation, reorganization or liquidation of the utility;
- setting procedures for property management;

- approval of the utility charter and making changes to it;
- approval and control of implementation of utility work plans, including strategic plans;
- setting rules for the use of profit and setting a portion of the profit, which should be transferred to the local budget.

The head of the local self-government body, e.g. city mayor, concludes a labor contract with the utility director.

Oblast administrations are responsible for provision of housing and communal services on the territories where local governments' powers are not exercised, e.g. small cities of rayon subordination. In addition, oblast state administrations are authorized to set prices for the services that are provided by non-communally owned utilities, e.g. privatized, leased ones. Oblast administrations may also set prices in case when several water and wastewater enterprises serve more than one municipality in a particular oblast. The latter situation is not yet well regulated and it is not clear if regulatory authority is assigned to the oblast administration on the territory of which the facilities are located, or to each local government administration where service is provided, and facilities are owned by local self-government body.

Despite utility ownership, water and wastewater services are provided by economically independent entities that are viewed as businesses, which are subject to enterprise taxes on profit. CSEs are responsible to ensure sufficient and safe supply of water to all customer groups and to provide wastewater collection, treatment and disposal.

There is a number of utilities, which are run by leased companies that are registered as separate legal entities. In 2003, for the first time in the WSS sector in Ukraine, a long-term (49 years) lease agreement has been concluded between the city of Odessa and a privately owned lease company. Several concessions with small private entrepreneurs for water, heat and housing are operating in rural areas in Crimea.

Since utilities are operating as independent legal entities and responsible for operations, implicitly, water and wastewater managers are responsible for capital investment and utilization of best financing options available. Among them are the following:

- User charges/tariffs;
- Funds from the State budget;
- Funds from SNG budgets;
- Ecology Funds Grants;
- Grants from IFIs;
- Debt financing: IFIs' loans, commercial bank loans, credit lines at FIs, corporate bonds, and leases.
- Energy Service Company (ESCO) scheme financing;
- Private equity financing.

SNG funding of water supply and wastewater infrastructure may include:

- Subsidies from the local budgets;
- Loans to communally owned CSEs from the Local budgets;
- Local Ecology Funds, e.g. City of Kiev Ecology Fund;
- Debt financing (within legal restrictions with respect to authority to borrow): IFIs' loans, Commercial bank loans or credit lines, municipal bonds.

Tariff Policy in the Water Supply and Wastewater Sector

Tariff Regulation in Water and Wastewater Sector

In Ukraine, the national government adopts general requirements related to the identification of costs that can be recovered through water and wastewater tariffs. These requirements are spelled out in the procedures and instructions of the central executive bodies, such as the SCHCS, Ministry of Economy and on the Issues of European Integration, Anti-Monopoly Committee, Ministry of Finance, and passed to the local level for implementation. National government takes control of the situation if there is no enforcement at the local level only in the issues related to quality, safety, labor, taxes, allocation and use of budget funding provided to the utilities and anti-monopoly legislation.

There are two schemes to regulate water and wastewater tariffs in Ukraine at the local level:

- The executive body of the *local government* should regulate tariffs for water and wastewater services, which are provided *by the communally owned utility.*

- If the entity is *state owned*, the authority to regulate tariffs lies with the *oblast administration.*

The system of price regulation is currently under review, to provide clearer guidance on regulatory authorities of oblasts and local governments in cases when several water and wastewater enterprises serve more than one municipality in a particular oblast, and facilities of such utilities are located in different cities; or in the cases when communally owned utility is operated by a lease company, which by definition is not owned by a territorial community.

By definition as "non-communally owned", private enterprises are subject to price regulation by oblast administrations. However, because there are few registered privately owned water and wastewater utilities in Ukraine, this issue is not being discussed broadly yet. In some instances, the regulatory powers remain with municipalities and some are exercised by oblasts. Odessa administration has announced that it reserves the power to set tariffs for the services, which will be provided by the private lease company over the term of the lease agreement, while in the city of Zolotonosha (Cherkasy oblast), the oblast administration sets tariffs for a closed joint stock water company Breeze.

One key issue which is being discussed with respect to strict division of regulatory authority between local governments and oblast state administrations, is subsidies. Subsidies have to be paid to utilities in case regulated tariffs are set at a level that do not cover full costs. In most cases, regulators set tariffs based on political considerations, below cost recovery level, in order to protect residential customers and to make tariffs affordable to the majority of the population.

Since Budget Code does not authorize oblast administrations to be responsible for the provision of housing and communal services in the oblasts, it is not clear whether oblast administrations can allocate subsidies for reimbursing utilities for losses created from inadequate tariff regulation. In complicated schemes of service provision on the territory of one oblast by utilities of various ownership and organizational forms, inefficiencies of tariff regulation become obstacles for financially viable operation of the utilities.

The absence of budget subsidies to compensate the gap between actual costs and the revenues based on tariffs set below cost recovery level results in sector under financing, deterioration of infrastructure, and poor supply of services. Utilities, which have to operate at a loss, cannot be treated creditworthy by the lenders; they fail to access capital market and to improve infrastructure and service quality. Lack of stability and predictability with respect to tariff levels and revenues is one of the greatest barriers to credit market activity.

Tariff Rules on Debt Service

Current water and wastewater tariff rules are very generous, they allow utilities to include all economically justifiable costs for recovery in tariffs. The utilities can include interest expenses resulting from their financing activities into tariff calculations. The Procedure on Water and Wastewaters Services[107] provides the list of financing activities, which include borrowing through bank loans, issuance of bonds and financial leasing. Based on the terms of agreements between lending and borrowing parties, the amounts of interest can be included in the cost basis for tariff setting.

The Procedure also provides for determining capital requirements in tariffs. Capital costs are defined as those associated with funding of capital

[107] Order of the SCHCS No. 139 of June 27, 2001.

investment programs, including acquisitions, construction, rehabilitation, modernization and other capital improvements of plant and facilities, and other costs related to acquisitions of non material assets, which are depreciated pursuant to the Law of Ukraine "On Enterprise Profit Tax".

Capital costs are viewed as funding that is required for implementation of capital investment programs during the budget year in excess of depreciation; the latter being also treated as allowable expense for tariff calculation purposes. The amount of capital costs in tariff is determined by the financing method that was chosen to support capital investment program and the amount of related costs which have to be recovered in the budget year. Annual capital requirements have to be based on a capital investment program and a long-term financial plan. Capital items that are funded through the capital investment program are capitalized for accounting purposes and depreciated over a defined period of time.

Capital investment costs can be allocated to customer classes on the basis of benefit or any other basis that would be chosen by the utility and approved by the regulators. Broad definition of capital costs allows flexibility in the choice of specific capital expenditures. However, the provisions of the Procedure leave some ambiguity which has to be clarified through guidelines.

The Procedure does not explicitly list the capital costs, which can be recovered through tariffs in excess of depreciation. For example, current methodology does not specify whether it is possible to make planned contributions to reserve of capital investment funds, which can be established to accumulate cash over extended periods for future investment into major facilities. It is assumed that long term financial planning will help utilities to identify future cash flow problems and they will figure out mechanisms for building up necessary reserves or accumulating capital funds. Meanwhile, utilities do not have experience with financial planning even for the budget year. At maximum, pro-forma profit and loss statement is prepared at request of the regulatory body. The Procedure could also be more specific on identification of costs associated with repayment of principle on bond issues or commercial loans, or return on equity capital.

Nevertheless, current legislation on tariff calculation is not treated as an obstacle for development of cost recovery tariffs. Tariff rules on cost identification are pretty straightforward and clear. Some improvements may be considered in the area of cost allocation and the choice of effective tariff structures.

The water and wastewater tariffs are charged separately since water supply and wastewater services are two separate types of services. Water supply normally includes water pumping, treatment and distribution to customers. Wastewater service includes wastewater collection, treatment and disposal. Each utility has its own procedure on charging customers for the services. One utility may show separate line items for water and wastewater service on the customer's bill, some may show it as one amount. Water or wastewater tariffs are charged only for those users who receive the service.

In Ukraine, tariffs for water or wastewater have uniform structure. That is why revenues corresponding to capital charges in the tariff are not set aside (dedicated) for capital investment purposes. It is up to utility to decide how to collect and to allocate revenues, between operation and investment expenditures. Very few utilities in the country plan for recovery of capital costs in the tariffs other than in the form of depreciation, which may constitute from 6 to 15% of the total costs depending on the overall cost structure of the services and level of depreciation of the fixed assets.

Despite the fact that the rules allow full cost recovery, regulators do not always follow the rules and do not increase tariffs to keep up with costs increase, so utilities are typically operating at a loss and have not enough resources to cover O&M costs, not speaking of capital costs.

Price cap regulation can also be viewed as a progressive regulatory option that is available in the sector. It is not currently used by the regulators due to lack of practical experience, but it can be considered as a good opportunity to create incentive regulatory mechanisms in the nearest future.

Grant vs. Market-rate Credit in the Water Supply and Wastewater Sector

Sector analysis, which has been performed based on the data provided to the SCHCS by the oblast center-municipalities, shows that with the transition from a centrally planned to a market-oriented economy, the share of central government finance in the WSS is falling down, compared to the finance provided by municipalities, and user charges (see table below). SCHCS statistics on the amount of investment into municipal infrastructure by 19 (out 26) oblast center-municipalities over 1996-2003 shows that the amount of funding from local budgets of municipalities exceeded amounts of State funding by almost 5 times, while in prior years this relationship was about 1 to 2 (for details, see Attachment 1). Such change is indicative of the process of decentralization of power and devolution of the important functions to local jurisdictions, especially after the Law of Ukraine "On Local Self-Government" has been enacted in 1997.

Meanwhile, state financing continues to be provided to the local governments and their respective water and wastewater utilities in the form of transfers called "target financing for capital investment". In 2004 State Budget, for the first time since 1995, the State has budgeted UAH 400 million (0.7 % of 2004 State Budget revenues) for investment into housing and communal economy to address issues requiring immediate solutions. There is no data yet available on the amount of overall budgetary financing that is planned for investment into water supply and wastewater sector. The State Budget funding will be granted to the cities in a form of subsidy. No subsidies with market-rate credit have been granted to the SNGs so far.

Table 42. Financing infrastructure investment in oblast centers of Ukraine, 1996-2003, 000 UAH

Source of Funding	1996-1997	1998-1999	2000-2001	2002-2003	Total
State Budget Total	120 661.9*	22 506.4	62 950.1	79 107.4	285 225.8
%, for WWS	*93*	*78*	*62*	*55*	*75*
City Budget Total	26 902.4	60 003.1	220 489.8	373 724.4	681 119.7
%, for WWS	*50*	*37*	*31*	*40*	*37*
User Charges Total	60 836.3	71 911.0	113 094.3	141 592.8	387 434.4
%, for WWS	*35*	*6*	*50*	*32*	*38*
Bank Loans Total	18 594.0	48 231.0	112 966.1	274 780.1	454 571.2
%, for WWS	*0*	*0*	*36*	*52*	*40*
Total	226 994.6	202 651.5	509 500.3	869 204.7	1 808 351
%, for WWS	*65*	*32*	*40*	*44*	*44*

*The data for 1996 may not be adjusted for UAH, and presented in karbovanets.

Source: SCHCS, Questionnaire Survey of the Oblast Centers of Ukraine in December 2003 - January 2004.

Another source of data, generated by the SCHCS for monitoring of the status of reforms in water and wastewater sector as a whole, represents information, which shows some discrepancies with the data supplied by the oblast center municipalities on the amounts of capital investment in water and wastewater sector during 2002 and 2003 (see table below). Oblast centers alone indicated higher amounts of investments than in the whole Ukraine for the same period. This is explained by the fact that both data sources were generated with incomplete information from the regions. Nevertheless, both sources of information show similar tendencies in the structure of capital investment finance, which indicate higher reliance of the CSEs on their own resources, coming from user charges; slight increase of the share of funding received from the local budgets, and increase of financing, attracted from other sources, which are assumed to be either grants or commercial loans.

Table 43. Financing of infrastructure capital investment in Ukraine, 2000-2003, 000 UAH

Indicator	2002		2003	
Total Amount of Capital Investment, including:	66,535	100%	140,367	100%
Utility Own-source Contributions	31,466	47%	80,886	58%
State Budget	18,226	27%	18,619	13%
Local budget	11,531	17%	25,356	18%
Other Sources	5,312	8%	15,735	11%

Source: SCHCS (Indicators on the Status of Reforms in the Housing and Communal Services Economy, January 2004).

In the table above, utility own-source contributions represent finance which is available from the operating budget surplus, which may result not only from profits, but from increase in accounts payable and adjustment for depreciation.

No parastatal agencies, such as Environmental Funds, as in Poland or Czech Republic, offer programs to provide below-market lending. Environmental Funds of Ukraine provide financing to the cities or their respective utilities exclusively in the form of subsidies (grants).

Use of Credit in Water Supply and Wastewater Sector

Available market data on SNG borrowing shows that little long-term credit has been used for financing of the Water Supply and Wastewater sector. Primary lenders, so far, have been IFSs, which provided loan financing to the cities of Zaporizhzhya (EBRD) and the city of Lviv (IBRD). No other experiences with SNG debt financing of WWS sector are known.

The data in Attachment 1 represents a summary of borrowing experience of various municipal CSEs with bank financing. Information reported by the cities shows that very few water utilities, operating in the oblast centers, obtained loan funding; among them are Zaporizhzhya, Dnipropetrovsk and Kirovohrad Vodokanals. Even assuming that the data is not fully representative of loan experiences of all water utilities in Ukraine, the fact that majority of oblast center utilities have not incurred debt financing for capital purposes is indicative of very weak debt financing activity in WWS, even compared to other sectors of municipal services economy, e.g. heat supply sector.

Private Participation in Water Supply and Wastewater Investment

There is no data available on the level of investment into WWS sector by private companies, mainly because private sector involvement is only beginning. Apart from a forty-nine year lease contract in Odessa with a national private company "Infox", several small concessions in Crimea, four joint stock companies operating in Donetsk, Kyiv and two cities of Chernihivska oblast, and nine limited liabilities companies (see Attachment 1), there is not much private sector participation observed[108].

Nevertheless, in 2003 private companies have started to express interest for entering municipal economy segment, and WWS sector in particular, as SCHCS officials remark. Private entities are mostly offering investment into municipal infrastructure over the time of a lease or concession agreement; however, no information on the type of financial instruments is available to public. Some investment companies have also conveyed SCHCS their willingness to invest into municipal services sector. In case of Odessa, it has been announced that Infox will invest UAH 500 million over seven years of operation.

Future Development of WWS Sector Credit Markets

Future of Credit Markets in the WWS Sector

National government's policy toward development of the credit market in the WWS sector is aligned with the overall goals that are set for achievement in the housing and communal economy as a whole. The Government's tasks are primarily focused on the development of economic stimuli for attracting investments in the entire communal services sector of Ukraine, which means that future financing of WWS sector will largely depend on achievement of these objectives.

---

[108] SCHCS reports 29 (2002) and 36 (2003) private operators of WWS utilities; however, detailed data on the organizational form of private utilities is available for 14 of them (For details, see Attachment 1, Table7).

Recognizing that tariffs alone cannot solve the huge financing needs of the water CSEs, developed credit markets are obviously going to play significant role in provision of long-term capital for the sector. There is no preference towards various types of debt instruments, both bank lending, municipal and corporate bond issuing can be considered as viable sources of financing, which will be competing with one another on cost basis.

Meanwhile, the Government of Ukraine is investigating various options which will allow to increase the level of investment into housing and communal economy and attract debt financing (which is currently used in critically low amounts). Technical assistance and actual project implementation by international consultants is playing a significant part in this process.

IFIs, which are pursuing business opportunities in Ukraine, are intensively promoting approval of a new Law on Local Borrowing, which could clarify confusing provisions in current legislation, define SNGs bankruptcy provision, and smooth market operation.

The World Bank's initiative on establishment of the UMDF facility for providing loans for development of infrastructure has been analyzed for several years before approval. Budget Code adoption was a catalyst in this process. Since UMDF facility is not yet operating, it is not possible to describe its impact on SNG debt market development. The most recent description of the UMDF structure has been assuming that the facility will be operating through a system of commercial banks with assigning them responsibility for credit analysis, risk assessment, and loan management.

The U.S. Agency for International Development currently implements Development Credit Authority (DCA) project for supporting credit financing in the municipal WWS and Heat Supply sectors in Ukraine. [109] Originally, USAID's DCA was created in 1998 to mobilize local private capital through the establishment of real risk sharing relationships with private financial institutions in USAID countries. It offers a vehicle for providing needed

[109] PADCO, Inc. is implementing this project in WWS and Heat Supply Sector.

credit for an array of enterprises and underserved sectors[110]. Under DCA project in Ukraine, the US Government will provide a five-year partial guarantees to commercial banks that will enable a number of communal service enterprises to finance municipal infrastructure improvement. The project will entail issuance of 50% loan guarantee in local currency to banks that provide loans to the selected CSEs (with focus on energy efficiency). Two water and wastewater CSEs have been selected so far for participation in a DCA project and the required documentation packages are under review of the project staff. Commercial banks, which were chosen by the CSEs and which agreed to provide loans under DCA framework, treat the U.S. government partial guarantee as a vehicle for reducing the amount of collateral normally required from the borrower and for considering reasonable reduction in the credit interest rate.

Additionally, in 2003, USAID has announced request for proposals for an Access to Credit project, the purpose of which is to mobilize credit in Ukraine for the use of small and medium businesses, prospective homeowners, farmers and municipalities. The core components of this project will be in the areas of mortgage lending, municipal bonds, and financial leasing and development of appropriate financial products to meet the needs of the Ukrainian SMEs, agriculture, and municipalities. The underlying objective of providing technical assistance for municipalities with municipal bond issuance is to increase the volume of local capital investment in support of essential municipal infrastructure and services, such as highways, water and sewage facilities, health care and education[111].

The future of credit market development in the water sector, as well as in the municipal services sector as a whole, will develop along with the needs of institutional investors, such as pension funds and insurance companies, which will have to match their funds with long term financing. In 2003, Ukrainian Supreme Council approved two major Pension Laws – The Law "On

[110] Best Practices of USAID's Development Credit Authority. USAID Office of Development Credit. Washington, DC. August 2002.

[111] The U.S. Agency for International Development's Mission to Ukraine, Belarus and Moldova (USAID/Kyiv). Request for Proposals (RFP) Number 121-03-009. Access to Credit in Ukraine, July 31, 2003.

Mandatory State Pension Insurance"[112] and the Law "On Non-State Pension Provision"[113], which set the basis for pension system reform and implementation of a three pillar pension system (solidarity system, mandatory accumulation system, non-state accumulation system). Corporate and municipal bonds with long-term maturities are expected to play an important part in the development of accumulated pension system in Ukraine. Pursuant to the Law "On State Pension Insurance", 20% of the State Accumulation Fund's of Ukraine assets can be invested in corporate bonds of Ukrainian issuers, and no more than 10% in municipal bonds. Under the Law "On Non State Pension Provision", no more than 40% of assets of non-state pension funds can be invested in Ukrainian corporate bonds, and no more than 20% in municipal bonds.

Further involvement of financially strong private sector participants into water supply and wastewater services provision and management is also treated as a step towards cheaper credit resources.

Since there is an urgent need to identify all possible sources of financing, the Ukrainian Government is reviewing all alternative financing options. For many years the Danish Government has been providing support to Ukraine on development of various initiatives in the water sector through DANCEE program. Within current DANCEE program, consultants provide technical assistance to SCHCS in studying mechanisms for priority rehabilitation investments and alternative financing mechanisms in the municipal sector using the water sector as an example. These include, but are not limited to, testing of various options for development of alternative financing mechanisms of water and wastewater sector investment. Analysis is conducted to assess whether, within the existing legislation, mechanisms for privileged investment activities such as techno-parks, priority development zones, etc. can be used for carrying out investment programs in the water sector.

[112] Law of Ukraine No. N 1058-IV of July 9, 2003 (Article 88).

[113] Law of Ukraine No. N 1057-IV of July 9, 2003 (Article 47).

Obstacles to Use of Credit in WWS Sector

Availability of debt financing sources to municipal economy, and water and wastewater sector in particular, will depend on a number of factors. Latest observations of sub national government credit market development showed that the principle constraints to greater use of credit in this sector lie both on the demand and supply sides. On the demand side, municipalities, as well as CSEs, find that loan terms are still insufficiently attractive for financing capital projects. Interest rates that are still ranging between 17-21% for three-year loans, as well as loan maturity, which is generally restricted by three years' tenure, pose difficulties to the utility managers in terms of finding projects with acceptable internal rate of return. No realistic alternative for pledging of physical assets as collateral is also viewed as an obstacle to greater use of credit.

In addition, there is a lack of managerial capacity and capital planning expertise at the municipal and utility level. Most of the mid and small size cities do not carry out short- or mid-term planning on regular basis. This results in the absence of project feasibility studies, and justified project return assessments. The most recent work performed on the issue of CSE borrowing has been sponsored by the U.S. Agency for International Development (USAID).[114] As observed by technical experts of US AID sponsored PADCO, Inc. "Tariff Reform and Communal Services Enterprises Restructuring Program in Ukraine", in many cases, CSEs channel scarce financial resources into low return and non priority investments, or make unreasonable technical decisions, which result in purchase of equipment with inadequate capacities that do not allow CSEs to achieve expected savings, which potentially would have been a source of debt repayment.

On the supply side, the banks are not yet willing to supply resources on long-term basis to municipalities or communally owned utilities. The tenor of the loans is nowhere close to depreciable lives of the fixed assets, which need to be replaced. With regard to CSEs, banks do not consider them to be creditworthy. Historically, this is a reasonable assessment. In 2002 and 2003, about 66% of water and wastewater utilities have been operating with

[114] USAID/PADCO, Inc. "Tariff Reform and Communal Enterprise Restructuring" Project (2003), USAID/PADCO, Inc. "Development Credit Authority" Project (2003).

losses[115]. Lack of confidence in the borrowers flexibility with tariff setting and the inability of CSEs to operate on a full cost recovery basis are the major reasons for high credit risk assessment associated with lending in the communal services sector, and consequently, low interest of lenders to get into this market. Those banks which get into business with CSEs apply very rigid collateral requirements that create obstacles for entering credit market for a majority of utilities and municipalities.

Among the key obstacles to building municipal creditworthiness, which are identified by municipal finance experts and representatives of local governments, is uncertainty and unpredictability of current system of intergovernmental finance. A number of municipalities, active in implementation of reforms in the municipal services sector, are concerned with their ability to support reforms and lack of incentives for increasing their revenue base. Pursuant to the Budget Code, theoretically, municipal government bodies can be guarantors of SNG debt, with revenues of the local budgets being pledged as SNG debt collateral. In practice, forming of local budget revenues is tied with serious risk factors, among which are the following[116]:

- *Low level of local budgets' revenues*. Revenues of the local budgets' (not including transfers of the State Budget) in 2002-2003 constituted about 8.8 % of the GDP, including revenues of the oblast and national level subordination cities – 3.7 % of the GDP (13,2 % of consolidated budget of Ukraine revenues)[117].

- *Limited taxing authorities of local governments*. Taxing authorities of SNGs are restricted only to setting of local taxes and fees on their respective territories (from the established list)[118] and establish local

[115] SCHCS, Indicators on the Status of Reforms in the Housing and Communal Services Economy, January 2004.

[116] Section prepared by Inna Lunina, Institute of Economic Projections, National Academy of Sciences of Ukraine.

[117] The data on the city budgets for 2002 and 2003 is not yet available.

[118] The Law of Ukraine "On the System of Taxation" defines the list of local taxes and fees.

tax rates (within determined ranges)[119], as well as establish tax rates of the single tax that is imposed on small businesses and private entrepreneurs (within UAH 20 - 200 range per month)[120]. The list of local taxes and fees includes 2 taxes and 13 fees. However, they contribute to less than 2% of local budgets' revenues, including some 3% of the revenues of the local budgets of the oblast and national level subordination cities. Single tax revenues make up about 2.5% of the local budgets' revenues, including 3.6% of revenues of the local budgets of the oblast and national level subordination cities.

- *Large share of State transfers in local budgets' revenues.* In 2003, share of transfers exceeded 34% as compared to 18.3% in 1999 (see next table); transfers exceed 25% of the budgets of the oblast and national level subordination cities (see table below).

- *Constant adjustments of the State transfers' formula***,** which means lack of stability and middle term predictability of local budgets' revenues. There have been 5 adjustments of the original transfer formula, which have been approved in September of 2001 by the Cabinet of Ministers of Ukraine (two adjustments in 2001, one - in 2002 and two – in 2003).

- *Methodology of transfer calculation lowers local governments' incentives to raise and improve own revenue base.* State transfers (so-called state budget equalization transfer funds) are based on the projected amount of revenues of the respective local budget, according to determined list of taxes[121], which include income tax, licensing fees, trade patent fees, single tax of small businesses. The

[119] Local tax and fees rates ranges are determined by the Decree of the Cabinet of Ministers of Ukraine "On Local Taxes and Fees".

[120] Possibilities for changing entrepreneur single tax rates are determined by the Presidential Decree " "On Simplified System of Taxation, Accounting and Reporting of Small Businesses" of July 3, 1998.

[121] The list of taxes, which are accounted for determine amount of interbudgetary transfers are specified in Articles 64 and 66 of the Budget Code of Ukraine. Projections of such tax revenues are made based on the actual data for three previous years.

> increase of revenue streams from these taxes means decrease of the amount of transfers from the State budget. Budget Code guarantees a certain level of local budgets' expenditures by allocating equalization transfers. In 2002, the minimum level of oblast local budgets' expenditures was reaching almost 90% of the oblast average level. In this context, local governments do not have incentives to create an environment beneficial for business development and for local economic activity; however there is an incentive to lobby for tax privileges and tax debt write offs for the businesses operating in the region.

In this respect, one of the key problems of intergovernmental finance is the problem of establishing stable base for increasing tax guarantees for local budgets.

Table 44. Revenue structure of SNGs Budgets, 1999-2002, %

	1999	2000	2001	2002	2003 *prior estimates*
Tax revenues	*68.1*	*62.9*	*59.1*	*58.3*	*54.3*
Residential income tax	19.3	34.1	35.1	38.3	39.4
Enterprise profit tax	30.0	11.3	8.5	4.4	0.4
Property taxes	1.8	2.8	2.2	2.1	1.8
Fees for specialized use of natural resources	7.3	7.8	6.5	6.4	6.0
Land tax	6.8	7.4	6.5	6.4	5.9
Internal taxes for goods and services	6.3	3.0	2.4	2.4	2.0
Local taxes and fees	2.7	2.6	2.1	1.9	1.7
Non-tax revenues	*3.4*	*9.5*	*8.7*	*7.3*	*7.0*
Proceeds from privatization	0.8	1.2	1.4	*	*
Own revenues of budgetary institutions		5.7	5.1	5.3	5.5
State special purpose funds	*10.1*	*4.0*	*2.7*	*1.0*	*1.5*
Total revenues (without transfers)	*81.7*	*76.6*	*71.0*	*68.8*	*65.8*
Transfers	*18.3*	*23.4*	*29.0*	*31.2*	*34.2*
Subsidy to Republican Budget of AR of Crimea, oblast and city of Sevastopol budgets	12.6	22.1	17.0	16.5	18.9
Cross-settlements	5.4	0.8	0.1	0.0	0.1
Subventions from the state budget	0.3	0.5	11.9	14.7	15.2
Total revenues	*100.0*	*100.0*	*100.0*	*100.0*	*100.0*

* revenues from privatization since 2002 are included in the section „financing“.

Source: Estimated based on the data of the Ministry of Finance of Ukraine.

Table 45. Revenue structure of the oblast and state subordination level cities, %

	1999	2001	2002
Tax revenues	*73.9*	*57.2*	*62.8*
Residential income tax	23.2	35.2	44.6
Enterprise profit tax	20.8	0.9	0.8
Property taxes	3.1	0.4	1.1
Fees for specialized use of natural resources	12.4	10.8	7.4
Internal taxes for goods and services	7.8	2.4	2.2
Local taxes and fees	5.3	3.9	3.2
Non-tax revenues	*5.1*	*11.5*	*8.2*
Proceeds from privatization	0.9	1.8	
Own revenues of budgetary institutions		6.4	6.0
State special purpose funds	*0.8*	*1.0*	*0.6*
Total revenues (without transfers)	*79.8*	*70.5*	*74.2*
Transfers	*20.2*	*29.5*	*25.8*
Subsidies	9.0	6.9	6.1
Cross - settlements	9.3	1.0	0.1
Subventions	1.9	21.6	19.6
Total revenues	*100.0*	*100.0*	*100.0*

Source: Estimated based on the data of the Ministry of Finance of Ukraine.

Recommendations and Technical Assistance

The principal issues, which the Ukrainian water sector has been facing for almost a decade, have now reached a point, critical for further development of municipal services sector as a whole. To avoid the collapse of many components of the physical infrastructure systems, the national government increased focus on the water sector by creation of various National Programs, to break a vicious circle of deteriorating service levels resulting from a nexus of problems both at service provider and at other stakeholders levels.

New Strategy for improvement efficiency of the national housing and communal services economy is presented in the Draft Law of Ukraine "The National Program of Reforming and developing Housing and Communal Economy for 2004-2010". It has summarized government's vision for the Ukrainian municipal sector development, which entails:

- To meet the demand of all water users for affordable housing-municipal services at appropriate service levels and quality complying with state standards approaching EU standards;

- To create conditions for sustainable and efficient operation and development of housing-municipal sector;

- To improve transparency of relations between housing-municipal service market agents;

- To decrease human-caused impact on natural objects;

- To encourage economic and rational use of resources and energy resources in particular.

The tasks, which Ukrainian Government sets for implementation in housing and communal services sector, show the need for utilization of best practices, which exist internationally, on creating conditions for sustainable and efficient operation and development of municipal services sector. Efficient use of financial resources attracted for investment into WWS sector has to be promoted in various ways and brought up to the national opinion leaders and water sector managers through a number of ways, among which are various training tools and technical assistance mechanisms.

Training

Develop training programs to institutionalize training process and share best practices in the area of municipal finance, utility financial and investment management, tariff regulation, private sector participation, strategic planning, citizen participation in the process of municipal infrastructure development and tariff setting etc.

This training initiatives can be delivered in various ways:

- by establishment of national or international training centers for water and wastewater managers, local government officials, regulators and other stakeholders from EECCA countries (donor grant funds may be used for this purpose; and possibilities for future operation on co-financing terms with the trainees may be considered in the future).

- through regional conferences of experts, service providers, and other stakeholders to identify ways of meeting developing capital market needs in a variety of fixed-income products with longer maturities.

Technical Assistance

At national level, technical assistance may include the following:

- Analysis of opportunities for mobilizing local capital and financial markets to support water and environmental infrastructure investments in Ukraine through various sources:
  - Commercial credit;
  - UMDF funding;
  - Utilization of co-financing mechanisms, e.g. grants with subsidized interest rates; grants with matching funds of local governments and CSEs; joint funding of several local governments through fund creation mechanisms, especially in rural areas; IFIs guarantees, issued with State funding, for SNG debt; environmental funds financing at subsidized interest rates, etc.
  - Alternative financial options.
- To solve current intergovernmental finance system problems, it is recommended to create a working group (of local governments' representatives, Association of Ukrainian cities, government officials of the Ministry of Finance of Ukraine, and other local and international stakeholders), with a mandate to reflect on:
  - the types of taxes which can be used to improve the revenue base of the local budgets;
  - opportunities to strengthen the tax authority of SNGs.

- Legal support with drafting legislation allowing increase of investment into municipal services infrastructure, including, but not limited to, the development of effective SNG debt security provisions.

- Assisting with the design of incentive regulation system in the area of municipal services provision in monopolistic markets.

At the local level, development of the local credit markets requires significant technical assistance to potential borrowers in various areas that will strengthen local governments' capacity to invest in environmentally related infrastructure.

Such areas include:

- design of municipal projects,

- financial/fiscal management,

- financial analysis and reporting,

- capital investment planning with assessment of the best possible use of the priority investment funding, taking into consideration energy conservation and water demand management,

- revenue forecasting, etc.

These technical assistance can be delivered in various ways:

- through requesting proposals from potential borrowers for technical assistance and tendering specific technical assistance to meet the potential borrowers' needs,

- by organizing a larger-scale technical assistance demonstration projects on a national-level using international and domestic experts in order to accumulate practical experience at the local level that allows to smooth implementation of newly approved legislation;

- by providing funds directly to potential borrowers so they can procure the specific technical assistance they require, etc.

Recommendation for Improving the Monitoring of SNG Capital Market Developments

Design and implementation of effective SNG debt markets will require improving the measurement and monitoring of key indicators on SNG financial markets development in Ukraine. In this context, collaboration between international donors and the Government of Ukraine may be needed to facilitate a program of regular statistical analysis on SNG capital market developments.

Reports would be used by the various stakeholders for decision making, including members of Inter-Agency Working Group representing Government of Ukraine, International Donor Agencies, International Finance Institutions, and municipalities that was created to assist in the development and implementation of financing mechanisms of local development projects, which are expected to be carried out by local self-governments without provision of sovereign guarantees.

Annex. statistics on local investment and finance

Table 46. Loan Agreements with International Financial Institutions

Period	Lender/Borrower	Total Loan Amount (in US dollars)	Repayment	Guarantees	Purpose
1999	EBRD/City of Zaporizhzhya	28 million	nd	Sovereign	Water and wastewater investment program in the city of Zaporizhzhya
1999	IBRD/Government of Ukraine	200 million (as of February 2004, 32.9 million utilized)	until 2018	Sovereign	Reconstruction and rehabilitation of heating system of the city of Kyiv
2000	IBRD/Government of Ukraine	18.29 million (as of February 2004, 9.7 million utilized)	12 years	Sovereign	Energy saving in administrative and public buildings of Kyiv.
2000	IBRD/Government of Ukraine*	Municipal Credit line On 01.2004 total loans provided for USD 5.66 million as of February 2004	Nd	Sovereign	Project Implementation on Softening Social Impacts of Reforms in Coal Industry of Ukraine (Luhansk, Donetsk, Lviv and Volyn oblsast)
2002	IBRD/Government of Ukraine	24.250 million	until 2021	Sovereign	Water and wastewater investment program in the city of Lviv
Total		276.2 million			

*Data provided by the Ministry of Finance of Ukraine, February 2004.

Source: Legislation of Ukraine.

Table 47. Volumes of securities registered by SSMSC, Billion UAH

Securities	1996	1997	1998	1999	2000	2001	2002	2003
Stock issues, per year	1.821	9.443	11.839	7.919	15.494	21.92	12.7957	6.508
Corporate Bond Issues, per year	0.013	0.116	0.008	0.132	0.070	0.694	4.275	3.352
Other securities, per year	nd	nd	nd	nd	nd	nd	0.0371	Nd
Total (cumulative since 1994)	nd	nd	nd	31.682	47.29	69.69	86.79	96.650

Source: SSMSC data, http://www.ssmsc.gov.ua/4/2002/2.2.2.1.shtml.

Table 48. Bank interest deposit and credit rates, % per annum[122]

Period	Total		In domestic currency		In foreign currency	
	Loans	deposits	Loans	Deposits	loans	deposits
1992	-	-	76.0	68.0	-	-
1993	-	-	221.1	187.3	-	-
1994	-	-	201.7	171.0	-	-
1995	-	-	107.1	61.2	-	-
1996	-	-	77.0	34.3	-	-
1997	-	-	49.1	18.2	-	-
1998	43.8	18.0	54.5	22.3	20.0	9.7
1999	43.3	17.1	53.4	20.7	21.0	9.0
2000	33.0	11.1	40.3	13.5	17.0	5.8
2001	26.1	9.9	31.9	11.2	13.1	5.6
2002	20.8	7.4	24.8	7.8	11.9	6.0
2003 (September)	14.2	6.4	17.2	6.7	11.7	5.5

Source: National Bank of Ukraine, http://www.bank.gov.ua/ENGL/Statist/PROCENT/prst_e.htm.

122 Interest rates are annualized without accounting of interbank market. Interest rates are calculated as average weighted on credits and deposits-portfolio. When calculating interest rates, the sums are not taken into account on which interest rates are not intended to total Before 1998 banks did not provide interest rate accounting on foreign exchange credits and deposits

Table 49. Bank lending to CSEs in the oblast centers of Ukraine, 1996-2003

Period	City	Short - term loans, (interest rate per annum)	Purpose of long-term loans (O&M or CI)	Long - term loans, (interest rate per annum)	Long - term loan term, (years)	Purpose of long-term loans (O&M or CI)
1996*						
1997	Cherkasy	no interest	CI (Housing)			
	Ivano-Frankivsk	60%	CI (Heat Supply)			
1998	Ivano-Frankivsk			75%	3	CI (Heat Supply)
1999						
2000	Mykolaiv	30%	O&M (Municipal electric transport)			
	Dnipropetrovsk	40%	CI (Water Supply)			
	Zaporizhzhya	36-35%	O&M (Water Supply)	Libor +1%	15	CI (Water supply and sanitation)
	Lviv	28%	O&M (Heat Supply)			
2001	Mykolaiv	27%	O&M, CI (Heat Supply, Municipal electric transport)			
	Ivano-Frankivsk			33%	1.5	O&M (Heat Supply)
	Kherson			18%	2	O&M (Heat Supply)
	Khmelnytsky	29 - 20%	O&M (Heat supply)			
	Zaporizhzhya	36 – 7%	O&M (Water supply and sanitation)	Libor +1%	15	CI (Water supply and sanitation)
	Lviv	30%	O&M (Heat supply)			

Period	City	Short - term loans, (interest rate per annum)	Purpose of long-term loans (O&M or CI)	Long - term loans, (interest rate per annum)	Long - term loan term, (years)	Purpose of long-term loans (O&M or CI)
2002	Mykolaiv	18%	O&M (Heat Supply)	18%	3	CI (Municipal electric transport)
	Dnipropetrovk	20%	O&M (Heat Supply)			
	Ivano-Frankivsk			28%	3	O&M (Heat Supply)
	Khmelnytsky	20-18%	O&M (Heat Supply)			
	Lviv	28 -20%	O&M (Heat supply)			
	Zaporizhzhya	36 – 7%	O&M (Water supply and sanitation)	Libor +1%	15	CI (Water supply and sanitation)
	Zaporizhzhya	24%	O&M (Heat Supply)	24%	2	O&M (Heat Supply)
2003	Mykolaiv			17%	5	CI (Road building)
	Dnipropetrovk	No interest	O&M (Heat Supply)			
	Chernivtsy			23%	3	CI, Purchase of transport
	Kirovograd	N/d	N/d(Water supply and sanitation)			
	Zaporizhzhya	14,6 - 11%	CI (Water supply and sanitation)	Libor +1%	15	CI (Water supply and sanitation)

*Some cities reported that they do not keep records on bank lending for the period of 1996-1999.

Source: State Committee on Housing and Communal Services of Ukraine, January 2004.

Table 50. Credits to economy of Ukraine, Million UAH[123]

Period	Total	Inclucing classif cation on							
		Currency		**credits**					
				short-term			*long-term*		
		domestic	Foreign exchange	total	domestic currency	foreign exchange	total	domestic currency	foreign exchange
1991	0.97	0.97	-	0.85	0.85	-	0.12	0.12	-
1992	27	24	3	26	23	3	1	1	-
1993	406	385	21	396	374	21	11	11	-
1994	1,558	1,199	359	1,381	1,022	359	176	176	-
1995	4,078	3,029	1,049	3,643	2,664	980	434	365	69
1996	5,452	4,102	1,350	4,845	3,653	1,192	607	449	158
1997	7,295	5,195	2,100	6,522	4,682	1,840	773	513	260
1998	8,873	5,117	3,756	7,240	4,438	2,801	1,633	679	954
1999	11,787	5,716	6,071	9,142	4,714	4,428	2,645	1,002	1,643
2000	19,574	10,568	9,006	16,060	8,903	7,157	3,514	1,665	1,848
2001	28,373	15,845	12,528	22,218	13,034	9,184	6,156	2,811	3,344
2002	42,035	24,463	17,572	30,185	18,689	11,497	11,849	5,774	6,076
2003**	60,491	35,791	24,700	36,226	24,198	12,028	24,265	11,593	12,672

*Excluding credits, granted by banks under liquidation.

** September.

Source: National Bank of Ukraine, http://www.bank.gov.ua/ENGL/Statist/CREDITS/kred_e.htm.

[123] Since April, 2003 the accrued interest is included. The corresponding indicators are updated since 2000 till March 2003

Table 51. Investment in housing and communal economy of oblast cities, 1996-2003, 000 UAH

Indicator	1996	1997	1998	1999	2000	2001	2002	2003	1996 - 2003
State Funding Total, including:	*110,440.4*	*10,221.5*	*10,495.0*	*12,011.4*	*34859.0*	*28,091.1*	*29,477.4*	*49,630.0*	*285,225.8*
Water supply	102,121.4	-	-	40.0	1034.2	1,197.0	2,131.0	150.3	106,673.9
Wastewater collection and treatment	4,819.0	5,791.3	6,895.0	10,669.1	27267.2	9,698.9	11,677.8	29,801.0	106,619.3
Heat Supply	-	-	-	-	-	803.8	899.0	-	1,702.8
Housing	3,500.0	4,430.2	3,600.0	1,302.3	6732.6	16,591.4	17,019.6	19,678.7	72,854.8
Solid waste treatment	-	-	-	-	-	-	-	-	-

Table 51. Investment in Housing and Communal Economy of Oblast Cities, 1996-2003, 000 UAH (continued)

Indicator	1996	1997	1998	1999	2000	2001	2002	2003	1996 - 2003
Municipal Budget Funding Total, including:	*11,570.2*	*15,332.2*	*23,913.4*	*36,089.7*	*98761.1*	*121,728.7*	*166,502.8*	*207,221.6*	*681,119.7*
Water supply	2,479.1	1,325.0	3,406.8	5,141.7	6850.8	7,955.1	15,002.9	24,041.6	66,203.0
Wastewater collection and treatment	5,489.5	4,110.4	9,192.8	4,546.8	29728.7	23,624.7	38,233.4	72,050.8	186,977.1
Heat Supply	937.9	1,374.0	2,015.0	1,480.2	4181.1	7,679.4	3,213.9	9,630.5	30,512.0
Housing	2,419.5	8,369.1	8,223.2	19,669.6	51435.3	80,652.2	107,409.4	93,134.8	371,313.1
Solid waste treatment	244.2	153.7	1,075.6	5,251.4	6565.2	1,817.3	2,643.2	8,363.9	26,114.5

Table 51. Investment in housing and communal economy of oblast cities, 1996-2003, 000 UAH (continued)

Indicator	1996	1997	1998	1999	2000	2001	2002	2003	1996 - 2003
CSE Funding Total, including:	*24,410.7*	*36,425.6*	*36,394.7*	*35,516.3*	*60917.4*	*52,176.8*	*78,701.0*	*62,891.8*	*387,434.4*
Water supply	4,645.3	9,352.9	8,732.0	9,259.9	32463.4	13,798.8	13,400.8	8,660.5	100,313.6
Wastewater collection and treatment	3,119.3	3,935.9	2,933.0	4,690.9	3591.7	6,852.4	12,639.1	9,970.5	47,732.8
Heat Supply	6,342.1	5,977.3	11,077.9	11,110.4	7808.4	11,247.3	4,364.4	4,329.2	62,257.0
Housing	10,279.0	17,159.5	13,651.8	10,660.5	17312.6	20,558.1	48,293.2	39,845.6	177,760.3
Solid waste treatment	25.0	,-	-	-	-	37.2	206.0	255.9	524.1

Table 51. Investment in housing and communal economy of oblast cities, 1996-2003, 000 UAH (continued)

Indicator	1996	1997	1998	1999	2000	2001	2002	2003	1996 - 2003
Commercial Bank Lending total, including:	*15,684.0*	*2,910.0*	*20,593.0*	*27,638.0*	*33482.9*	*79,483.2*	*138,591.3*	*136,188.8*	*454,571.2*
Water supply	-	-	-	-	10881.9	29,772.2	78,725.3	64,277.5	183,656.9
Wastewater collection and treatment	-	-	-	-	-	-	-	-	-
Heat Supply	-	-	-	-	1200.0	9,300.0	21,266.0	5,624.0	37,390.0
Housing	15,684.0	2,910.0	20,593.0	27,638.0	21401.0	40,411.0	38,600.0	66,627.3	233,864.3

Source: SCHCS, Questionnaire Survey of the Oblast Center Municipalities, December 2003- January 2004

Table 52. List of non-communally owned WWS utilities in Ukraine, 2003[124]

Oblast	Name of Utility	Organizational form
Donetsk oblast	Snizhnyanskvodokanal (City of Snizhne)	Ltd
	Donvuglevodokanal (City of Donetsk)	OJSC
Zaporizhzhya oblast	Azov –Servis (City of Kyrylivka)	Ltd
City of Kyiv	Kyivvodokanal	OJSC
Sumy oblast	Vodotorgprylad (City of Ohtyrka)	Ltd
	Akvaservis (City of Putivl)	Ltd
Ternopil oblast	Olimp (City of Zalischiki)	Ltd
Cherkasy oblast	Breeze (City of Zolotonosha)	CJSC
Chernihivska oblast	Komunalnyk (City of Koryukivka)	CJSC
	Komunalnyk (residential area Lyubych)	Ltd
	Komunalnyk (City of Novgorod Siversky)	Ltd
	Komunservis (residential area Ripky)	CJSC
Chernivetska oblast	Brok- blons (residential area Beregomet)	Ltd

Source: Association "Ukrvodoecologia", Ukrainian Water Association, Kyiv 2003.

[124] The latest data of SCHCS indicated that the number of utilities with PSP is 36, no details are available

Table 53. Municipal bond issues

Issuer	Term			Nomination	Value of Bond Offer (Hryvna)	Value Bonds Sold	Percentage of Interest Bearing Bond/Bond Issue Purpose
	Date of Issue	*Date of Maturity*	*Tenure of Bond (months)*				
Dnipropetrovsk City Council	July 1 1995	June 30 1998	-	1000 Hr. each	21,000,000	-	small privatization objects
	LOAN IS SUSPENDED						
Kyiv City Council	July 1 1995- July 1 1996	Nov. 14 1995- Dec.26 1995, Jan. 23 1996- Feb.27 1996, Mar. 12 1996- Apr. 9 1996	3	500 Hr. each	51,320,000	Hr.1, 842,750	10%
Donetsk oblast, Donetsk City Council and Committee on Cap. Construction	Nov. 1 1995	June 30 1998	32	50 Hr. each	1,952,050	532,139.74	Housing Construction

Table 53. Municipal bond issues (continued)

Issuer	Term			Nomination	Value of Bond Offer (Hryvna)	Value Bonds Sold	Percentage of Interest Bearing Bond/Bond Issue Purpose
	Date of Issue	*Date of Maturity*	*Tenure of Bond (months)*				
Donetsk oblast, Maryupil City Council Department of Capital Construction	December 1996	July 1998	20	50 Hr. each	5,000,000		Housing Construction
Kharkiv City Council	Dec. 1 1995	Jan.1 1997- Jan.31 1997	14	300	1,200,000	1,200,000	average rate of refinancing
				30	300,000	300,000	
				Total	1,500,000	1,500,000	
	Dec. 1 1996	Jan.1 1999- Jan.31 1999	26	300	3,700,200	2,029,800	average National Bank of Ukraine rate
				30	300,000	206,070	
				Total	4,000,000	2,235,870	
Komsomolsk City Council	Dec. 25 1995	May 15 1997- August 15 1997	20	24.5	1,500,135	-	Housing Construction
			LOAN IS TERMINATED				

Table 53. Municipal bond issues (continued)

Issuer	Term			Nomination	Value of Bond Offer (Hryvna)	Value Bonds Sold	Percentage of Interest Bearing Bond/Bond Issue Purpose
	Date of Issue	*Date of Maturity*	*Tenure of Bond (months)*				
Poltava City Council	Mar. 1 1996	June 1 1998	27	40	1,000,000	69,174.50	Housing Construction
Lviv City Council	April 1996	Dec. 30 1998	31	40	2,000,000	1,996,680	3 months deposit rate of state savings bank;
Zaporizghzhya City Council	June 1 1996-June 31 1996	2 months after the end of circulation period	12 months after the date of the placement of issue	10	2,000,000	2,000,000	0.7 of National Bank of Ukraine discount rate during the tenure of bonds
Autonomous Republic of Crimea Government of CR	Oct. 15 1996	Oct. 15 2000	48	100	120,000,000	120,000,000	70% of National Bank of Ukraine discount rate

Table 53. Municipal bond issues (continued)

Issuer	Term			Nomination	Value of Bond Offer (Hryvna)	Value Bonds Sold	Percentage of Interest Bearing Bond/Bond Issue Purpose
	Date of Issue	*Date of Maturity*	*Tenure of Bond (months)*				
Kremenchug (Poltava oblast) City Council	Dec. 1 1996	Dec. 1 1997- Nov. 30 2001	66	500	9,000,000	76,500	Housing Construction
		Dec. 1 2001- May 1 2002	66	50	4,500,000	10,050	Housing Construction
				Total	13,500,000	86,550	
Autonomous Republic of Crimea	Jan. 1 1997	Jan. 1 1998	3,6,9,12 months	100	5,000,000	3,243,500	60% per annum
Autonomous Republic of Crimea	Apr. 15 1997	Apr. 15 1998	12	100	7,500,000	7,500,000	75% of National Bank of Ukraine discount rate

Table 53. Municipal bond issues (continued)

Issuer	Term			Nomination	Value of Bond Offer (Hryvna)	Value Bonds Sold	Percentage of Interest Bearing Bond/Bond Issue Purpose
	Date of Issue	*Date of Maturity*	*Tenure of Bond (months)*				
Odesa * City Council	May 1 1997	May 1 1998- June 15 1998	13.5	10	2,000,000	61,000,000	50%
				20	4,000,000		
				50	5,000,000		
				100	10,000,000		
				200	10,000,000		
				500	10,000,000		
				1000	20,000,000		
				Total	61,000,000		
aporizhzhya City Council	June 1 1997- Nov. 30 1997 Final date of issue placement - June 11 1997	2 months after the end of circulation period	12 months after the beginning date of issue placement	10	5,000,000	5,000,000	0.7 of National Bank of Ukraine discount rate during the tenure of bonds

Table 53. Municipal bond issues (continued)

Issuer	Term			Nomination	Value of Bond Offer (Hryvna)	Value Bonds Sold	Percentage of Interest Bearing Bond/Bond Issue Purpose
	Date of Issue	*Date of Maturity*	*Tenure of Bond (months)*				
Kherson City Council	July 1 1997	July 1 1998	12	50,000	10,000,000	10,000,000	3.40%
Brovary City Council Kiev Oblast	Apr. 14 1998- Apr. 28 1998	Apr. 14 1999- Apr. 28 1999	12	1,000	200,000	25,000	27%
				5,000	800,000	475,000	
				Total	1,000,000	500,000	
Ukraine Total					***314,272,185***	***156,506,664.24***	

* As of November 1, 2003, 253, 281 bonds have been redeemed. 436,719 bonds are still in circulation, the outstanding debt is UAH 45,723,650, outstanding debt on interest is UAH 22,861,825.

The data does not include the bonds issue of Kiev City Council of November 15, 2003 for the amount of UAH 150 million.

Source: PADCO, Ukraine, based on the data of SSMSC, December 2003.

Table 54. Capital investment in water supply and sanitation sector by source of funds, 2002-03, 000 UAH

№	Indicator	Total for Ukraine		Including by oblast													
				AR Crimea		Vinnitsa		Volyn		Dnipropetrovsk		Donetsk		Zhytomyr			
		2002	**2003**	2002	2003	2002	2003	2002	2003	2002	2003	2002	2003	2002	2003		
1	*2*	*3*	*4*	*5*	*6*	*7*	*8*	*9*	*10*	*11*	*12*	*13*	*14*	*15*	*16*		
1	Total Amount of Capital Investment, including:	**66 535**	**140 596**	825	3501	1806.7	2984.7	1970.4	2434.1	0	0			370	1570		
2	Utility own-source contributions	**31 466**	**80 886**			1043.6	524.2	251.6	687.6	0	0						
3	State Budget	**18 226**	**18 619**	404	2282	335	50	748.0	490.0	0	0			100	200		
4	Local budget	**11 531**	**25 356**	421	1219	174.1	1884	938.0	956.5	0	0			270	980		
5	Other Sources	**5 312**	**15 735**			254	526.5	32.8	300.0	0	0				390		

Table 54. Capital investment in water supply and sanitation sector by source of funds, 2002-03, 000 UAH (continued)

№	Indicator	Including by oblast													
		Zakarpattya		Zaporizhzhya		Ivano-Frankivsk		Kyiv		Kirovohrad		Luhansk		Lviv	
		2002	2003	2002	2003	2002	2003	2002	2003	2002	2003	2002	2003	2002	2003
1	2	*17*	*18*	*19*	*20*	*21*	*22*	*23*	*24*	*25*	*26*	*27*	*28*	*29*	*30*
1	Total Amount of Capital Investment, including:	3847.6	3144.9	30999	75740	1882.6	6158.1	1634	2602	3884.7	6699.2				
2	Utility own-source contributions	241	376.5	26963	52331	188.3	566.9	330	1010		5741.2				
3	State Budget	1719	500	2000	4167.9	100	2250	520	580	3687.3					
4	Local budget	1466.6	1670.7	2036	7521	695.8	2557.6	774	875	197.4	958				
5	Other Sources	421	597.7	0	11720	898.5	783.6	10	137						

Table 54. Capital investment in water supply and sanitation sector by source of funds, 2002-03, 000 UAH (continued)

№	Indicator	Including by oblast													
		Mykolaiv		Odesa		Poltava		Rivne		Sumy		Ternopil		Kharkiv	
		2002	2003	2002	2003	2002	2003	2002	2003	2002	2003	2002	2003	2002	2003
1	2	*31*	*32*	*33*	*34*	*35*	*36*	*37*	*38*	*39*	*40*	*41*	*42*	*43*	*44*
1	Total Amount of Capital Investment, including:			5049.9	17404			472	1029.5	3065	3934	1315	1564		
2	Utility own-source contributions			406	15929			5.5	104.7	1363	2751	165	205		
3	State Budget			3190	50			350	525	694	540	400	805		
4	Local budget			1250	1268			51.4	340.1	1008	643	180	214		
5	Other Sources			203.9	157.1			65.1	59.7			570	340		

Table 54. Capital investment in water supply and sanitation sector by source of funds, 2002-03, 000 UAH (continued)

№	Indicator	Including by oblast											
		Kherson		Khmelnytsk		Cherkasy		Chernivtsy		Chernihiv		City of Sevastopol	
		2002	2003	2002	2003	2002	2003	2002	2002	2003	2002	2003	2002
1	2	*45*	*46*	*47*	*48*	*49*	*50*	*51*	*52*	*53*	*54*	*55*	*56*
1	Total Amount of Capital Investment, including:	918.3	1618.1	2028	4321.9			620	504.4	5180.1	5210	667	176.6
2	Utility own-source contributions	12.3	20.5	371.6	549.5					125.5	89.22		
3	State Budget	500	798	610	996.1			150		2051.4	4208.2	667	176.6
4	Local budget	406	799.6	1041.7	2719.3			440	489.4	180.9	261.1		
5	Other Sources			4.7	57			30	15	2822.3	651.55		

Source: SCHCS (Indicators on the Status of Reforms in the Housing and Communal Services Economy, January 2004).

OECD PUBLICATIONS, 2, rue André-Pascal, 75775 PARIS CEDEX 16
PRINTED IN FRANCE
(97 2006 02 1 P) ISBN 92-64-03595-8 – No. 54993 2006